Conversations with Gore Vidal

Literary Conversations Series
Peggy Whitman Prenshaw
General Editor

Photo credit: © 2004 Nancy Crampton

Conversations with Gore Vidal

Edited by
Richard Peabody and Lucinda Ebersole

University Press of Mississippi
Jackson

www.upress.state.ms.us

The University Press of Mississippi is a member of the Association of American University Presses.

First edition 2005
∞
Library of Congress Cataloging-in-Publication Data

Vidal, Gore, 1925–
  Conversations with Gore Vidal / edited by Richard Peabody and
Lucinda Ebersole.—1st ed.
    p. cm. — (Literary conversations series)
  Includes bibliographical references and index.
  ISBN 1-57806-672-7 (alk. paper) — ISBN 1-57806-673-5 (pbk. : alk. paper)
  1. Vidal, Gore, 1925– —Interviews. 2. Authors, American—20th century—Interviews.
I. Peabody, Richard, 1951–. II. Ebersole, Lucinda. III. Title. IV. Series.

PS3543.I26Z464   2005
818′.5409—dc22   2004059554

British Library Cataloging-in-Publication Data available

Books by Gore Vidal

Williwaw. NY: Dutton, 1946.

In a Yellow Wood. NY: Dutton, 1947.

The City and the Pillar. NY: Dutton, 1948. Rev. ed., Boston: Little, Brown, 1965.

The Season of Comfort. NY: Dutton, 1949.

Dark Green, Bright Red. NY: Dutton, 1950. Rev. ed., NY: New American Library, 1968.

A Search for the King: A Twelfth-Century Legend. NY: Dutton, 1950.

A Star's Progress. NY: Dutton, 1950. [Katherine Everard pseudo.]

Death in the Fifth Position. NY: Dutton, 1952. [Edgar Box pseudo.]

The Judgment of Paris. NY: Dutton, 1952. Rev. ed., Boston: Little, Brown, 1965.

Death Before Bedtime. NY: Dutton, 1953. [Edgar Box pseudo.]

Thieves Fall Out. Greenwich, CT: Fawcett/Gold Medal, 1953. [Cameron Kay pseudo.]

Death Likes It Hot. NY: Dutton, 1954. [Edgar Box pseudo.]

Messiah. NY: Dutton, 1954. Rev. ed., Boston, Little Brown, 1965.

A Thirsty Evil: Seven Short Stories. NY: Zero Press, 1956.

Visit to a Small Planet and Other Television Plays. Boston: Little, Brown, 1956.

Visit to a Small Planet: A Comedy Akin to a Vaudeville. Boston: Little, Brown, 1957.
[Broadway Version] Rev. ed., 1959.

The Best Man: A Play about Politics. Boston: Little, Brown, 1960.

On the March to the Sea: A Southern Tragedy. NY: Grove Press, n. d. Evergreen Playscript
Series.

Three: Williwaw, A Thirsty Evil, Julian the Apostate. NY: Signet/New American Library,
1962.

Rocking the Boat. Boston: Little, Brown, 1962.

Romulus: A New Comedy. Adapted from a play by Friedrich Durrenmatt. NY: Dramatists
Play Service, 1962.

Three Plays. London: Heinemann, 1962.

Julian: A Novel. Boston: Little, Brown, 1964.

Washington, D.C.: A Novel. Boston: Little, Brown, 1967.

Myra Breckinridge. Boston: Little, Brown, 1968.

Sex, Death, and Money. NY: Bantam, 1968.

Weekend: A Comedy in Two Acts. NY: Dramatists Play Service, 1968.

Reflections upon a Sinking Ship. Boston: Little, Brown, 1969.

Two Sisters: A Memoir in the Form of a Novel. Boston: Little, Brown, 1970.

An Evening with Richard Nixon. NY: Random House, 1972.

Homage to Daniel Shays: Collected Essays, 1952–1972. NY: Random House, 1972.

Burr: A Novel. NY: Random House, 1973.

Myron: A Novel. NY: Random House, 1974.

1876: A Novel. NY: Random House, 1976.

Matters of Fact and Fiction (Essays 1973–1976). NY: Random House, 1977.

Kalki: A Novel. NY: Random House, 1978.

Three by Box. NY: Random House, 1978.

Sex Is Politics, and Vice Versa. Los Angeles: Sylvestre & Orphanos, 1979.

Views from a Window: Conversations with Gore Vidal. Ed. Robert Stanton. Secaucus, NJ:
    Lyle Stuart, 1980.

Creation: A Novel. NY: Random House, 1981.

The Second American Revolution and Other Essays (1976–1982). NY: Random House, 1982.

Pink Triangle and Yellow Star and Other Essays (1976–1982). London: Heinemann, 1982.

Duluth: A Novel. NY: Random House, 1983.

Lincoln: A Novel. NY: Random House, 1984.

Vidal in Venice. NY: Summit/Antelope, 1985.

The Ladies in the Library and Other Stories. Helsinki: Eurographica, 1985.

Armageddon? Essays, 1983–1987. London: Andre Deutsch, 1987.

Empire: A Novel. NY: Random House, 1987.

At Home: Essays 1982–1988. NY: Random House, 1988.

Hollywood: A Novel of America in the 1920s. NY: Random House 1990.

A View from the Diner's Club: Essays 1987–1991. London: Andre Deutsch, 1991.

Live from Golgotha: The Gospel According to Gore Vidal. NY: Random House, 1992.

Screening History. Cambridge, MA: Harvard, 1992.

The Decline and Fall of the American Empire. Berkeley: Odonian Press 1992.

United States: Essays 1952–1992. NY: Random House, 1993.

Palimpsest: A Memoir. NY: Random House, 1995.

The City and the Pillar and Seven Early Stories. NY: Random House, 1995.

Virgin Islands: Essays 1992–1997. London: Andre Deutsch, 1997.

The American Presidency. Monroe, ME: Odonian Press, 1998.

The Smithsonian Institution: A Novel. NY: Random House, 1998.

Gore Vidal: Sexually Speaking: Collected Sex Writings. Ed. Donald Weise. San Francisco:
    Cleis Press, 1999.

The Essential Gore Vidal. Ed. Fred Kaplan. NY: Random House, 1999.

The Golden Age: A Novel. NY: Doubleday, 2000.

The Last Empire: Essays 1992–2000. NY: Doubleday, 2001.

Perpetual War for Perpetual Peace: How We Got to Be So Hated. NY: Thunder's Mouth Press/Nation Books, 2002.

Dreaming War: Blood for Oil and the Cheney-Bush Junta. NY: Thunder's Mouth Press/Nation Books, 2002.

Inventing a Nation: Washington, Adams, Jefferson. New Haven, CT: Yale, 2003.

Imperial America: Reflections on the United States of Amnesia. NY: Thunder's Mouth Press/Nation Books, 2004.

Contents

Introduction

"If Gore Vidal had not existed, some deity with an instinct for the elegant, the per-verse and the unclassifiable would have had to invent him. In the jumbled playroom of American lit, he is the malevolent jack-in-the-box."

—*Gary Kamiya,* Salon.com

No other living American writer has been as widely interviewed as Gore Vidal, nor has any played as large a role as social critic, provocateur, gadfly, and acerbic wit when it comes to the state of American society. Few have had his connections to the upper class world of power and money, and fewer still having those connections have risked censure by so ably biting the hand that fed them. "We laugh nervously as he intelligently exposes stupidity and hypo-crisy in American politics, religion, education, the arts, and even our lifestyles."[1] Vidal has not been afraid to be controversial, to chastise America's failings, or to ask us to change our ways. One of the most prolific and commercially successful authors of the last century, he has paid a considerable price for being so outspoken—enduring decades of dismissal and critical neglect—a trend that may at last have been righted by his winning the National Book Award in 1993 for *United States: Essays 1952–1992.*

Despite being a golden boy after the publication of *Williwaw,* his first novel in 1946, two years later he was a pariah owing to the publication of *The City and the Pillar,* a novel whose frank homosexual subject matter was ahead of its time in this country. The critics may have turned on him but the read-ing public embraced his plays, his screenplays, his pseudonymous mysteries, and his historical novels and essays. Indeed, Vidal has been a popular writer for most of his career, one who has enjoyed devout cult followings for his more satiric novels and science-fiction books alone.

---

1. Robert L. Stanton, *Views from a Window: Conversations with Gore Vidal* (Secaucus, NJ: Lyle Stuart, 1980) 13.

That public support has generated hundreds of light magazine profiles and pages of interviews. The more you search for Gore Vidal interviews the more you will find. It's as though Donald Windham's statement about Gore Vidal in the *New Yorker* back in 1960 was absolute truth—"Nothing's easier nowadays than to get the feeling of being entirely surrounded by Gore Vidal."[2] Little has changed since then where Vidal's concerned—forty-four years later Gore Vidal is again seemingly everywhere—in print, on the web, on the air, and on TV in the American Masters series.

How can it be possible that Gore Vidal has been writing at such a consistently high level for close to sixty years? He's still writing and publishing despite suffering in recent years from Epstein-Barr syndrome and glaucoma. He's upturned the applecart more than once in literary and high society circles. His refusal to be what others would have him be makes him contrary and unique in a world where lesser writers aspire to be media darlings. He's been called everything from the Elegant White Knife, to the Gifted Bitch, from the Apostate Angel to the Last Defender of the American Empire.

The sheer output of his multifaceted career is Olympian—his fiction, his essays, his screenplays, his guest appearances as a talking head through the years (on everything from *60 Minutes* and *Charlie Rose*, to the *Dick Cavett Show* and *What's My Line?*), several campaigns for political office, and above all his elegant wit and razor-sharp mind. Autodidact, inventor of the Peace Corps, fox in the hen house, betrayer of secrets from the U.S. upper class, Vidal often seems like Prometheus, bringing mankind the fiery torch.

An international celebrity, Gore Vidal always gives good interviews, seemingly loving the role of educator. He shocks, he jokes, he feeds, he elucidates. He seems to have an endless source of information available to be drawn from at any moment. He has refined the art of the *bon mot* and even the least of the hundreds of interviews he's done for radio, TV, and print mediums possess one or more gems. Selecting the interviews for this volume was a decidedly unenviable task simply due to the vast quantity of interviews his work has generated.

Yet, for somebody who has featured in as many interviews as he has, there are surprisingly few which really examine in depth Vidal's writing process, his characters, plots, techniques, with anything approaching critical analysis. The majority of his interviewers have taken the easy path, grilling him on the

---

2. Donald Windham, *The New Yorker*, 23 April 1960.

same repetitive questions on politics, sex, and history, which seems to belittle his achievements as a relentless working writer, and one of the highest quality.

"It is as a novelist of ideas and a satirist that Gore Vidal differs most noticeably from the other major writers of his generation. His imagination is powered by his intellect, and his high seriousness is expressed with wicked wit in an elegantly aphoristic prose style."[3]

Perhaps his swipes at the academic world and the powers that be, combined with his decision to write novels that focus on creatures of history or religion or politics, fall outside the purview of those ivory towered critics who embrace only the "serious academic novel." While the 1968 publication of his wickedly comic masterpiece *Myra Breckinridge* helped solidify his reputation as a literary bad boy, it also won him a lifelong following among readers with a taste for the outrageous and authentic. As Italo Calvino wrote, "One cannot speak of the revival of the novel's form in the last fifteen years without turning back to what may be his most famous novel, *Myra Breckinridge*. That satirical and grotesque burlesque, made up of a collage of the language and myths of the mass-culture, inaugurated a new phase in the way to present our era, which is comparable to pop art, but much more aggressive and with an explosion of expressionistic comedy."[4] Leave it to Vidal to spend the majority of the past forty years in Italy and always manage to keep his finger on America's pulse.

The interviews collected here cover a span of forty-three years. The first substantial interview with Vidal regarding his work, and a departure from what up to that point had been features where quotes from Vidal were decidedly sparse, something Vidal calls "book chat," was Eugene Walter's interview published in the *Transatlantic Review* in the summer of 1960. Vidal had already published sixteen books but this interview is a template for most that followed—his talking-head persona, the shrewd, self-confident, subversive wit, in fine form. Here he says, "Do I make myself seem a dark literary prince? More sinned against, etc.? I certainly mean to!" He calls *The Judgment of Paris* his best book to this point, admires Lawrence Durrell's *Alexandria Quartet* and the work of Paul Bowles, and William Golding. How does he write? "Novels in longhand, plays on the typewriter, the morning hours. I begin with a vague idea of the knot to be tied or untied."

3. Fred Kaplan, *The Essential Gore Vidal* (New York: Random House, 1999) xix.
4. Italo Calvino, "Imagining Vidal," *Threepenny Review* #17, Spring 1984.

The *Fag Rag* interview allows Vidal to discuss sexual issues, to confess that he's never allowed the word "gay" to pass his lips and that he's a generalist who rejected the role of main flag-waver for the gay movement as he had no desire then or now to be diminished or placed in a box. Gore Vidal has never allowed others to define him. He prefers to seduce and will not be seduced. He talks about the role of the writer as entertainer and delivers a delightful Faulkner *bon mot* re. Hemingway, "You know, Hemingway's problem is that he never takes chances." Vidal believes you have to keep pushing the boundaries as much as possible. And then closes by saying that American literature has always been second-rate.

Vidal speaks eloquently about writers, influences, and revisions in Gerald Clarke's lengthy *Paris Review* interview. He comes down in favor of Brigid Brophy, Anthony Burgess, Philip Roth, Evelyn Waugh, and P.G. Wodehouse, and surprisingly also likes works by Robert Coover and William H. Gass. However, he does ridicule Richard Brautigan. Of F. Scott Fitgerald, Vidal says, "Books will be written about him long after his own work has vanished— again and again we shall be told of the literary harvest god who was devoured at summer's end in the hollywoods."

The *American Film* interview presided over by Hollis Albert best captures Vidal's television and film script career. (He's written more than a hundred scripts.) Vidal has an encyclopedic mind when it comes to the cinema. He derides the *auteur* theory that directors are more important than writers and argues that film is all about the script, calls Casanova one of the most inter- esting men who ever lived, and marvels that good films seem to be made from secondary books but that great books always fail when rendered as movies. In talking about the debacle that was the movie *Caligula*, he states that "one of the things I have discovered as I proceed along the great road of life is that you make the same goddamned mistakes over and over and over again."

Vidal has always carried himself as though he were a great statesman (political or literary) ever since he was at his grandfather Thomas P. Gore's knee. In the Charles Ruas interview he clarifies, "I never wanted to be a writer. I mean, that's the last thing *I* wanted. I expected to be a politician." But writers write so, for good or ill, the political arena lost a unique and creative thinker.

Jon Wiener's interview, the longest in the volume, gives Vidal a forum from which to bemoan the lack of historical knowledge or consciousness in

America as a whole. He surprises by saying that the National Security State was already out of JFK's control in 1961–1962. He also lambastes the rich for ripping off the country, for their history of diversionary politics, while destroying the quality of life, education, et al., and for manufacturing enemies one after the other to grow their war machine, and he even half-jokingly claims to have created President Ronald Reagan. (If Vidal had picked Reagan over Melvyn Douglas to star in *The Best Man* in 1960, it would have revived Reagan's movie career and he might never have become president.) Vidal is the ultimate insider. His discovering JFK designing the Green Beret uniform and insignia (Green Beret for the Irish) is one of those moments that only he would seem privy to. But best of all, this interview reveals Vidal's brilliant program for education reform in the U.S. (Something akin to the St. John's College Great Books Program but beginning at age six.)

Jay Parini, whose role as Gore Vidal's literary executor gives him a unique knowledge of what's missing vis-à-vis Vidal and his work, edited the first substantial look at the writer and his career—*Gore Vidal: Writer Against the Grain*, which features essays and appreciations by Harold Bloom, Italo Calvino, Thomas M. Disch, Stephen Spender, and others. Parini considers Vidal an innovator, a writer whose oeuvre includes both realism and experimental writing. "One steps back from Gore Vidal's vast opus—surely one of the largest and most intellectually and artistically substantial of any American writer in our time—with mingled awe and exhaustion . . . Vidal is, most centrally, a writer. One of the premier essayists this nation has produced, he is also one of its most gifted novelists."[5] Parini's interview aptly follows up on unfinished threads from previous interviewers and fills in many gaps.

Harry Kloman, creator of "The Gore Vidal Index" on the World Wide Web, had the opportunity to interview Vidal in Pittsburgh in 1991, while Vidal was in town during the shooting of the movie *Bob Roberts*. Here Vidal praises Jeanette Winterson as one of the writers worth reading today and mentions that Mike Nichols wanted to film *Myra Breckinridge* with Anne Bancroft in the titular role.

Larry Kramer's 1992 interview covers all things gay as he tries to claim Vidal for the greater gay movement, something that Vidal has always deflected. Vidal never discusses his private life, considers himself an "objective and classical writer," and preaches "Don't be ghettoized, don't be categorized."

---

5. Jay Parini, *Writer Against the Grain* (New York: Columbia University Press, 1992) 29.

Vidal also believes that presidents Abe Lincoln, James Buchanan, and Franklin Pierce were gay.

The later interviews occur after Vidal's critical reputation has been resurrected and assured. He is no longer the outcast writer, erased from reference books or lists of American novelists. From now on he is the political voice of reason.

In *Gadfly*, a small Charlottesville-based magazine, he is appalled that "Americans hate history." He also surprises by being something of a Luddite—he doesn't use a computer or the internet.

The last interview in this volume is by Amy Goodman, one of the toughest no-holds barred reporters in America, as well as producer and host of the *Democracy Now!* radio show. Vidal has by now become one of the most outspoken critics of what's going on in the bowels of the National Security State. Here Vidal tackles Opus Dei, a Catholic order that has ties to many current world leaders and even Supreme Court justices. He also focuses on the role religion plays in Bush's foreign policy and talks about his correspondence with Timothy McVeigh, the Bronze Star-winning Gulf War veteran who was executed for his alleged role in the Oklahoma City bombing.

The series of interviews reprinted here should convey something of the width and breath of Gore Vidal's multifaceted intelligence. He is not just a gifted writer and essayist, but an extraordinary talker. He may, like Oscar Wilde, be remembered generations from now more for what he said than for what he wrote. Few writers have accomplished as much in their lifetimes. There are easy comparisons to Mark Twain and Henry James, distinguished men of letters who traveled, lived abroad, and whose essays and nonfiction vied with their literary creations for shelf space. In the end, Vidal's has been a lifetime of achievement which cannot be dismissed. "If I live to an old age I dread to think of all the work I shall have done,"[6] Vidal said in a January 1950 *NY Times* interview.

And now as we go to press in 2004, a two-CD set of interviews on WBAI-FM entitled *Gore Vidal Speaks Heresy (and backs it up)* has just been released by the WBAI-Pacifica radio station.

It does appear that Gore Vidal will get the last laugh.

We are grateful to the interviewers and publishers who granted permission, and to Beth Fisher and Carl Hahn for their help with the bibliographical info. Plus special thanks to Keith Kahla at St. Martin's Press and to Harry Kloman the mastermind of "The Gore Vidal Index."

6. *New York Times* January 1950.

Richard thanks Lucinda for her energy, laughter, and consummate good taste. He also thanks Margaret Grosh for love and endurance, for allowing him the time necessary to complete this project, and for always being there through the rough times. And where would he be if not for his sweet daughters—Twyla and Laurel?

Lucinda would like to thank Richard who, like Job, persevered through floods, pestilence, vermin, and exceptional chaos to bring this book to fruition. And to Gore Vidal, who reminds her every day, "write something, even if it's just a suicide note."

LE
RP

Chronology

1925   Born Eugene Luther Vidal, Jr., on October 3 in the Cadet Hospital at the United States Military Academy in West Point, New York, the only child of Nina Kay Gore and Eugene Luther Vidal. His father was an aeronautics instructor and later worked for the Roosevelt administration as Director of Air Commerce from 1933 until 1937. By the end of 1925 they had moved to Washington, D.C., to live with Nina's father, Senator Thomas Pryor Gore, at his home in Rock Creek Park.

1935   Attends Sidwell Friends School (after brief stints at Potomac School and Landon School) from 1934–1936. In May his parents divorce. Nina and Gore settle into a two-room flat at Washington's Wardman Park Hotel. By October his mother marries Hugh D. Auchincloss, one of the wealthiest men in Washington. (They will have a daughter and son.) Gore and Nina move into Merrywood, Auchincloss's Virginia mansion on the Potomac River.

1936   Attends St. Alban's School in Washington from 1936–1939. From his dormitory window he can see the Washington Monument. He falls in love with fellow pupil Jimmie Trimble, who was later killed in action on Iwo Jima in 1945.

1939   Baptized in order to be confirmed in February at the Washington Cathedral as Eugene Luther Gore Vidal. During the summer he sails for Europe aboard the *Ile de France* on a school trip. They are fortunate to make one of the last trains out of Italy before Mussolini closes the border. His mother removes him (against his wishes) from St. Alban's School and enrolls him at the Los Alamos Ranch School in New Mexico (1939–1940). By the end of the year his father marries Katharine Roberts. (They will have two children.)

1940   Attends Phillips Exeter Academy, where he reads, writes, sculpts, and makes his first appearance on the debate platform. One of his younger classmates is John Knowles.

1941   He drops "Eugene," "Luther," and "Jr." from his name in homage to
        his blind grandfather (whom he had read to since the age of ten) to
        become Gore Vidal. His mother and Hugh Auchincloss are
        divorced.

1943   In July 1943, after graduation, he enlists in the army. He is too
        young for active service and is sent for three months to a special
        army engineering program at Virginia Military Institute.

1944   His poor eyesight keeps him out of officer training school
        and West Point. He becomes instead a junior-grade warrant
        officer aboard the freight supply ship *FS-35*, stationed in
        the Aleutian Islands. He serves from December 1944 to
        March 1945.

1945   At the end of March he's hospitalized for acute rheumatoid arthri-
        tis, relieved of duty, but not discharged. He finishes his first novel,
        Williwaw, while recovering at Camp Gordon Johnston in Florida.
        The novel included an openly gay character. The success of the
        novel was helped in part by the support of Eleanor Roosevelt in
        her influential newspaper column. By the end of the year he's
        working as an associate editor at E.P. Dutton (his publisher) and
        meets Anaïs Nin.

1946   Officially discharged from the army in February, he lives at his
        father's Manhattan apartment and works at Dutton until he
        resigns in the spring in order to write full time. *Williwaw* is pub-
        lished in June to great success. Meets Paul Bowles. Vidal has an
        uncredited acting role in Maya Deren's film *Ritual in Transfigured
        Time*. Buys a writing retreat in Antigua, Guatemala, where Anaïs
        Nin is a visitor.

1947   Second novel, *In a Yellow Wood*, is published. The June issue of *Life
        Magazine* runs an article on young U.S. writers, including Vidal
        along with Truman Capote, Thomas Heggen, Jean Stafford, Calder
        Willingham, and six others.

1948   Travels through Italy with new friend Tennessee Williams. *The City
        and the Pillar*, one of the first American novels to present homo-
        sexuality as perfectly normal, is published. Critics vow to ignore
        Vidal's future efforts. Meets Christopher Isherwood, André Gide,
        Jean Cocteau, Samuel Barber, and the remnants of Bloomsbury.

1949   *The Season of Comfort* is published. Senator Gore dies in March.

1950   Conceives and helps edit Victor Weybright's literary magazine
        New World Writing. Publishes *Dark Green, Bright Red*. Purchases
        Edgewater, a run-down Federal-period house on the Hudson River
        near Rhinebeck, New York. In September, he meets Howard
        Austen, who will become his closest friend.

1952   *The Judgment of Paris* is published.

1954   *Messiah* is published. Over the next few years he writes close to
        thirty original scripts and adaptations for television including
        1954's *Dark Possession*.

1955   His most successful 1955 scripts are *Summer Pavilion, Sense of
        Justice, The Death of Billy the Kid*, and the satirical teleplay *Visit to
        a Small Planet*, which is broadcast live to millions. Vidal signs a
        five-year contract to write scripts for MGM. Moves into the Chateau
        Marmont in Los Angeles where he becomes friends with Paul
        Newman and Joanne Woodward, also contract players fresh to the
        Coast.

1957   Adapts *Visit to a Small Planet* for the stage. The play runs on
        Broadway for 338 performances.

1958   Rents a flat at Chesham Place in London, where he is joined
        by his mother and Austen. After a falling out with his mother,
        he never sees her again. In Rome writes script for *Ben Hur*
        with Christopher Fry. In New York he becomes friendly with
        the Kennedys. (Jacqueline Bouvier's mother had married
        Hugh Auchincloss.) Introduces Tennessee Williams to JFK
        and Jackie.

1959   Wins a New York Film Critics Circle nomination for Best
        Screenwriting for his adaptation of *Suddenly, Last Summer*.

1960   *The Best Man* runs on Broadway for 520 performances. Vidal
        accepts the Democratic Party nomination for Congress in his
        Duchess County New York District. Becomes friends with Eleanor
        Roosevelt. Runs far ahead of the Democratic national ticket in his
        heavily Republican district, but loses nonetheless.

1962   His play *Romulus* runs at the Music Box Theatre for sixty-nine
        performances. *Rocking the Boat*, his first collection of essays,
        appears. Heinemann, in London, publishes *Three Plays*. He
        considers a run for a New York Democratic Senate seat but
        declines.

1963   Moves with Howard Austen to Rome, taking an apartment on
        Via Giulia. Gore works on *Julian*, about the fourth-century Roman
        Emperor Julian the Apostate. Breaks with the Kennedys.
1964   *Julian* is published and becomes a number one bestseller. Film
        version of *The Best Man* opens.
1965   Revises *The City and the Pillar* with a new ending.
1966   Moves to a penthouse apartment in Via di Torre Argentina, his
        Roman residence until 1993. *Washington, D.C.* is published, the
        first novel of what Vidal calls his "narratives of empire."
1967   Writes the uproarious satire *Myra Breckinridge*.
1968   *Myra* is published and immediately becomes a bestseller. His play
        Weekend opens in New Haven, breaks attendance records at the
        National Theatre in Washington, D.C., and disappears from
        Broadway after a disappointing twenty-two performances. He
        covers both the Republican and Democratic conventions as a TV
        commentator. The infamous William F. Buckley-Gore Vidal feud
        erupts on the *Dick Cavett Show*. Joins with Eugene McCarthy
        supporters to create the New Party.
1969   His father dies in Los Angeles. Vidal takes a five-year lease
        on a vacation apartment in Klosters, Switzerland, where
        the rich and famous gather. He sells Edgewater by the end
        of the year.
1970   *Two Sisters* is published. Jason Epstein convinces him to leave
        Little, Brown, for Random House, where Epstein becomes his
        editor.
1971   Purchases La Rondinaia, a Cliffside villa in Ravello, Italy. *An
        Evening with Richard Nixon* runs on Broadway for thirteen
        performances.
1973   *Burr* is published and becomes a number one bestseller.
1974   Appears on *60 Minutes* with Mike Wallace. *Myron* is published.
1976   *1876* is published. *Time Magazine* (March 1) cover story on Vidal's
        life and work. Purchases a house on Outpost Drive in the
        Hollywood Hills.
1978   His mother, whom he has not seen since 1958, dies. *Kalki* is
        nominated for a Nebula and a Locus award.
1981   *Creation*, which focuses on religion in the fifth century B.C., is
        published.

1982   Becomes a candidate for the Democratic nomination for Senator
          from California. Loses to Governor Jerry Brown in primary, com-
          ing in second in a field of nine candidates, earning approximately
          half a million votes. Wins the National Book Critics Circle Award
          for criticism for *The Second American Revolution and Other Essays*.
1983   The satirical novel *Duluth* is published.
1987   *Lincoln* is published and becomes a bestseller.
1987   Gives a speech at the Kremlin in Moscow, on the origins of the
          Cold War. *Empire* is published. A *South Bank Show* on the BBC is
          devoted to Vidal. His essay on the forgotten novelist Dawn Powell
          is published in the *NY Review of Books*.
1988   ABC airs a miniseries based on *Lincoln*.
1988   Writes *Gore Vidal's Billy the Kid* for TNT cable and has an uncred-
          ited part in the film. Honored at the Edinburgh Festival.
1990   *Hollywood* is published. The BBC films *Gore Vidal's Gore Vidal*.
          Writes a script for Martin Scorsese based on the lives of Theodora
          and Justinian. Presides over the Venice Film Festival. Writes the
          screenplay for *To Forget Palermo* directed by Francesco Rosi.
1991   Gives the Massey lectures in the History of American Civilization
          at Harvard, April 1–3.
1992   Plays Senator Brickley Paiste in the film *Bob Roberts*. Harvard pub-
          lishes the Massey Lectures as *Screening History. Live from Golgotha*
          is published and becomes a bestseller.
1993   *United States: Essays 1952–1992* is published and wins the National
          Book Award. Gives up his Rome apartment for year-round resi-
          dency at La Rondinaia. Plays Prof. Pitkannan in the film *With
          Honors*.
1994   Filmed in Washington, D.C. for two documentaries.
1995   *Palimpsest*, Vidal's memoir, is published on his seventieth birthday.
          The BBC two-hour documentary on his life is aired in the U.S. to
          coincide with the occasion.
1996   Records a three-part program on the history of the American pres-
          idency for British television.
1997   Plays Congressman Page in the film *Shadow Conspiracy*. Plays
          Director Josef in the film *Gattaca*.
1998   *The Smithsonian Institution* is published and becomes a bestseller.
1999   *Gore Vidal: Sexually Speaking: Collected Sex Writings* is published.

2000   *Golden Age*, the final novel in Vidal's "narratives of empire," is pub-
        lished. *The Best Man* is revived on Broadway and stars Chris North,
        Spalding Gray, Charles Durning, and Elizabeth Ashley.
2001   *The Last Empire: Essays 1992–2000* is published.
2002   *Dreaming War: Blood for Oil and the Cheney-Bush Junta* and
        Perpetual War for Perpetual Peace are published. He has an uncred-
        ited role in the film *Igby Goes Down*, written and directed by step-
        sister Nina's son, Burr Steers.
2003   *The Education of Gore Vidal*, a documentary special is aired in
        February as part of the American Masters series on Public
        Television.
2004   Records two-CD set, *Gore Vidal Speaks Heresy (and backs it up)*, a
        two-hour "Fireside Chat" on George W. Bush and 9/11, for the
        New York City Pacifica radio station WBAI (99.5 FM).

Conversations with Gore Vidal

Conversations with Gore Vidal

Eugene Walter / 1960

From *Transatlantic Review*, Summer 1960, pp. 5–17.

I first saw Gore Vidal on Umnak Island, in the Aleutians, during the war, in the midst of a roaring blizzard. He caught my attention at once by his self-possession. He had just landed on the island, which is remote, desolate, sad. What I remember most is that he was very young, and that he kept looking about, taking everything in, while the other soldiers, mostly older, were grumbling and cursing and pulling their fur parkas about their faces. I watched him as he stamped his boots in the snow and turned his head this way and that. (An observer observed!) Later, in New York in 1946 when *Williwaw* was published, I bought the novel at once on the peculiarly Aleutian recommendation of the name (that of a howling wind that comes from the Bering Sea and crosses the islands) and recognized the photograph of the author. I was impressed by the tightly-written, unpretentious quality of the book, and followed the work of Vidal from then on. *In a Yellow Wood* came in 1947, *The City and the Pillar* in 1948, *The Season of Comfort* in 1949, and two books in 1950: *A Search for the King* (an historical novel on the Richard-Blondel theme) and *Dark Green, Bright Red*. Then came a breathing spell before *The Judgment of Paris* in 1952, and a longer pause before *Messiah* in 1954. (Since then there has been a collection of short stories, a book of television plays, and the comedy, *Visit to a Small Planet*.) The last two novels had small success, to my complete mystification, for they are of high excellence, balanced, intuitive, witty, and with a distinctive and unforgettable acid flavor all their own. *The Judgment of Paris* is an account of a young American's *wanderjahr* in Europe, crowded with amusing characters and incidents. *Messiah* is black satire: an image of America dominated by a television god; it has a Jacobean consciousness of mortality, a dry style—moreover, the reader is not invited to identify himself with any of the characters. All is lucid, understated, bitter. When I read it, I thought, "If this had been translated from the French, how the reviewers would fall out in a dead faint, and how the readers would argue over it." But it was home-grown and somehow got lost in the shuffle, while several big slovenly novels from semi-literate writers made the news. When I heard Vidal was coming to Italy, I couldn't wait to see him. We had been acquainted briefly in New York in 1946, but now, years and books later, I was full of questions to ask. We met in Rome, and he agreed to an interview.

I

A small salon in the Grand Hôtel, Rome.

Interviewer: Shall we do the statistics and so forth? Your frame of reference?
Gore Vidal: I was born October 3, 1925, at West Point, New York. Within a year my family moved to Washington, D.C. I was raised there and in nearby Virginia.

Int: And your name: were you named after your grandfather, the Senator?
GV: He was Thomas Pryor Gore of Oklahoma; my name is Eugene Luther Gore Vidal. I wasn't named for him, although he had a great influence in my life. He was blind from the age of ten; I read to him on and off for seventeen years.

Int: He was a very interesting figure, wasn't he? What did you read to him?
GV: Oh, yes, he brought Oklahoma into the Union in 1907, and he was the first Senator. What did we read? Well, I read him Constitutional History and British common law mostly; for pleasure we had Brann's *The Iconoclast* and the Victorian poets. In his attic in Rock Creek Park, D.C. (I describe that house in a short story, "A Moment of Green Laurel") there were seven or eight thousand books. The first that I could read by myself was called *The Duck and the Kangaroo*. My favorites were Lane's *Arabian Nights* and a 19th century *Stories from Livy*.

Int: Your education . . . ?
GV: Lots of schools. From 11 until 14 I was in St. Alban's, in Washington. I was a year at Los Alamos, then 3 years at Exeter which were among the happiest of my life. You know, getting away from the family and its problems.

My first novel was written at Exeter when I was 15. At least, part of a first novel, because I had a terrible problem for years: I could finish nothing. But I did about 100 pages of that one, all about Mussolini, his mistress, spies, very florid—the result of a trip to Rome in 1939. I wrote quite a few short stories, too.

Int: And verse?
GV: Some rather didactic verse. As a poet I was a profound moralist with a resolute metre—terrible, thumping stuff.

Int: Then you always knew you were cut out to be a writer?
GV: Oh, no! There was an awful crisis in my mind—the choice between politics and literature. I was brought up with the idea of going into politics; all the family were in politics. Even my father, an aviation man, was in Roosevelt's Little Cabinet as Director of Air Commerce. And the Gores are forever running for office all around the South. The family was originally from Mississippi.

Int: Did you write a great deal then? When did you first publish?
GV: In the *Exeter Review*, of which I was an editor. I published three stories before I graduated in June, 1943; went into the army in July, 1943, was sent to Army Training Group at V.M.I. for one term, where I wrote part of another novel. The writer I had read and studied and chosen for my model was—this may surprise you, but then I was an unworldly seventeen!—Somerset Maugham. I had also met, in the bridge-playing world of my mother, Michael Arlen who knew Maugham, so the novel I was trying to write was really *Cakes and Ale* all over again, with Maugham instead of Hardy, Arlen instead of Hugh Walpole, and myself as Maugham writing it. It was a beautifully weary book, in what is now the grand tradition of adolescent novel-writing.

Int: You must have started *Williwaw* about then . . .
GV: Well, let's see: when I left hospital I was dumped into the infantry, and then got into the air force, then into crash boats, then passed an examination as a First Mate, knowing nothing of navigation save what I learned from memorizing a book on the subject. Finally, I was sent to the Aleutian Islands as First Mate of the F.S.35. Fortunately, it was so foggy that no one ever

discovered I couldn't set a course. We relied on Point to Point navigation:
a symbol? Anyway, up there making a regular run between Chernowski Bay
and Dutch Harbor, in December, 1944, I wrote half of *Williwaw* in pencil in
a grey ledger marked *Accounts*; then, for the fourth time I gave up, convinced
I couldn't finish anything. Meanwhile, I had slyly contracted arthritis, was
hospitalized in Los Angeles. After, I was sent to Florida to train 18-year-olds.
One night alone in Headquarters—I was Officer of the Day—there was
hurricane warning up, and everything was shuttered against the coming
storm—I had just seen Boris Karloff in *Isle of the Dead*—that night I finished
Williwaw.

Int: How did *Williwaw* come to be published?
GV: I first took the novel and a bunch of poems to Roger Linscott at Random
House who liked the poems but wouldn't read the novel because it was in
longhand. He seemed to lack dedication. But I had the book typed. There was
a woman doing a life of Amelia Earhart, and when she came to interview my
father, who had known the flyer, I showed her the manuscript. She suggested
I take it to Nicholas Wreden of Dutton's. I did and we got on well; he said
he'd publish it, and offered me a job when I got out of the army. I worked at
Dutton six months, until *Williwaw* came out in April, 1946, and I quit on the
strength of the notices. Couldn't stand going to an office. I have never gone
to an office since. So, having attained some recognition, I fled to Guatemala
where I lived off and on for three years and wrote *In a Yellow Wood* and
The City and the Pillar. Those three books were written between the ages of
19 and 21. And it is depressing to think that I am still known primarily
for such green work. My later books are a good deal more right, and very
different. But literary reputations change slowly.

II

Amalfi. We had driven down—a party of four—in an ancient Mercedes
touring car suitable for a retired or deported gangster. We spent the night
wandering about the deserted streets, hearing only the stream that tumbles
down the mountain and rushes through the city to the sea. Vidal used the
town for an episode in *The Judgment of Paris*, but he had not visited it for
some years. The next morning we breakfasted on a terrace overlooking the
sea and continued our conversations.

Int: If you please, I should like a bit of history on *The City and the Pillar*. One has heard so many contradictory statements concerning it, why you wrote it, whether or not it's autobiographical, all that.

GV: Well, first of all, it is not "about" homosexuality. The actual theme is not unlike Alain-Fournier's: if one continues always to look back, to relate everything to a first affair, one is emotionally, even humanly destroyed. The pillar of salt. Oh, I realize that the ending of *The City and the Pillar* smacks of *Tosca*, but it was inevitable. I think now that if I had not written the novel so realistically, I could have made that ending work. But I deliberately chose a flat grey style which I thought would give immediacy to certain human facts which up till then had not been frankly handled in America. I wanted an undecorated, a graphic effect. And I did very much want to shock. As for autobiography, the book, like all of my work, is invented, down to the last detail. There were absolutely no originals of the characters.

Int: You rely on imagination more than observation then?

GV: What Thackeray called the "fancy." I am incapable of reporting anything. For me, the fact that something *happened* is quite enough, and needs no further comment. The act of writing is creating something that was *not*, and to make it *real*. A novelist, as I see it, must invent the truth.

Int: What effect did the publication of the book have on your life, literary and personal?

GV (*pauses, then smiles slowly*): Let me take a deep breath and tell you. First, I was at that time the author of two books embarrassingly admired— embarrassingly because I was under 21 and newspaper praise is a false thing at best, though, I suspect now, preferable to blame. I was the Huck Finn of the younger novelists, photographed against ships for *Life Magazine*, boyishly scowling. I seemed as safe as . . . who? Herman Wouk? I was in the running. Then came the bomb: *The City and the Pillar*. I remember I read it through once before it was sent to the printer, and I thought that if I ever read it again I'd never publish it . . . So I sent back a hardly-corrected proof. Then the reviews, what few there were, began and I discovered what happens in America if you tamper with the fragile—people avert their eyes, and go on talking. Half of my former admirers did not review it at all. *The New York Times* refused to advertise it—and when the publishers took the matter directly to Mr. Sulzberger, he decided to uphold his censor. Of the reviews received, a few were thoughtful and lengthy, most quite bad. Two words popped up to haunt that book, and all my writing ever since: "clinical" and "sterile." "Clinical" is used whenever one writes of relationships which are not familiar—I dare say that if the story had dealt with a boy and a girl instead of two boys the book would have been characterized as "lyrical." "Sterile" is an even deadlier curse upon the house, and comes from a dark syllogism in the American *zeitgeist*: the homosexual act does not produce children therefore it is sterile; Mr. X's book is concerned with the homosexual act therefore the book is sterile. (This syllogism was first proposed by the Russians when they turned on André Gide and it used to be a standard Stalinist line.) But despite the absence of reviews and no advertisements in *The New York Times*, the book was a bestseller. Aesthetically, the book was very youthful, very naïve, hasty but "felt," and I suppose in a way that the rudeness of its execution was part of its strength and the reason why it goes on year after year being read. I still think publishing it was a virtuous act and I would do it again, hard fate though it has been in some ways. One quite lost the newspaper reviewers, which was sad because their gentle twittering was always a great comfort; after all, I belong to no literary clique; I am outside the Academy; I have no friends who slyly review me . . . the business of literary politics has never figured in my life. Do I make myself seem a dark literary prince? More sinned against, etc.? I certainly mean to! And one does get what one wants, despite the querulous tone, the occasional misgivings. Forcing the world to adjust to oneself has always seemed to me an honorable life work . . . that one fails in the end is irrelevant.

Int: Did you receive many letters from readers?
GV: Just before the book was published *The Kinsey Report* came out, and I received a charming letter from Dr. Kinsey complimenting me on "my work in the field"! But I also received about 2000 letters, mostly of a confessional nature, from every corner of the world (the book was translated into French, Italian, Dutch, Norwegian, German, etc.).

Int: Do you still have echoes of it?
GV: Oh, yes. Letters still come. Critically . . . well, for instance, there was a young critic who began a distinguished critical career by particularly

admiring and celebrating the heterosexual love scenes of *In a Yellow Wood* but then later, after the appearance of *The City and the Pillar*, declared that I was unable to write convincingly of the man-woman relationship: a *volte-face* which I forgive him but which I find continuously burdensome as I proceed upon my "clinical" and "sterile" way. One could write *Anna Karenina* now and get the same reaction.

Int: Let's see, you finished that book in Guatemala: where did you go next?
GV: I finished *The Season of Comfort* down there, too. I lived in the ruins of a 16th-century Carmelite convent in Antigua. Well, after *The City and the Pillar* was published, I came to Europe in March, 1948. I went straight to Rome where I had a friend, Frederic Prokosch. Then I met Tennessee Williams and we drove all around Italy in a Jeep. All this time I was writing *A Search for the King*. Then back to Paris, to the U.S., a last trip to Guatemala (to write *Dark Green, Bright Red*), then Paris again, and back to the U.S.

Int: I'm dizzy. What year are we now?
GV (*chuckling*): 1950 was a crucial year—when I published two novels: *A Search for a King* which had good reviews and no sales, and *Dark Green, Bright Red* which had bad notices and no sales—and optimistically bought the house at Barrytown on the Hudson River where I still live; went broke; wrote in an absolute explosion of delight *The Judgment of Paris*, a picaresque which is my best book. It was quite well received; sold pretty well enough. To support myself, I took to lecturing—colleges, ladies' clubs—a chilling experience. Then at my wit's end, I wrote three mystery stories under a pseudonym. And, as is usual with works of the left hand, they were all successful. Meanwhile, I was working on *Messiah*, which was published in 1954, to sink serenely beneath the waves, although it was well regarded in Europe. Survival was now a desperate matter. So I hit upon a kind of five-year plan: an all-out raid upon television, which could make me enough money to live the rest of my life. It's been a fascinating, wearying experience. The plan was finished two years ago, and barring the unexpected I am, in a modest way; financially set for life. If one has the stamina, there's a lot to be said for piracy.

Int: Will you write more novels?
GV: Oh, yes. I have one in my head now but curiously enough whereas I could never think of ideas for plays a few years ago, now I think of nothing but ideas for plays: the old novel instinct has gone temporarily into the theatre. One tends to invent in one form or the other. The unexpected thing about my five-year plan is that I came to enjoy play-writing and as one enjoys it one respects it, which I didn't at first.

Int: Which gives you greater satisfaction, your novels or your plays?
GV: The novel. If only because I don't get the play deep enough or the characters rich enough for my purposes. I think this failure has to do with language. I'm not happy with naturalistic dialogue: I don't much use it, as you'll see, in those books I've written since 21, and yet I haven't found an alternative to the terrible naturalistic gabble in our theatre, the racket of "Do come in," "Drink?" "Yes," "Where'd you leave it?" "Upstairs," "Well, go look, etc." I don't do it much better than the others, but what I have done, and what interests me, is to clown, to be funny, bizarre—I enjoy comedic invention, both high and low, there is almost nothing quite so satisfying as making an audience laugh while removing their insides.

Int: Tell me about your television adaptations, about dealing with Faulkner, James, etc.?
GV: I did them for money of course—but I always tried to pick a writer I respected—or at least that I thought I could do something respectable with. I was most successful with Faulkner and James. I have a considerable affection for James, but not much for Faulkner. I failed entirely with Hemingway, and so has nearly everyone else, which makes one wonder about the original . . . or at least about its viability in *our* time.

Int: You were saying you invented everything, but weren't there some characters in *In a Yellow Wood* who were recognizably well-known New York literary and social figures?
GV: Well, let's say sometimes I drew small caricatures in the margin . . . peripheral doodling. The thing accomplished is "made," not recorded. Odd how people—even knowing ones—think it's always one's own life. I suppose they are so accustomed to the self-obsessed Thomas Wolfe sort of thing that the whole idea of invention is both discredited and disbelieved.

Int: Interesting, too, how *The City and the Pillar* was considered scandalous in America, and considered a moral work in Europe.

GV: I am, and don't entirely understand why, a moralistic writer in a very American way. I seem always to be writing about a moral choice and . . . well, that's for the critics to worry about.

III

On the terrace of the Trattoria Paris, in the Trastevere section of Rome. The motorbikes roared and blasted past us, a thin hedge away, as we dined and talked.

Int: Do you feel that your early interest in history and politics has done a great deal in shaping you as a novelist?

GV: Yes. You know Bernard Shaw used to say that religion and politics . . . in the large sense . . . are the only things that should concern a man; they certainly fascinate me though they are currently unfashionable preoccupations. The contemporary novel has split: on the one hand there is the private universe novel, unrelated to the society around it, unrelated to the fact of death. I suppose Nathalie Sarraute has taken it quite as far as anyone in our period . . . the anti-novel (old-fashioned actually . . . the Goncourts used to write them, and very glum they were). Then there are the busy popular novels. All that concern over who divorces whom and why this marriage failed and who's to get custody of those children and finally, who cares? Even Maisie has got to know a very great deal to save that sort of novel. And love! Dear God, the horror Love has become in our culture! Mr. X. don't write so good, but he does feel Love is the only thing which matters, and Compassion, too . . . and everyone gets a warm glow from Mr. X's stylized compassion. It is the stunning cliché of our literature, and the largest lie about man's estate. Whitehead once wrote that the way to assess a society is not by what it says of itself but those things it does not say, the never-mentioned, the taken-for-granted. Well, it seems to me that the underlying assumption of our society is that Love (something vague, anodyne, splendid) is every man's due and of course not only is it not every man's due, it is not always desirable. Flaubert was fascinated by that theme! Bovarism . . . Only his Emma was a woman of meagre intelligence while some of our very best writers are neatly impaled on this same folly. A satire on the Romantic assumption is in order now.

How wonderful to be the first contemporary novelist *not* to tack the ensign of Love to his mast. Paul Bowles of course attempted the reverse in *Let It Come Down*; at the end, his protagonist achieves perfect alienation . . . I suppose it's the same thing turned inside out but it was amiable to read.

Int: Then you would deal with the grand problems?
GV: Yes! the great emotions, the great crises . . . anything to keep from surrendering to the idea that we are all victimized by the hugeness of society. Even if this is true, one should still attack the giant head-on; the alternative is paralysis or, worse, deliberate smallness. *We all know so much more than we write.* And why don't we write it? Because we are afraid of being thought stupid or wicked or . . . unlovable.

IV

Bricktop's Club, under the Via Veneto, Rome. After Bricktop sang her definitive version of "Miss Otis Regrets," we settled down in a corner for some quiet drinking, and to finish our interview.

Int: Could you tell me a little of your working methods?
GV: Novels in longhand, plays on the typewriter, the morning hours. I begin with a vague idea of the knot to be tied or untied. I always think of every writer having in his head a repertory theatre with a resident company of players. Some play themselves over and over again, some are more protean. When I decide the knot, I "cast" the novel, using the actors I need. Sometimes I mis-cast. Sometimes I curse the short-comings of my company but I can't fire them: they are aspects of one's own personality . . . they have term contracts.

Int: Do you rewrite much?
GV: I write first drafts with great speed but the older I get (a familiar observation, I know) I rewrite more and more. When I first started, it was like working in egg-tempera—flat, quick-drying, on a wall, one got it right or one didn't. In shorter works like *Williwaw* I got it right. In others I got it wrong. I'm more an oil-painter now. More deliberate. A good deal less certain.

Int: Do you make notes or outlines: keep a notebook?
GV: No, I always lose them, because I hate to re-read them. I jot things down occasionally, then never look at them again. Never have more than one page of random notes for an entire novel.

Int: What would you consider the perfect novel: the novel you'd most wish to read?

GV: The terrible thing is, I don't want to read *a* novel—I never have. When I read fiction with any delight it has always been when I've the time to read the whole of a man's work, rather than one book.

Int: Who gives you greatest pleasure?

GV: Well, different works at different times and in different moods. I suppose my greatest pleasure still comes from Apuleius and Petronius, "the bright pagan world." Then I've read all of Flaubert, Proust, Henry James, Meredith, and Peacock, who for a certain kind of thing I often try to do, is the most relevant model. The novel of ideas: a most imprecise designation. Everybody, of course, would like to have written *Le Grand Meaulnes*.

Int: Any others who have been signposts for you?

GV: I don't know. One's tendency is to fake influences later, to rearrange history. I suppose Gibbon has had as profound an effect on me as any writer. I don't mean stylistically so much as the effect of his attitude. Then one goes through phases: Lawrence's *Women in Love*, and Mann's *The Magic Mountain* and *Tonio Kröger*. When I was very young the greatest influence—don't know if I dare say it—was Shakespeare. I read all Shakespeare when I was 14 at Los Alamos. *The Yale Shakespeare*, a play to a volume, I read the lot.

Int: And contemporaries?

GV: I am much drawn to the moral fabulists William Golding (*The Lord of the Flies*) and John Bowen (*After the Rain, The Truth Shall Not Help Us*), to Paul Bowles in his short stories. Or to mention someone doing what I try to do: Lawrence Durrell in his Alexandria novels—*Justine, Balthazar*, etc.—it is dazzling work.

Int: Now a question of style: what led from the documentary style of your first books to the extravagance of *The Judgment of Paris*?

GV: I found that naturalism wasn't natural for me. When I began at 19 to write in a hard flat style it was because that seemed to me the only way to write; it was the national manner. Not till I finished my third book did I realize the style was inadequate for my purposes, and that I must find my own voice and tone. *The Season of Comfort* was the midway work, an experiment and a debacle.

Int: That historical romance, *A Search for the King*, how did that pop up in the list of your books?

GV: A *jeu d'esprit*. I like the fabulous, the invented, and I dislike repeating myself. I am not captive to one region nor to one unflinching attitude toward life. I am always conscious that we live, in Sir Thomas Browne's phrase—"in divided and distinguished worlds," and I should never be so presumptuous as to say finally, "That is it!"

Int: Have you consciously designed the different pitch, or tone, of each of the books?

GV (*thoughtfully*): It comes out of the subject and out of oneself at the time. I am a dry clown who has often miscast himself in the drama; when I've gone wrong in novels it has usually been that my view was not, simply, the useful one of the subject . . . It seems to me, when I am playwriting seriously, that I'm not writing. Yet the emotional concentration is the same. Final relief is more gratifying, yet it's like doing charades. Cousin germane to prose yet not prose.

Int: A couple of last points . . . didn't you stir up a hornet's nest in America a year or so ago . . . some opinions on the novel . . . ?

GV: Yes. I wrote in *The New York Times*, and again in *The Reporter* articles stating very tentatively the proposition that the novel as a popular art form was ended. Now its decline, from the point of view of general interest, is a fact, and I took the line that the fault (this is the reverse of the busy review-ers) is the public's, not the writer's. We have never had more interesting writ-ers than we do today. But the public has sneaked off, and I suggested that the novel, which after all is only 300 years old in our language, was perhaps an inter-regnum form, and that the public, from the Greek mysteries to televi-sion, had always preferred the dramatic event.

Int: Your contemporaries mounted high horse over this?

GV: Yes. Yet no one bothered to argue the central premise: the brief life of the novel in our language—of which we can observe the origins, flowering, and decline. But then they don't read too carefully, which rather proves the point. Anyway, from what I have seen of the young today, the bright ones are inter-ested in sociology, philosophy at second hand, and of course, criticism.

Int: Ah-ha, and now we come to the inevitable question. What about criticism in America?

GV: It's either a monkish avocation conducted in the Academy or it is simply garrulous newspaper writing, and that perfect justice of which we all dream (even if it is summary execution!) is denied us.

Int: Have you noted any critical ideas of any importance in America?

GV: I wouldn't know! I read a good deal of criticism, but only as a vice, not so good as reading science fiction, rather better than reading mystery stories. But I do admire the confidence of our nobler critics. They've got it made, and they know it!

Int: Do you think writing for movies, television and so forth is corroding to a writer's more serious work?

GV: Unfortunately, one has to earn a living. For me it was less compromising to write for films than to teach, or review other people's books. Or journalism. Yet there is a destructive element in writing for hire and it is, simply, indifference: a man's defense when he believes or is made to believe that he is misusing his talent (and the world which was indifferent to the talent itself is usually eager to point out its misuse). The sullen response—and especially if he is successful in a worldly way—is indifference. And it must be fought against in the dark hours for indifference is death to the artist. Somewhere in that is a peculiarly American tragedy.

Gore Vidal: The *Fag Rag* Interview

John Mitzel, Steven Abbott, and the Gay Study
Group / 1974

Fag Rag: Have allegations of homosexuality ever been used to ruin anyone in politics in your lifetime as far as you know?

Gore Vidal: The senator from Massachusetts, David Ignatius Walsh, tried to make my father when my father was a West Point cadet. Chased my father and his roommate, who had been down for the inauguration of Woodrow Wilson. Senator Walsh picked them up. They were both very innocent West Pointers. My father said it was just appalling. He chased them around the room. West Point was very innocent in those days. When my father joined Roosevelt's administration, he went absolutely to pieces when he had to go before a Senate committee. I always told him that way in the back of his mind there was the memory of his bad experience of Senator Walsh. So he regarded all senators as potential rapists and pederasts. Walsh was caught during the war in a boy whorehouse, supposedly frequented by Nazi sympathizers, in Brooklyn, with a man who will be nameless—Virgil Thomson. Not together, but Virgil was also caught. One newspaper started to break the story. Walsh was chairman of naval affairs, as well as the master of Massachusetts, and he was the Cardinal's business man. Roosevelt, under his wartime powers, said that any newspaper that printed this would be prosecuted and shut down. The *New York Post* printed it in the first edition, then got the word. Nothing ever appeared. And Walsh? Nothing ever happened to him. He was re-elected in due course. There wasn't anybody in Massachusetts from the little birds on the Common who didn't know what David Walsh was up to.

FR: The Jenkins thing made such an enormous scandal. At the same time you apparently have no problem.

GV: I stay away from YMCA men's rooms, for one thing.

FR: We understand that J. Edgar Hoover actually sent him a bouquet of flowers. He was the only one in Washington who showed Jenkins any sympathy.
GV: Hoover cared.

FR: He was helping to give Hoover work.
GV: After all, I dedicated *An Evening with Richard Nixon* to "J. Edgar Hoover and . . .

FR: Clyde Tolson . . .
GV: With appreciation."

FR: You've said that you didn't think that anyone was a homosexual.
GV: I've always said it was just an adjective. It's not a noun, though it's always used as a noun. Put it the other way. What is a heterosexual person? I've never met one. When you say Lyndon Johnson and Adlai Stevenson behaved like two typical heterosexuals over the weekend, in their response, well, I don't know what they had in common. To me, it's just descriptive of an act.

FR: What about faggot or fag, the way we use it today? For example, in the title of the paper *Fag Rag*?
GV: I prefer the word faggot which I tend to use myself. I have never allowed actively in my life the word "gay" to pass my lips. I don't know why I hate that word.

FR: I think it's because *The Advocate* and the bourgeois press have picked up on it and made it into a noun.
GV: Also, I mean, historically it meant a girl of easy virtue in the seventeenth century. They'd say: "Is she gay?" Which meant: "Is she available?" And this, I don't think, is highly descriptive of anybody. It's just a bad word. You see, I don't think you need a word for it. This is what you have to evolve. These words have got to wither away in a true Hegelian cycle.

FR: A lot of homosexuals seem to be very concerned about whether they are called gays, faggots, fairies, or homosexuals.
GV: I would give it as a general warning: it may not apply to anybody in your generation, but certainly in the case of mine that I could have been, from

1948 on, The Official Spokesman. But I have no plans to be so limited. I'm a generalist, and I'm interested in a great many other things. Knowing the mania of the media, they want everybody to be in a pigeonhole. Oh, yes. He's The Official Fag. Oh, yes. He's The Official Marxist. And I have never allowed myself to be pigeonholed like that. Also I don't regard myself as one thing over another. The point is, why not discard all the words? Say that all sexual acts have parity. Which is my line.

FR: In *Fag Rag 5* we reprinted an article by Robert Duncan, "The Homosexual in Society," from Dwight Macdonald's old magazine *Politics*. Duncan used the word "jam" and I had never heard it.
GV: "Jam" was a much-used word. Kind of trade, but not really trade. Pretty hard to get. Perhaps when the fact was removed the word withered away too. No one seemed to be impossible. "Jam" only referred to boys. You'll find "jam" in *The City and the Pillar*, I think. I did a little glossary in there in my World Almanac way. "Dirt" was a word; that was for a bad piece of trade. I'm supposed to have coined the phrase "Last year's trade is this year's competition." That's in *The City and the Pillar*. I noticed it was quoted in *Fag Rag 6*. I don't think it was original with me, but I get the credit because I was the first to write it.

FR: Something that strikes me in the *Gay Sunshine* interviews is that at some point or other, the interviewees deal with the issue of their own homosexuality and their writing. They act as though homosexuality, the desire for sex, particularly sex with youth—which may not be at all an issue with you—is an obstacle to writing. During the period of sexual activity there is a great deal less writing.
GV: I don't understand that at all. But Hemingway said something very much like that. He always liked to maintain sexual continence when he was writing seriously.

FR: Are you sexually active when you write?
GV: The more active I am the better I write. I'm much more interested in economics and class than sex. All this is part of the middle class, part of the Puritan work ethic. You keep your seed in your bank and it collects interest; you have too many drafts on it you weaken it. This is a Protestant, work ethic,

middle-class thing. It was my very good fortune not to be born middle class. So I'm at a completely different vantage point.

FR: Do you think you're similar to the working class, in this respect?
GV: Well, that's what's always been claimed by the British, and I think so. The fact is that for us there was really no fuss about sex. You did as much as you could. I'm fascinated by this book about Vita Sackville-West and Harold Nicolson, *Portrait of a Marriage.* That's really mind-blowing to middle-class Americans. Harold Nicolson was a relentless chaser of Guardsmen and Vita Sackville-West of cunt. This is the condition of people who are not trapped into that economic middle-class tightness, and the worry of always keeping up appearances, the worry that they're always going to be "done in" by somebody. The working class, God knows, they're filled with terrible passion and prejudice, but give them a sexual act to perform that seems amusing . . . In Texas—that relentless Bible belt—there's nobody who's not available. It's like Italy.

FR: How do you contrast the sort of decadent Puritanism with sensuality— of which you've always been an advocate—in Italy?
GV: The Italians are naturally sensual and opportunistic about sex. They don't fuss. That's one of the reasons why there are really no queer bars.

FR: The interviews that writers give to *Gay Sunshine* seem to dwell on promiscuity. Your life seems to be very different.
GV: As promiscuous as I can make it.

FR: Yeah, but you have more style than almost any other writer. I loved that story in one of your essays about your going to bed with Kerouac.
GV: [*Laughs.*]

FR: So much for the "Tell—
GV: "Tell It Like It Is" school.

FR: You have been very open in your life in dealing with taboo. First in *The City and the Pillar*, in many of your essays, and then with *Myra Breckinridge.* Where do you draw the line? Is the line constantly shifting?

In the interview you gave to *Viva* you were asked: "Was your first sexual experience with a man or a woman?"
GV: I think I had a very funny answer. I don't think she got it right. I said: "I was much too polite to ask."

FR: Were you younger than eighteen when you had your first experience?
GV: Oh my God! I was eleven! And I was brought up in the South.

FR: You loved your father very much, didn't you?
GV: I adored him, yes.

FR: And Hugh D. Auchincloss was your stepfather?
GV: Yeah. I liked Hughdie. But he's a magnum of chloroform.

FR: Do you still see the Auchinclosses much?
GV: I see my sister. There are so many Auchinclosses around you are bound to see some. They're always around.

FR: Were you an only child?
GV: I was an only child until I was about thirteen.

FR: Even though you were not middle class, was there ever a time in that whole period that you felt you worried about your sexuality?
GV: Never. Absolutely never.

FR: No identity crisis? No breakdown?
GV: I did exactly what I wanted to do all the time.

FR: You were very beautiful when you were young. You're good-looking now, too, but pretty in your youth.
GV: So I read in all these memoirs of my great beauty.

FR: Yes. Truman Capote said you took him to the Everard Baths.
GV: I did take Truman to the Everard. Couldn't have been funnier. "I just don't like it." [*Mimics Truman Capote.*]

FR: Does Truman go to the trucks? What does he do?
GV: He falls in love passionately with air-conditioning repair men. He had a tragic affair recently with an air-conditioning repair man.

FR: There's one thing you said about Capote's writing: "So like Faith Baldwin." If that's true about his life, he's got the inspiration.
GV: I can't read him because I'm diabetic.

FR: Regarding youth, are you never attracted by younger people?
GV: Oh, yes. I said I don't flatter the young, either as a writer or as a performer. And I don't flatter them sexually. That doesn't mean I don't like them.

FR: Do you enjoy being seduced as much as seducing?
GV: No. I hate it.

FR: Getting back to the right-wing, closet, repressed mentality—*Point of Order* has been playing here in theatres. The David Schine-Roy Cohn thing is intriguing. We've heard stories of them naked snapping towels in hotels. Did that come out at the time?
GV: We used to sing "Come Cohn or Come Schine." Sure. [*Laughter*]. Senator Flanders of Vermont, noble old boy, tried to not only knock them off with it but McCarthy himself.

FR: The whole Army-McCarthy hearings were meant as a cover-up for this homosexual relationship?
GV: Yeah. McCarthy himself was homosexual. This sort of wing of "preverts."

FR: Do you have a conscious feeling about your writing and politics? Do you feel you've got a political role?
GV: No.

FR: Even though you're not in politics per se, you have a base. When I saw you on *The Dick Cavett Show* the other night, after you destroyed that poor Jesuit [John McLaughlin, a speech writer and deputy special assistant to Nixon], I remarked that what's so refreshing about seeing you compared to others on the tube is that you come out with the truth very casually.
GV: I'm not running for office. I don't have to worry about the unpleasant mail. I made the decision in '64 that I was not going to go to Congress. It was very plain that I would have been elected if I had run. And, I turned down, in the beginning of '68, the nomination and support for the Senate.

FR: You were thinking of running in '68?
GV: As late as '68. This was before *Myra Breckinridge* came out. I finally told them. I said: "Look kids, I think without this book we might do it, but with this book, we won't be able to get through."

FR: Have you thought much about the Bicentennial and the country remembering its beginning—I know your essays in *Homage to Daniel Shays.*
GV: Bicentennial? I wrote *Burr* as my meditation on the political process.

FR: Politically, do you see any opportunity for using the whole remembrance of the origins of the country in a political way?
GV: One tactic which is useful: you can always promote radical causes under the guise of Going Back to the Constitution. And sometimes quite legitimately. The Bill of Rights is still a radical document. I find sometimes when I'm trying to be an advocate, trying to convince a really difficult audience, you can always refer back to the origins and tell them that this is the way it was meant to be.

FR: When you've got Daniel Shays, Tom Paine, and all the rest of them, you've got some rich potential.
GV: Yes.

FR: What do you think of the talk show circuit?
GV: There's a whole technique to it. You just have to study how to do it. Use it to your own purposes.

FR: How do you get through mass media with what is essentially an anti-mass message?
GV: You have to become an explainer. You have to make up your mind before you go on that you are going to make the following points. Don't make too many because they can't remember them. You are going to say: if I want to get the sex laws changed, I will then have thought it out in my head how I'll lead the conversation. It doesn't make any difference what they ask; you just go right on. "Yes, that's interesting," and go right on to the point you were going to make. It's like any other kind of skill. You have to learn how to do it. It's very useful.

FR: But the media itself. It's a sort of reverse from McLuhan.
GV: It's better than nothing. People don't listen. All day yesterday and the day before in Chicago, little old ladies, cabdrivers who I know hate my guts, all came up and wanted to talk about the exchange with the priest on Cavett's show. They were all very pleased by it.

FR: Did you talk with the Jesuit after the show?
GV: He told me that Walter Cronkite is a notorious left-winger.

FR: The nature of the bourgeois press, the very fact that they teamed you with someone like that, does this make you feel compromised having to deal with slime? That you're on a par with slime?
GV: No! I'm the detergent!

FR: I think you did an "Inouye." [Senator Daniel K. Inouye] You said: "Lies. Lies. Priest."
GV: No, no. I said: "You are lying, priest. Think to your immortal soul." The Brother gulped on that.

FR: The thing that bothers me is that every other elite—you come out of the liberal elite—in Germany, France, etc., produces leaders, phenomenal people.
GV: No revolution ever came from the bottom.

FR: Exactly. But the United States, just in the last ten years, has had an attempt on the part of many people who come out of the elite—
GV: An attempt to do what? Change things?

FR: Yes. From the left. We have no leadership. The media have taken every figure in the movement, just to take one example.
GV: And used them up. I watched Abbie Hoffman from the beginning since the first time he appeared on the scene—at a debate between Tom Hayden and me. Abbie was in the audience. He got up and harangued. I could see they loved him on television. "Freako!" "Wild man!" I said to myself: If that man is around in three years I'll be surprised. They'll use him up. And then there will be another wild man, and he will be on a different kick.

FR: David Bowie now.
GV: Yeah. Survival in the United States is not easy whether it is for a writer or a singer or anyone else. Certainly is a critical society. It's not easy at all.

FR: You didn't make the "Enemies List."
GV: That's not true! I was number 212. I can't remember. I wasn't in the top twenty, which was one of their ways of destroying me.

FR: Have you ever had IRS, passport, or FBI trouble?
GV: I've been broken into twice by the FBI when I was with the People's Party. As was Spock. You can always tell because they never take anything. They should at least take the TV set, but they're so damn lazy and it's heavy.

FR: These are agents?
GV: Yeah. Then they would go through papers, papers, papers.

FR: Was this under Johnson or Nixon?
GV: Nixon.

FR: Have they ever tried to talk with you?
GV: No. I am on the FBI list of people never to talk to about anything, because I went after Hoover about twelve years ago.

FR: Before it was fashionable.
GV: Yeah. And really let him have it.

FR: Did you ever meet the man?
GV: Yes.

FR: Did he look you in the eye? My brother always told me you can always tell a queer because he'll never look you in the eye.
GV: Somebody was asking me. Said he thought Richard Nixon was obviously homosexual. I said: "Why do you think that?" He said: "You know, that funny, uncoordinated way he moves." I said: "Yeah. Like Nureyev."

FR: What was your motivation behind the People's Party with Spock?
GV: I didn't have any. I was just sort of riding along with it. We started the New Party in '68. The idea was simply to try and make a representative party. It wasn't worth doing. It was nothing but young group therapists who believe in "elitism" or "structure." It was pointless.

FR: *Fag Rag* tries to see homosexuality in America at this point as being a vehicle for radical expression.
GV: Yet when you get with any radical blacks or any radical anything, forget it.

FR: Remember the quote: "The place for a woman in the movement is on her back?" One wonders if there isn't room now for what Hofstadter did with paranoia in American politics, something to do with sexual repression. I think *Myra B.* is the tip of the iceberg.
GV: There is considerable work to be done. Every intelligent person in the country knows the thing is a joke.

FR: I don't know. I'm very skeptical. Though I identify with your literary works, I sometimes wonder why you still have this tropism towards belief in the faith. Perhaps they could be manipulated in the right direction. When it comes to personality and style and reason and argument against the 4.4 percent and their money, you're going to lose.
GV: Well, I don't know. I have seen attitudes change a good deal since I began. This magazine of yours would not have existed twenty-five years ago. I think the 4.4 percent changes in its own inscrutable way, but I do not think I believe it will be done by intelligent advocacy. I have said if it is going to change, it is going to be collapse. The system will collapse. It does not work now. The government does not work. And the economic system is not working. Something will crash. Who picks up the pieces? I would want a social democracy as my replacement. I just want to get the goddamn population down by about two-thirds. Then there's plenty of room for everybody and plenty of wealth for everybody.

FR: The point that continues to plague me is the lack of leadership. I do not see any positive political strategy.
GV: You need a new party. You come back to it again. I made my effort along with these others in '68 and again in '72.

FR: But what is the base?
GV: If you saw the manifesto I did ["A Dialogue with Myself," *Esquire*, October 1968], you have got to have a party of human survival.

FR: Regarding the issue of censorship, I'm doing an article on John Horne Burns, particularly the job the critics did on him. Did you know him?
GV: Yes.

FR: I find in researching him that there are only three pieces still extant since his death: your piece in the *New York Times Book Review*, Brigid Brophy's piece in the Sunday *London Times* magazine, and a piece in *One* magazine, a Los Angeles-based homophile publication.
GV: He was obliterated by the press.

FR: In rereading him, there is a certain circumspection that comes through.
GV: He's being careful.

FR: Very careful. The homosexual passion is there, breaking through.
GV: He was careful in the first one, *The Gallery*. *Lucifer with a Book*, however, is when the critics let him have it. I think *The Gallery* is certainly the best of the "war books." It was much applauded, much admired. You see, he did six or seven books before *The Gallery*. He was an awful man. Monster. Envious, bitchy, drunk, Bitter. Which was why *The Gallery* was so marvelous. It was his explosion into humanity at a fairly late date. I think he was in his early thirties, after a half-assed career as an English teacher and writing unprintable novels.

FR: Have you ever seen any of the manuscripts?
GV: No. But I've been told about them by Freddie Warburg who published him in England who said they were all pretty bad. They must be around somewhere.

FR: How did he die? I can't find that out. Was he killed?
GV: No, no, no. He was drinking himself to death in Florence. Every day he would go to the Grand Hotel and stand in the bar and drink Italian brandy, which is just about the worst thing in the world. And chew on fruit drops candy. He always said that it would counteract the drunkenness. He was

living with a doctor, an Italian veterinarian. They had a rather stormy relationship but nothing sinister about it. One day he was drunk at a bar, wandered out in the hot midday sun and had a stroke. Cerebral hemorrhage.

FR: At age thirty-seven?

GV: I think he wanted to die. They really wiped him out on *Lucifer with a Book*. We were both, in 1947, the leading writers in the country. The ineffable John W. Aldridge began his career with a piece in *Harper's* magazine, out of which came his book *After the Lost Generation*. He reversed all his judgments later. He began his career as our great admirer. He discovered we were dealing with the horrors of homosexuality. He then exactly reversed himself and began to applaud the Jewish giants who are still with us today. Aldridge is nothing if not a rider of bandwagons. So Burns was absolutely at the top then. We were both admired as War Writers. To be a War Writer was pretty gutsy. You can't knock a War Writer. Then *City and the Pillar*. Then *Lucifer with a Book*. They said: "Oh, my God! What is this we've been admiring?"

FR: Did the straight critics pick up on the homosexual themes in *Lucifer with a Book* and *The Gallery*?

GV: They got it in *Lucifer with a Book*. He hit you on the head with it.

FR: One never knows the mentality of reviewers.

GV: We wrote differently in those days, but it was perfectly plain what was going on at that school.

FR: And was that reason to condemn the book?

GV: Entirely. Any writer suspected of being homosexual. When Norman Mailer met me in 1950, he said: "You know, Gore, I thought you were the Devil." Just terrible but true. The only thing that they respect, that they put up with, is a freak like Capote, who has the mind of a Kansas housewife, likes gossip, and gets all shuddery when she thinks about boys murdering people.

FR: So Mailer went after you?

GV: They all did. However, Capote never really touched on the subject. He is a Republican housewife from Kansas with all the prejudices. Just as Norman Mailer is a VFW commander in Schenectady.

FR: It's rather amazing that just as you were accepted, really, for something like *The City and the Pillar*, just as it was becoming acceptable to deal with homosexuality as such, you came out with *Myra Breckinridge* which even among homosexuals is controversial.

GV: I always remember a remark Faulkner made about Hemingway. Faulkner was very guarded in talking about his contemporaries. He once said to me: "You know, Hemingway's problem is that he never takes chances." You have got to keep going as far out as you can, as far as your imagination will take you.

FR: That is the chasm I see in your life and work. While on the one hand you have a fascination with power, you know more accurately than almost any other writer or politician in America the kind of mediocrities the American electorate coughs up, quashing out any kind of leadership. On the other hand you're such an avant-garde writer, capturing the sensibility so exquisitely at any given time. You should understand that in America there is no true way of jiving them. You can't publish *Myra* without getting the housewife at the supermarket to go: No. Unh-uh. No way. Look at the job they did on Rocky when he married Happy.

GV: Never underestimate their corruption. If you can amuse them, they will forgive you just about anything. And if you are a success, they will crown you.

FR: What kind of success?

GV: Money.

FR: Is that why the historical novels?

GV: I'm fascinated with the origins of the United States and Christianity, which were the two subjects I took on.

FR: Do the historical novels make more money than the earliest ones like *Williwaw* and *In a Yellow Wood*?

GV: Oh yes.

FR: Why did you publish three mysteries in the Fifties under the pseudonym "Edgar Box"?

GV: I was broke. I needed money. I wrote each of them in a week. Except one of them. I wrote half of it in three days and the house burned down. I had to go back to it, and I had forgotten who was the murderer. So I had to think of a whole new plot halfway through it. Try to figure out which one I had in mind. Ten thousand words a day, seven days.

FR: Did you have little charts on the wall? Esther here and Warren in the window?
GV: No. When you're young, it is the most amazing thing. You can do formidable things.

FR: Formula or formidable?
GV: Formidable. Formula takes maturity.

FR: It seems like the other way around. It seems that someone who's such a craftsman as you would avoid formula.
GV: I think you will find it takes a long time to find your tone of voice. I didn't until *Judgment of Paris*. I published five or six books before I really got it. I wouldn't say got it right, but got it accurate. I was now coming through. For us, it was very difficult to overcome Hemingway and *The New Yorker*. That style was just so oppressive. One hardly knew of anything else. Anything else sounded affected in your own voice.

FR: Did you know Paul Goodman in the Fifties?
GV: Yes. I'd see him around. I never knew him well.

FR: How do you measure his impact in terms of the sexual thing?
GV: Well, I haven't read that diary or journals he kept or anything, but he was obviously very daring considering that he made himself the guru of the middlebrow educationalists.

FR: True. It was not until Sputnik that he almost nurtured his own following.
GV: Yes. I was rather startled that in a way he had that much integrity. I always thought he was a bitter man. Playing up to a constituency. There is nothing worse than playing up to the young, a game I will never get into.

FR: Of course he was fascinated by the young. Perhaps that explains a part of his sexual fascination.
GV: Yes. You can be sexually fascinated by them and still not flatter them. I think flattery had a lot to do with his sexual techniques. It has nothing to do with mine.

FR: In *Burr*, you mention a Senator Breckinridge who was Buchanan's vice president. And in the 1940s there was a famous transsexual—
GV: In San Francisco?

FR: From a very rich family. She was supposedly the biggest queen in the world. And her name was Breckinridge. Is that true?
GV: Well. It is true. Bunny Breckinridge. [*Laughter.*] Now this is the most extraordinary thing. I was reminded years later that I had never met Bunny Breckinridge, but that everybody that I knew had known him and talked to me about him. This was in the Forties. Then it just went right out of my head, and Breckinridge came into my head. I just wanted a very solid-sounding name with lots of syllables. Myra would not be content with just being Smith.

FR: But the rumor was that she was related to the famous former V.P., Vice President Breckinridge.
GV: Oh well.

FR: We figured: Vidal's into politics; he'll know that.
GV: No. I didn't know that.

FR: It's documented, I'm told, in a book called *Queer Street, USA*.
GV: About Bunny Breckinridge?

FR: Yes. Was she a transsexual or just a big queen?
GV: Just a big queen. Very rich.

FR: Why did you choose not to go to college?
GV: I was supposed to go to Harvard. It occurred to me. I went into the army at seventeen, got out at twenty. What was the point of going into another institution when I had already written my first novel?

FR: But did you know that "education" was a fraud then, too? Or just a drag on your career?
GV: No. In those days we thought you could actually go to a place like Harvard and it would be worth doing. But only if you wanted to lead a conventional life and rise in a law firm or something. I had the great pleasure of lecturing at

Harvard while all my classmates from Exeter were undergraduates. Greatest moment of my life, I mean I really rubbed it in. It's all been downhill since.

FR: What about the poetry you wrote while at Exeter? Has it ever been published?
GV: I hope not. There's a book coming out about me. A professor has gone and read it all.

FR: I suppose literary criticism is one of the penalties for being prolific when you're young. By middle age, you have to start dealing with critical biographies.
GV: Writers younger than I am like Updike and Harold Pinter. There are more books about Harold Pinter than there are about Chekhov. Most extraordinary thing.

FR: It's Sputnik again. It's all the college-educated *Time* subscribers who buy books now and belong to book clubs.
GV: Nobody reads these books. It is make-work so you can get tenure in universities. Who's not been done from the Forties? Ah, there's Vidal. Willingham. Let's do Willingham.

FR: I saw a Susskind show recently where he had all the old stable of Philco Playhouse writers.
GV: Oh, really?

FR: Chayefsky. And who is the Australian who writes novels now?
GV: Sumner Locke Elliot. A great wit. Very charming.

FR: Were you part of that stable?
GV: Sure. I did *Visit to a Small Planet.*

FR: Chayefsky said he did *Marty* for $900. He wasn't bitter about it now because he's making lots of money, but the other guests did a little complaining. Now David Susskind and all the critics—
GV: David was their agent.

FR: My impression is that you did well. *Visit* went on to become a movie and a Broadway play.
GV: Yeah. Chayefsky went on. He made several movies.

FR: Did you make money out of your television plays?
GV: I never seemed to be able to make more than $7000 a year, year in and year out.

FR: But you were published before you went and they were not.
GV: Oh yes.

FR: They were just sort of Kitchen Writers from Brooklyn.
GV: Radio men. Radio joke writers.

FR: You do a lot of projects. It was mentioned in *Atlantic* that you were doing a screenplay entitled *Plaza*. I looked for this and never saw it.
GV: That was Robert Aldrich. Rather not a bad idea. He blew the financing. It never got made.

FR: Also, I read in *Life* that you were doing a novel called *Dreams*. Then I never read anything else about this.
GV: I wrote part of it. I never finished it. I think it's mostly going into *Myron*.

FR: Concerning your relationship with Howard Austen. What is the financial arrangement and/or how will you leave your money?
GV: I have lived twenty-three years with the same person. Presumably because I am older I will die first and just leave it to him. That's all.

FR: Do you know anything about other "gay" authors who died and left money?
GV: Somerset Maugham left Alan Searle very well provided for.

FR: Wasn't there a big scandal with the Maugham estate?
GV: Maugham was just so ga-ga. He was making trouble all over the place. He tried to cut his grandson out by saying that his daughter was not really his daughter, and she was—curiously enough.

FR: Gide was married. Did he have a family?
GV: He had no children. I don't know where Gide's money went. Probably to Marc Allegret, the director.

FR: Will Capote be very rich when he dies?
GV: Capote has no money.

FR: Really? Living at UN Plaza?
GV: This is one of the reasons *why* he has no money. He thinks he's Bunny Mellon—to get back to another Bunny. He thinks he's a very rich Society Lady, and spends a great deal of money.

FR: Where does Auden's money go?
GV: He had no money.

FR: He leaves an estate, though.
GV: If he left $10,000, I would be very surprised.

FR: What will Isherwood do?
GV: He would leave it to Don Bachardy, and to anyone he wants to.

FR: Do you enjoy the historical novel? Or is it a drudge so that you can do something mad in between?
GV: No. I really like them very much.

FR: Among American fiction writers, who do you read for enjoyment?
GV: Calder Willingham. Southern writer. Very funny.

FR: I couldn't get through *Providence Island*.
GV: No. That's bad. But *Rambling Rose* is new and rather good. I love *Geraldine Bradshaw*. They're pussy novels, you're right. Just this terrible, relentless quest for pussy. Just full of failure, which is like life, which is what I like about it.

FR: Did you get through *Gravity's Rainbow*?
GV: I don't think I'm going to get to that. I have tried the academic writers. There is a sort of division of literature which I cast a benign eye upon.

I'm sure there is a place for it: novels which are written to be used in the classroom. Since I think that's where the novel is going to end up, I think of myself as an anachronism, and *that* is the future. Someone like John Barth to me is just cement. Pynchon. I read *V.* Some of it is fun, but so heavy-handed. The jokes are so heavy, such awful names. Nabokov remembers him. He was in one of Nabokov's classes at Cornell. Nabokov thinks rather highly of him. Nabokov I usually enjoy, though not as much as he enjoys himself. I like old Saul Bellow. I find him cranky but true.

FR: Do you mind being exploited? For example, I just read Dotson Rader's new book *Blood Dues.*
GV: A little cunt. A real cunt.

FR: In *Blood Dues*, if it had not been for you and Tennessee Williams, there would be no book, except for his bloody nose at the end.
GV: I have no intention of reading that book. I read something he wrote in *Esquire* about me and Tennessee; that I had not gone to the church because I was afraid Tennessee would upstage me. Imagine a mind that would conceive that. Tennessee is one of my oldest friends. Vain as I am, that is not the sort of thing that would ever cross my mind.

FR: The whole Southern mentality is so foreign to me in a way. You had one foot into it. Is it easy to patronize Southern writers?
GV: When I began to write, they were the center of American literature. Much overpraised. Now they're rather underpraised. And the Jewish writers came along, bringing with them their stern patriarchal attitudes.

FR: What is the prospect for women's liberation, gay liberation and sensuality in America?
GV: I keep coming back to economics. I keep thinking about the collapse of the currency, the shortages in the world.

FR: It occurred to me a while ago that your whole prophecy of what is going to happen in this country would indicate that American literature as well as politics is gone, going. It has got to be replaced with something.
GV: I don't think it has to be replaced with anything. American literature has always been second-rate. The schools in America, which are also second-rate,

could never discuss this because their mandate rests upon pretending
that since we were briefly a great world empire, therefore we were a great
civilization. When you compare Mark Twain to George Eliot, or compare
Dostoevsky to Stephen Crane, or poor Hemingway to Proust, my god! Henry
James, a great novelist, became English.

FR: I think all of your work is in print except *A Season of Comfort*. This is
remarkable, and proof that you are saying something. My final question is:
Are queens different today in the Seventies then they were in the Forties?
GV: Ahhh, I don't know. That's an interesting thought, though it seems to me
that everything is the same always. Certain things are more open now than
they were then. But they were pretty open in the sort of ghetto life of the
Forties. And New York, Lexington Avenue, was very royal.

FR: Do you keep a diary?
GV: I kept one in '48. I sealed it and gave it to the University of Wisconsin
with my papers.

FR: To be opened after your death?
GV: After my death or the Second Coming, whichever comes first.

The Art of Fiction L: Gore Vidal

Gerald Clarke / 1974

From *Paris Review*, Fall 1974. Reprinted by permission of *The Paris Review*.
© *The Paris Review*.

Gore Vidal lives in a run-down penthouse above Rome's Largo Argentina: reconstructed temples from the pre-Augustan era are set incongruously in the middle of what looks to be Columbus Circle without the charm. It is August. Rome is deserted. The heat is breathtaking during the day, but at sundown a cool wind starts and the birds swarm in the blue-gold Tiepolo sky. He sits on a large terrace lined with plants in need of watering.

In photographs, or on television, Gore Vidal appears to be dark-haired and somewhat slight. He is neither. He stands six feet; his chest is broad and deep (a legacy of Alpine ancestors); despite constant attendance at a gymnasium, the once flat stomach is now reorganizing itself as a most definite paunch. He regards his own deterioration with fascination: "After all, in fifteen months I shall be fifty," he declares, apparently pleased and disturbed in equal parts.

His hair is light brown, evenly streaked with white. His teeth are meticulously capped. The agate-yellow eyes are myopic, and when he does not wear glasses he tends to squint. The voice . . . well, everyone knows the voice. He sits now in a broken wicker armchair; the baroque dome of San Andrea della Valle appears to float above his head. He wears a blue shirt, gray trousers, sandals. Although he talks naturally in complete sentences, he is not at ease talking about his own work . . . he prefers that others be the subject of his scrutiny. An accomplished debater, he tends to slip away from the personal, the inconvenient.

Interviewer: When did you first start writing?

Gore Vidal: I would suppose at five or six, whenever I learned how to read. Actually, I can't remember when I was *not* writing. I was taught to read by my grandmother. Central to her method was a tale of unnatural love called "The Duck and the Kangaroo." Then, because my grandfather Senator Gore was blind, I was required early on to read grown-up books to him, mostly constitutional law and, of course, the *Congressional Record*. The later continence of my style is a miracle, considering those years of piping the additional remarks of Mr. Borah of Idaho.

Int: When did you begin your first novel?
GV: At about seven. A novel closely based on a mystery movie I had seen, something to do with "the blue room" or "hotel" (not Stephen Crane's). I recall, fondly, that there was one joke. The character based on my grandmother kept interrupting everybody because "she had not been listening." Merriment in the family during the first reading. It doesn't take much to launch a wit. Then I wrote a great deal of didactic poetry, all bad. With puberty the poetry came to resemble "Invictus," the novels *Of Human Bondage*. Between fourteen and nineteen I must have begun and abandoned six novels.

Int: How far did you get on these novels?
GV: A few chapters, usually. I did get halfway through the one written before *Williwaw*. All about someone who deserted from the army—no doubt reflecting my state of mind, since I was in the army during the war (from seventeen to twenty). Unfortunately, my protagonist deserted to Mexico. Since I had never been to Mexico, I was obliged to stop.

Int: What were the other five about? School?
GV: No. I began the first really ambitious one when I was fourteen or fifteen. I had gone to Europe in the summer of '39 and visited Rome. One night I saw Mussolini in the flesh at the Baths of Caracalla—no, he was not bathing but listening to *Turandot*. The baths are used for staging operas. I thought him splendid! That jaw, that splendid emptiness. After all, I had been brought up with politicians. He was an exotic variation on something quite familiar to me. So I started a novel about a dictator in Rome, filled with intrigue and passion, Machiavellian *combinazione*. But that didn't get finished either, despite my close study of the strategies of E. Phillips Oppenheim.

Int: Finishing *Williwaw* at nineteen broke the barrier; it was published and you wrote three novels in quick succession.

GV: Yes. Every five minutes it seemed. Contrary to legend, I had no money. Since I lived on publishers' advances, it was fairly urgent that I keep on publishing every year. But of course I *wanted* to publish every year. I felt no strain, though looking back over the books I can detect a strain in the writing of them. Much of the thinness of those early novels is simply the pressure that I was under. Anyway, I've gone back and rewritten several of them. They are still less than marvelous but better than they were.

Int: What do you feel about going back and rewriting? Don't you think in a way that you're changing what another person, the younger Vidal, did?

GV: No. You are stuck with that early self for good or ill, and you can't do anything about it even if you want to—short of total suppression. For me, revising is mostly a matter of language and selection. I don't try to change the narrative or the point of view, except perhaps toward the end of *The City and the Pillar*. I felt obligated to try a new kind of ending. But something like *Dark Green, Bright Red* needed a paring away of irrelevancies— the fault of all American naturalistic writing from Hawthorne to, well, name almost any American writer today. I noticed recently the same random accretion of details in William Dean Howells—a very good writer, yet since he is unable to select the *one* detail that will best express his meaning, he gives us everything that occurs to him and the result is often a shapeless daydream. Twain, too, rambles and rambles, hoping that something will turn up. In his best work it does rather often. In the rest—painful logorrhea.

Int: You once said that the test of a good work, or a perfect work, is whether the author can reread it without embarrassment. How did you feel when you reread your early books?

GV: Sometimes less embarrassed than others. Rereading *Williwaw*, I was struck by the coolness of the prose. There is nothing in excess. I am still impressed by that young writer's control of his very small material. When I prepared the last edition, I don't suppose I cut away more than a dozen sentences. The next book, on the other hand, *In a Yellow Wood*, is in limbo forever. I can't rewrite it because it's so bad that I can't reread it. The effect, I fear, of meeting and being "ensorcelled" by Anaïs Nin. Or Jack London meets Elinor Glyn. Wow!

Int: What about your first "successful" novel, *The City and the Pillar?*
GV: A strange book because it was, as they say, the first of its kind, without
going into any great detail as to *what* its kind is. To tell such a story then was
an act of considerable moral courage. Unfortunately, it was not an act of very
great artistic courage, since I chose deliberately to write in the flat, gray,
naturalistic style of James T. Farrell. Tactically if not aesthetically, this was
for a good reason. Up until then homosexuality in literature was always
exotic: Firbank, on the one hand; green carnations, on the other. I wanted to
deal with an absolutely ordinary, all-American, lower-middle-class young
man and his world. To show the dead-on "normality" of the homosexual
experience. Unfortunately, I didn't know too many lower-middle-class,
all-American young men—except for those years in the army when I spent
a good deal of time blocking out my fellow soldiers. So I made it all up. But
the result must have had a certain authenticity. Tennessee Williams read it in
1948 and said of the family scenes, "Our fathers were very much alike."
He was surprised when I told him that Jim Willard and his family were all
invented. Tennessee also said, "I don't like the ending. I don't think you
realized what a good book you had written." At the time, of course, I thought
the ending "powerful."

Int: Now you've changed the ending to have the young man—Bob—not
killed by Jim, as he was originally.
GV: Yes. Twenty years ago it was thought that I had written a tragic ending
because the publishers felt that the public would not accept a happy
resolution for my tale of Sodom, my Romeo and his Mercutio. But this
wasn't true. The theme of the book which, as far as I know, no critic has ever
noticed, is revealed in the title, *The City and the Pillar*. Essentially, I was
writing about the romantic temperament. Jim Willard is so overwhelmed by
a first love affair that he finds all other lovers wanting. He can only live in
the past, as he imagined the past, or in the future as he hopes it will be when
he finds Bob again. He has no present. So whether the first love object is a
boy or girl is not really all that important. The novel was not about the city
so much as about the pillar of salt, the looking back that destroys. Nabokov
handled this same theme with infinitely greater elegance in *Lolita*. But I was
only twenty when I made my attempt, while he was half as old as time.
Anyway, my story could only have had a disastrous ending. Obviously, killing
Bob was a bit much even though the original narrative was carefully vague on

that point. Did he or didn't he kill him? Actually, what was being killed was the idea of perfect love that had existed only in the romantic's mind. The other person—the beloved object—had forgotten all about it.

Int: What is the procedure once a book is revised? Do publishers accept this with grace? Are the old books recalled from libraries?
GV: *Williwaw* and *Messiah* were only slightly altered, *The City and the Pillar* was much revised. *The Judgment of Paris* was somewhat cut but otherwise not much altered. *Dark Green, Bright Red* was entirely rewritten. Except for *The City and the Pillar*, the new versions first appeared in paperback. Later the revised *Messiah* and *The Judgment of Paris* were also reissued in hardcover. I have no idea what the publishers thought of all this. It is not wise to solicit the opinions of publishers—they become proud if you do. As lovers of the environment, I suspect they were pleased that the new versions were so much shorter than the old, thus saving trees. The original editions can also be found in the libraries, margins filled with lewd commentaries, and the worms busy in the binding.

Int: Has anyone else done such a wholesale revision of his past work?
GV: I shouldn't imagine that any American writer would want to do anything that reflected on the purity and the spontaneity of his genius at any phase of his sacred story. In the land of the free, one sentence must be as good as another because that is democracy. Only Henry James set out methodically to rewrite his early books for the New York edition. Some works he improved; others not. Tennessee, come to think of it, often rewrites old plays, stories . . . it's sort of a tic with him. Returning to an earlier time, different mood.

Int: You have said that *The Judgment of Paris* was your favorite of the early books.
GV: It was the first book I wrote when I settled in on the banks of the Hudson River for what proved to be twenty years of writing, my *croisée.* . . . Certainly *The Judgment of Paris* was the novel in which I found my own voice. Up until then I was very much in the American realistic tradition, unadventurous, monochromatic, haphazard in my effects. My subjects were always considerably more interesting than what I was able to do with them.

This is somewhat the reverse of most young writers, particularly young writers today.

Int: You mean they're proficient technically but don't have much to say?
GV: They appear to rely on improvisation to get them to the end of journeys that tend to be circular.

Int: Which works and which authors are you thinking of?
GV: Well, as I was talking I was thinking of a book—any book—by someone called Brautigan. I can never remember the titles. The last little book I looked at is about a librarian. Written in the see-Jane-run style. Very cheerful. Very dumb. Highly suitable for today's audience. But he's not exactly what I had in mind. There is one splendid new—to me—writer. Robert Coover. He, too, is circular, but the circles he draws enclose a genius of suggestion. Particularly that story in *Pricksongs and Descants* when the narrator creates an island for you *on the page*. No rude art his. Also *Omensetter's Luck* by William H. Gass. A case of language doing the work of the imagination, but doing it very well.

Int: What is there in writing except language?
GV: In the writing of novels there is the problem of how to shape a narrative. And though the search for new ways of telling goes on—I've written about this at terrible length*—I don't think there are going to be any new discoveries. For one thing, literature is not a science. There is no new formula. Some of us write better than others; and genius is never forced. There are signs that a number of writers—University or U-writers, as I call them—are bored with the narrative, character, prose. In turn they bore the dwindling public for novels. So Beckett stammers into silence, and the rest is cinema. Why not?

Int: But in the forties . . .
GV: In the forties I was working in the American tradition of straight narrative, not very different from John P. Marquand or John Steinbeck or

---

* "On the French New Novel," *Encounter* (December, 1967). Also, collected in *Homage to Daniel Shays* (Random House, 1972).

Ernest Hemingway. For me it was like trying to fence in a straitjacket. In fact, my first years as a writer were very difficult because I knew I wasn't doing what I should be doing, and I didn't know how to do what I ought to be doing. Even interestingly conceived novels like *Dark Green, Bright Red* or *A Search for the King* came out sounding like poor Jim Farrell on a bad day. Not until I was twenty-five, had moved to my house in the country, was poor but content, and started to write *The Judgment of Paris*, that suddenly I was all there, writing in my own voice. I had always had a tendency to rhetoric—Senator Borah, remember? But fearing its excess, I was too inhibited to write full voice. I don't know what happened. The influence of Anaïs Nin? The fact that I had stopped trying to write poetry and so the poetic line fused with the prose? Who knows? Anyway, it was a great release, that book. Then came *Messiah*. Unfortunately, my reputation in '54 was rock bottom. The book was ignored for a few years, to be revived in the universities. Dead broke, I had to quit writing novels for ten years—just as I was hitting my stride. I don't say that with any bitterness because I had a very interesting ten years. But it would have been nice to have gone on developing, uninterruptedly, from *Messiah*.

Int: What voice are you using now?
GV: My own. But I confess to a gift for mimicry. The plangent cries of Mrya are very unlike the studied periods of Aaron Burr, but the same throat, as it were (deep, deep), sings the song of each. I envy writers like Graham Greene who, year in and year out, do the same kind of novel to the delight of the same kind of reader. I couldn't begin to do that sort of thing. I have thrown away a number of successful careers out of boredom. I could have gone on after *The City and the Pillar* writing shocking John Rechy novels, but chose not to. My first two Broadway plays were successful, and I could have continued for a time to be a popular year-in, year-out playwright. Chose not to. Chose not to keep on as a television playwright. Then once *Julian* did well, I could have gone on in *that* genre. The same with *Washington, D.C.*, when I, inadvertently, captured the mind and heart of the middle-class, middle-aged, middle-brow lady who buys hardcover novels—not to mention the book clubs. But then I let *Myra* spring from my brow, armed to the teeth, eager to lose me ladies, book clubs, book-chat writers—everything, in fact, except her unique self, the only great "woman" in American literature.

Int: And *Burr*? You seem to have got them all back again.

GV: Doubtless a misunderstanding. I had assumed that *Burr* would be unpopular. My view of American history is much too realistic. Happily, Nixon, who made me a popular playwright (the worst man in *The Best Man* was based on him), again came to the rescue. Watergate so shook the three percent of our population who read books that they accepted *Burr*, a book that ordinarily they would have burned while reciting the pledge of allegiance to the flag.

Int: Is it true that you were thinking of putting out *Myra Breckinridge* under a pseudonym?

GV: No. Oh, well, yes. I wanted to make an experiment. To publish a book without reviews or advertising or a well-known author's name. I wanted to prove that a book could do well simply because it was interesting—without the support of book-chat writers. Up to a point, the experiment worked. The book was widely read long before the first reviews appeared. But for the experiment to have been perfect my name shouldn't have been on the book. I didn't think of that till later. Curious. Twenty years ago, after *Messiah* was published, Harvey Breit of *The New York Times* said, "You know, Gore, anything you write will get a bad press in America. Use another name. Or do something else." So for ten years I did something else.

Int: Why will you always get a bad press?

GV: That's more for you to determine than for me. I have my theories, no doubt wrong. I suspect that the range of my activity is unbearable to people who write about books. Lenny Bernstein is not reviewed in *The New York Times* by an unsuccessful composer or by a student at Julliard. He might be better off if he were, but he isn't. Writers are the only people who are reviewed by people of their own kind. And their own kind can often be reasonably generous—*if* you stay in your category. I don't. I do many different things rather better than most people do one thing. And envy is the central fact of American life. Then, of course, I am the Enemy to so many. I have attacked both Nixon and the Kennedys—as well as the American Empire. I've also made the case that American literature has been second-rate from the beginning. This caused distress in book-chat land. They *knew* I was wrong, but since they don't read foreign or old books, they were forced to write things like "Vidal thinks Victor Hugo is better than Faulkner." Well,

Hugo *is* better than Faulkner, but to the residents of book-chat land Hugo is just a man with a funny name who wrote *Les Misérables*, a movie on the late show. Finally, I am proud to say that I am most disliked because for twenty-six years I have been in open rebellion against the heterosexual dictatorship in the United States. Fortunately, I have lived long enough to see the dictatorship start to collapse. I now hope to live long enough to see a sexual democracy in America. I deserve at least a statue in Dupont Circle—along with Dr. Kinsey.

Int: You often refer to critics.
GV: Reviewers . . . actually newspaper persons who chat about books in the press. They have been with us from the beginning and they will be with us at the end. They are interested in writers, not writing. In good morals, not good art. When they like something of mine, I grow suspicious and wonder.

Int: One of the comments sometimes made is that your real position—your greatest talent—is as an essayist. How would you answer that?
GV: My novels are quite as good as my essays. Unfortunately, to find out if a novel is good or bad you must first read it, and that is not an easy thing to do nowadays. Essays, on the other hand, are short, and people do read them.

Int: You once said the novel is dead.
GV: That was a joke. What I have said repeatedly is that the *audience* for the novel is demonstrably diminishing with each passing year. That is a fact. It is not the novel that is declining, but the audience for it. It's like saying poetry has been declining for fifty years. Poetry hasn't. But the audience has. The serious novel is now almost in the same situation as poetry. Eventually the novel will simply be an academic exercise, written by academics to be used in classrooms in order to test the ingenuity of students. A combination of Rorschach test and anagram. Hence, the popularity of John Barth, a perfect U-novelist whose books are written to be taught, not to be read.

Int: As long as we're on Barth, let me ask you what you think of your contemporaries, people in your generation, people in their forties?
GV: You must realize that anything I *say* (as opposed to write) about other novelists is governed by my current mood of jaunty disgust—which is quite impartial, cheerful, even loving. But totally unreliable as

criticism—putting me in the great tradition of American journalism, now
that I think of it.

Int: Do you read your contemporaries? Do you read their new works as they
come out?
GV: I wouldn't say that I am fanatically attentive. There's only one living
writer in English that I entirely admire, and that's William Golding. Lately
I've been reading a lot of Italian and French writers. I particularly like Italo
Calvino.

Int: Why do you think Golding good?
GV: Well, his work is intensely felt. He holds you completely line by line,
image by image. In *The Spire* you see the church that is being built, smell the
dust. You are present at an event that exists only in his imagination. Very few
writers have ever had this power. When the priest reveals his sores, you see
them, feel the pain. I don't know how he does it.

Int: Have you ever met him?
GV: Once, yes. We had dinner together in Rome. Oxford don type. I like his
variety: each book is quite different from the one before it. This confuses
critics and readers, but delights me. For that reason I like to read Fowles—
though he is not in Golding's class. Who else do I read for pleasure? I always
admire Isherwood. I am not given to mysticism—to understate wildly,
but he makes me see something of what he would see. I read P. G. Wodehouse
for pleasure. Much of Anthony Burgess. Brigid Brophy. Philip Roth when he
is at his most demented. I like comic writers, obviously. I reread Evelyn
Waugh. . . .

Int: Were you influenced by Waugh?
GV: Perhaps. I was given *Scoop* in 1939 and I thought it the funniest book I'd
ever read. I used to reread it every year. Of the American writers—well,
I read Saul Bellow with admiration. He never quite pulls off a book for me,
but he's interesting—which is more than you can say for so many of the
other Jewish Giants, carving their endless Mount Rushmores out of halvah.
Calder Willingham I've always liked—that frantic heterosexuality. There
must be a place for his sort of thing in American literature. I've never
understood why he was not an enormously popular writer.

Int: You have known a good many writers. Is there anything to be got from knowing other writers personally?

GV: I don't think so. When I was young I wanted to meet the famous old writers that I admired. So I met Gide, Forster, Cocteau, and Santayana. I sent Thomas Mann a book. He sent me a polite letter with my name misspelled. I never expected to "learn" anything from looking at them. Rather it was a laying on of hands. A connection with the past. I am perhaps more conscious of the past than most American writers, and need the dead for comfort.

Int: Do you enjoy being with other writers? Henry James once said, for example, that Hawthorne was handicapped because he was isolated from other writers.

GV: Yes, I like the company of other writers. Christopher Isherwood, Tennessee Williams, and Paul Bowles have been friends. But I am not so sure James meant that Hawthorne's isolation had to do with not knowing other writers. I think James meant that the American scene was culturally so thin that it was hard to develop intellectually if you had nobody to talk to. This explains the solipsistic note in the work of so many American writers. They think they are the only ones in the world to doubt the existence of God, say—like Mark Twain, for instance.

Int: Who was the first writer you ever met?

GV: Well, growing up in Washington, a lot of journalists came to the house. Walter Lippmann, Arthur Krock, Drew Pearson . . . but I did not think much of journalists. I was more interested in Michael Arlen, who used to come and play bridge. A splendid, rather ornate, Beerbohmesque dandy. And by no means a bad writer. I was fascinated recently by *Exiles*, his son's book about him. One summer before the war we were all at the Homestead Hotel in Hot Springs, Virginia, where Michael and Atalanta Arlen were much admired by everyone, including my mother and her husband, Hugh Auchincloss. But to my astonishment, I now read that the boy was embarrassed by them—they were too dark, flashy, exotic, not pink and square like the American gentry. Like us, I suppose. Life is odd. Michael's son wanted for a father a stockbroker named Smith, while I would've given anything if his father had been my father—well, *step* father.

Int: But later, on your own, whom did you meet, know. . . .

GV: I was still in uniform when I met Anaïs Nin in 1945. I refer you to the pages of her diary for that historic encounter. I thought she was marvelous but didn't much like her writing. Years later, reading her journals, I was horrified to discover that she felt the same about me. In '48 I met Tennessee in Rome, at the height of his fame. We traveled about in an old Jeep. I have never laughed more with anyone, but can't say that I learned anything from him or anyone else. That process is interior. Paradoxically, in the ten years that I wrote for television, theater, movies, I learned how to write novels. Also, writing three mystery novels in one year taught me that nothing must occur in narrative which is not of use. Ironic that the lesson of Flaubert—which I thought that I had absorbed—I did not really comprehend until I was potboiling.

Int: You have described meeting E. M. Forster at King's College. . . .

GV: I met him first at a party for Isherwood. London '48. Forster was very excited at meeting Tennessee and not at all at meeting me—which I considered unfair, since I had read and admired all his books while Tennessee, I fear, thought that he was in the presence of the author of *Captain Horatio Hornblower*. Part of Tennessee's wisdom is to read nothing at all. Anyway, Forster, looking like an old river rat, zeroed in on Tennessee and said how much he admired *Streetcar*. Tennessee gave him a beady look. Forster invited us to King's for lunch. Tennessee rolled his eyes and looked at me. Yes, I said quickly. The next day I dragged Tennessee to the railroad station. As usual with Tennessee, we missed the first train. The second train would arrive in half an hour. Tennessee refused to wait. "But we *have* to go," I said, "He's sitting on one of the lions in front of the college, waiting for us." Tennessee was not moved by this poignant tableau. "I can't," he said, gulping and clutching his heart—when Tennessee does not spit blood, he has heart spasms. "Besides," said Tennessee primly, wandering off in the wrong direction for the exit, "I cannot abide old men with urine stains on their trousers." I went on alone. I have described that grim day in *Two Sisters*.

Int: You seem to still see this scene vividly. Do you think of the writer as a constant observer and recorder?

GV: Well, I am not a camera, no. I don't consciously watch anything and I don't take notes, though I briefly kept a diary. What I remember I remember— by no means the same thing as remembering what you would like to.

Int: How do you see yourself in an age of personality-writers, promoting themselves and their work? For instance, Capote says he is an expert at promoting books and gaining the attention of the media.
GV: Every writer ought to have at least one thing that he does well, and I'll take Truman's word that a gift for publicity is the most glittering star in his diadem. I'm pretty good at promoting my views on television but a washout at charming the book-chatters. But then I don't really try. Years ago Mailer solemnly assured me that to be a "great" writer in America you had to be fairly regularly on the cover of the Sunday *New York Times* book section. Nothing else mattered. Anyway, he is now what he wanted to be: the patron saint of bad journalism, and I am exactly what I set out to be: a novelist.

Int: Where do you place Nabokov?
GV: I admire him very much. I'm told he returns the compliment. We do exchange stately insults in the press. Shortly after I announced that I was contributing a hundred dollars to the Angela Davis defense fund in Nabokov's name—to improve his image—he responded by assuring an interviewer from *The New York Times* that I had become a Roman Catholic. It is curious that Russia's two greatest writers—Nabokov and Pushkin— should both have had Negro blood.

Int: Have you read *Ada*?
GV: No one has read *Ada*. But I very much admired *Transparent Things*. It is sad that the dumb Swedes gave their merit badge to Solzhenitsyn instead of Nabokov. Perfect example, by the way, of the unimportance of a writer's books to his career.

Int: How about some of the younger writers? What do you think of John Updike, for example?
GV: He writes so well that I wish he could attract my interest. I like his prose, and disagree with Mailer, who thinks it bad. Mailer said it was the kind of bad writing that people who don't know much about writing think is good. It is an observation that I understand, but don't think applies to Updike. With me the problem is that he doesn't write about anything that interests me. I am not concerned with middle-class suburban couples. On the other hand, I'm not concerned with adultery in the French provinces either. Yet Flaubert commands my attention. I don't know why Updike doesn't. Perhaps my fault.

Int: Are there others of the younger generation who are perhaps less well known whom you like?
GV: Alison Lurie. Viva's autobiography . . .

Int: Andy Warhol's superstar?
GV: Yes. And it's marvelous. Part fiction, part tape recording, part this, part that, gloriously obscene. Particularly interesting about her Catholic girlhood in upstate New York. Her father beating her up periodically beneath the bleeding heart of Jesus. And those great plaster Virgins that he had all over the lawn, lit up at night with three thousand candles. That kind of thing appeals to me more than stately, careful novels.

Int: You came out of the Second World War. What do you think of the writers of the previous generation—Hemingway, for example?
GV: I detest him, but I was certainly under his spell when I was very young, as we all were. I thought his prose was perfect—until I read Stephen Crane and realized where he got it from. Yet Hemingway is still the master self-publicist, if Capote will forgive me. Hemingway managed to convince everybody that before Hemingway everyone wrote like—who?—Gene Stratton Porter. But not only was there Mark Twain before him, there was also Stephen Crane, who did everything that Hemingway did and rather better. Certainly *The Red Badge of Courage* is superior to *A Farewell to Arms*. But Hemingway did put together an hypnotic style whose rhythm haunted other writers. I liked some of the travel things—*Green Hills of Africa*. But he never wrote a good novel. I suppose, finally, the thing I most detest in him is the spontaneity of his cruelty. The way he treated Fitzgerald, described in *A Moveable Feast*. The way he condescended to Ford Madox Ford, one of the best novelists in our language.

Int: What are your feelings about the so-called great writers of the twentieth century, Hemingway aside? You didn't like Faulkner, I take it.
GV: I like mind and fear rhetoric—I suppose because I have a tendency to rhetoric. I also come from a Southern family—back in Mississippi the Gores were friends of the Faulkners, all Snopeses together. In fact, when I read Faulkner I think of my grandfather's speeches in the Senate, of a floweriness that I have done my best to pluck from my own style—along with the weeds.

Int: How about Fitzgerald?

GV: If you want to find a place for him, he's somewhere between Maurice Baring and Evelyn Waugh. I like best what he leaves out of *The Great Gatsby*. A unique book. Incidentally, I think screenwriting taught him a lot. But who cares what he wrote? It is his life that matters. Books will be written about him long after his own work has vanished—again and again we shall be told of the literary harvest god who was devoured at summer's end in the hollywoods.

Int: You said you thought you had been influenced by Waugh, but weren't quite sure how. Who else has influenced you? Either now or years ago.

GV: Oh, God, it's so hard to list them. As I said, by the time I got to *The Judgment of Paris* I was myself. Yet I'm always conscious that literature is, primarily, a chain of connection from the past to the present. It is not reinvented every morning, as some bad writers like to believe. My own chain or literary genealogy would be something like this: Petronius, Juvenal, Apuleius—then Shakespeare—then Peacock, Meredith, James, Proust. Yet the writers I like the most influenced me the least. How can you be influenced by Proust? You can't. He's inimitable. At one point Thomas Mann fascinated me; thinking he was imitable, I used to compose Socratic dialogues in what I thought was his manner. One reason for rewriting *The City and the Pillar* was to get rid of those somber exchanges.

Int: How much do you think college English courses can influence a career? Or teach one about The Novel?

GV: I don't know. I never went to college. But I have lectured on campuses for a quarter-century, and it is my impression that after taking a course in The Novel, it is an unusual student who would ever want to read a novel again. Those English courses are what have killed literature for the public. Books are made a duty. Imagine teaching novels! Novels used to be written simply to be read. It was assumed until recently that there was a direct connection between writer and reader. Now that essential connection is being mediated—bugged?—by English departments. Well, who needs the mediation? Who needs to be taught how to read a contemporary novel? Either you read it because you want to or you don't. Assuming, of course, that you can read anything at all. But this business of taking novels apart in order to show bored children how they were put together—there's a madness to it. Only a literary critic would benefit, and there are never more than ten good critics in the United States at any given moment. So what is the point to these desultory autopsies performed according to that little set of instructions at the end of each text? Have you seen one? What symbols to look for? What does the author mean by the word "white"? I look at the notes appended to my own pieces in anthologies and know despair.

Int: How would you "teach" the novel?
GV: I would teach world civilization—East and West—from the beginning to the present. This would occupy the college years—would be the spine to my educational system. Then literature, economics, art, science, philosophy, religion would be dealt with naturally, sequentially, as they occurred. After four years, the student would have at least a glimmering of what our race is all about.

Int: If you were teaching one of those "desultory" courses, how would you describe your style?
GV: As a novelist I have a certain mimetic gift. I can impersonate a number of characters. In *Myra Breckinridge* there are two different voices. One for Buck Loner, one for Myra—neither mine. On the other hand, when I write an essay, the style is my own—whatever that is, for the subject often imposes its own rhythm on my sentences. Yet I can usually spot my own style, and tell if a word's been changed.

Int: *Two Sisters* is hard to categorize and put in any tradition. You call it a memoir in the form of a novel, or novel in the form of a memoir. What led you to write in that form?
GV: It created its own form as I went along. I didn't feel that a straightforward memoir would be interesting to do. On the other hand, I don't like romans à clef. They're usually a bit of a cheat. You notice I keep talking not about the effect my writing is going to have on others but the effect it has on me. I don't really care whether I find a form that enchants others as much as I care about finding something that can delight me from day to day as I work it out. I was constantly fascinated and perplexed while writing that book. It's done with mirrors. One thing reflects another thing. Each of the three sections is exactly the same story, no different, but each section *seems* to be different. Each section contains exactly the same characters, though not always in the same guise.

Int: It's typical of your newer novels that you make such use of interjected letters, tape recordings, and diaries. Do you find that technique easier, or better or preferable to a straight narrative?

GV: It makes for immediacy. I know how difficult it is for the average American to read anything. And I'm speaking of the average "educated" person. It is not easy for him to cope with too dense a text on the page. I think the eye tires easily. After all, everyone under thirty-five was brought up not reading books but staring at television. So I am forced to be ingenious, to hold the reader's attention. I think I probably made an error using the screenplay form for part of *Two Sisters*.

Int: Why?

GV: I'm told it was hard to read. Poor Anthony Burgess, following me, has just made the same mistake with *Clockwork Testament*. Also, I kept saying all through the book what a bad screenplay it was. Predictably, the reaction was, well, if *he* says it's a bad screenplay, why, it really must be a bad screenplay and so we better not read the bad screenplay. One must never attempt irony this side of the water.

Int: But you do in your work, on television . . .

GV: Yes. And it has done me no good. In America the race goes to the loud, the solemn, the hustler. If you think you're a great writer, you must say that you are. Some will disagree, of course, but at least everyone will know that you're serious about your work. Speak of yourself with the slightest irony, self-deprecation, and you will be thought frivolous—perhaps even a bad person. Anyway, the playing around with letters and tapes and so on is just . . . I keep coming back to the only thing that matters: interesting myself.

Int: What about writing in the third person?

GV: I wonder if it is still possible—in the sense that Henry James used it. *Washington, D.C.* was my last attempt to write a book like that—and I rather admire *Washington, D.C.* After all, that was the time I got into the ring with Proust, and I knocked the little fag on his ass in the first round. Then I kneed old Leo T. the Great and on a technical KO got the championship. Funny thing, this being the best. . . . But even the world champ had a tough time licking *Washington, D.C.* The third person imposed a great strain on me, the constant maneuvering of so many consciousnesses through the various scenes while trying to keep the focus right. It was like directing a film on location with a huge cast in bad weather.

Int: Do you feel more at home with the first-person novel now? Do you think you'll continue with it?
GV: Since I've done it recently in *Burr* and again in *Myron*, I'll probably *not* do it again, but who knows? The second person certainly holds few charms. Perhaps no pronouns at all!

Int: What sets you apart, do you think, from other American writers?
GV: My interest in Western civilization. Except for Thornton Wilder, I can think of no contemporary American who has any interest in what happened before the long present he lives in, and records. Also, perhaps paradoxically, I value invention highly, and hardly anyone else does. I don't think I have ever met an American novelist who didn't sooner or later, say when discussing his own work, "Well, I really knew someone exactly like that. That was the way it happened, the way I wrote it." He is terrified that you might think he actually made up a character, that what he writes might not be literally as opposed to imaginatively true. I think part of the bewilderment American book-chat writers have with me is that they realize that there's something strange going on that ought not to be going on—that *Myra Breckinridge* might just possibly be a work of the imagination. "You mean you never knew *anyone* like that? Well, if you didn't, how could you write it?"

Int: *Two Sisters*, however, does invite that intense search for clues you abhor. You meant for it to, didn't you? You wonder who is who and what's what.
GV: It would be unnatural if people didn't. After all, it is a memoir as well as a novel. But mainly it is a study in vanity and our attempts to conquer death through construction or through destruction. Herostratus does it in one way, and I do it in another—at least, the self that I use in the book. Eric does it in yet another way. Those girls, each has her own view of how she's going to evade death and achieve immortality. And it's all a comedy from the point of view of a stoic writer like myself.

Int: Can you tell me about your work habits? You must be enormously disciplined to turn out so much in such a relatively short time. Do you find writing easy? Do you enjoy it?

GV: Oh, yes, of course I enjoy it. I wouldn't do it if I didn't. Whenever I get up in the morning, I write for about three hours. I write novels in longhand on yellow legal pads, exactly like the First Criminal Nixon. For some reason I write plays and essays on the typewriter. The first draft usually comes rather fast. One oddity: I never reread a text until I have finished the first draft. Otherwise it's too discouraging. Also, when you have the whole thing in front of you for the first time, you've forgotten most of it and see it fresh. Rewriting, however, is a slow, grinding business. For me the main pleasure of having money is being able to afford as many completely retyped drafts as I like. When I was young and poor, I had to do my own typing, so I seldom did more than two drafts. Now I go through four, five, six. The more the better, since my style is very much one of afterthought. My line to Dwight Macdonald "You have nothing to say, only to add" really referred to me. Not until somebody did a parody of me did I realize how dependent I am on the parenthetic aside—the comment upon the comment, the ironic gloss upon the straight line, or the straight rendering of a comedic point. It is a style which must seem rather pointless to my contemporaries because they see no need for this kind of elaborateness. But, again, it's the only thing I find interesting to do.

Hungover or not, I write every day for three hours after I get up until I've finished whatever I'm doing. Although sometimes I take a break in the middle of the book, sometimes a break of several years. I began *Julian*—I don't remember—but I think some seven years passed between the beginning of the book and when I picked it up again. The same thing occurred with *Washington, D.C.* On the other hand, *Myra* I wrote practically at one sitting—in a few weeks. It wrote itself, as they say. But then it was much rewritten.

Int: Do you block out a story in advance? And do characters ever run away from you?
GV: When I first started writing, I used to plan everything in advance, not only chapter to chapter but page to page. Terribly constricting . . . like doing a film from someone else's meticulous treatment. About the time of *The Judgment of Paris*, I started improvising. I began with a mood. A sentence. The first sentence is all-important. *Washington, D.C.* began with a dream, a summer storm at night in a garden above the Potomac—that was Merrywood, where I grew up. With *Julian* and with *Burr* I was held to historical facts. Still, I found places where I could breathe and make up new things. My Burr is not the real Burr any more than Henry Steele Commager's

Jefferson is the real Jefferson. By and large history tends to be rather poor fiction—except at its best. The *Peloponnesian War* is a great novel about people who actually lived.

Int: In your novel *Messiah* . . .
GV: I didn't know the end of the book when I started writing. Yet when I got to the last page I suddenly wrote, "I was he whom the world awaited," and it was all at once clear to me that the hidden meaning of the story was the true identity of the narrator, which had been hidden from him, too. *He* was the messiah who might have been. When I saw this coming out upon the page, I shuddered (usually I laugh as I write), knew awe, for I had knocked both Huxley and Orwell out of the ring. Incidentally, ninety percent of your readers will not detect the irony in my boxing metaphors. And there is nothing to be done about it.

Int: Except for me to interject that you are playing off the likes of Hemingway and Mailer in the use of them. Shall I go on? Do you keep notebooks?
GV: I make a few pages of notes for each novel. Phrases. Names. Character descriptions. Then I seldom look again at the notes. At the end of each workday I do make notes on what the next day's work will be. I've a memory like a sieve. Under a pseudonym (Edgar Box) I wrote three mystery books in 1952—I was very broke. Halfway through the last one I forgot who the murderer was and had to find a substitute.

Int: What do you start with? A character, a plot?
GV: *Myra* began with a first sentence. I was so intrigued by that sentence that I had to go on. Who was she? What did she have to say? A lot, as it turned out. The unconscious mind certainly shaped that book.

Int: Do you find any difficulties in writing about America and Americans when you are out of the country so much?
GV: Well, I think others would notice my lapses before I did. Anyway, I come back quite often and my ears are pretty much attuned to the American . . . scream. But then I've been involved in one way or another with every election for nearly twenty years. And I spend at least two months each year lecturing across the country.

Int: Besides the pleasures of living, are there any advantages in terms of perspective for the writer who lives outside the country?

GV: For me, every advantage. If I lived in America, I would be a politician twenty-four hours a day, minding everybody else's business and getting no work done. Also, there are pleasures to this sort of anonymity one has in a foreign city. And it's nice to be always coping with a language you don't speak very well. Occasionally I regret it when I'm with someone like Moravia, who speaks so rapidly and intricately in Italian that I can never follow him.

Int: What do you think generally about the writer engagé? Should a writer be involved in politics, as you are?

GV: It depends on the writer. Most American writers are not much involved, beyond signing petitions. They are usually academics—and cautious. Or full-time *literary* politicians. Or both. The main line of our literature is quotidianal with a vengeance. Yes, many great novels have been written about the everyday—Jane Austen and so on. But you need a superb art to make that sort of thing interesting. So, failing superb art, you'd better have a good mind and you'd better be interested in the world outside yourself. D. H. Lawrence wrote something very interesting about the young Hemingway. Called him a brilliant writer. But he added he's essentially a photographer and it will be interesting to see how he ages because the photographer can only keep on taking pictures from the outside. One of the reasons that the gifted Hemingway never wrote a good novel was that nothing interested him except a few sensuous experiences like killing things and fucking—interesting things to do but not all that interesting to write about. This sort of artist runs into trouble very early on because all he can really write about is himself and after youth that self—unengaged in the world—is of declining interest. Admittedly, Hemingway chased after wars, but he never had much of anything to say about war, unlike Tolstoy or even Malraux. I think that the more you know the world and the wider the net you cast in your society, the more interesting your books will be, certainly the more interested you will be.

Int: Do you think of your novels as *political* novels?

GV: Of course not. I am a politician when I make a speech or write a piece to promote a political idea. In a novel like *Burr* I'm not composing a polemic about the founding fathers. Rather, I am describing the way men who want power respond to one another, to themselves. The other books, the inventions like *Myra*, are beyond politics, in the usual sense at least.

Int: Are you interested in the other arts at all? In painting, sculpture, music, opera, dance?

GV: Architecture, for one. I'm fascinated by the ancient Roman Empire amongst whose ruins I live. I've been in every city and town of Italy, and I suppose I've been into nearly every Roman church. I particularly like mosaics. I am not musical. This means I very much like opera. And baroque organ music, very loud. I like ballet, but in Rome it's bad. In painting, I'm happiest with Piero della Francesca. I hate abstract painting. In sculpture, well, the Medici tombs—I had a small talent for sculpture when I was young.

Int: Does it help a writer to be in love? To be rich?

GV: Love is not my bag. I was debagged at twenty-five and turned to sex and art, perfectly acceptable substitutes. Absence of money is a bad thing because you end up writing "The Telltale Clue" on television—which I did. Luckily, I was full of energy in those days. I used to write a seventy-thousand-word mystery novel in ten days. Money gives one time to rewrite books until they are "done"—or abandoned. Money also gave me the leisure to become an essayist. I spend more time on a piece for *The New York Review of Books* than I ever did on, let us say, a television play. If my essays are good it is because they are entirely voluntary. I write only what I want to . . . except, of course, in those money-making days at MGM—composing *Ben Hur*.

Int: But how about the movies? You're still writing for movies, aren't you?

GV: Yes. I love movies, and I think a lot about movies. Recently I thought I would like to direct. More recently, I have decided it's too late. I am like the Walter Lippmanns. I saw them a few years ago. They were euphoric. Why? "Because," she said, "we have decided that we shall *never* go to Japan. Such a relief!"

Int: Why do you prefer movies to the theater?

GV: I'm embarrassed by live actors. They're always having a much better time than I am. Also, few plays are very interesting, while almost any movie is interesting—if just to watch the pictures. But then I'm typically American. We weren't brought up with theater like the English or the Germans. On the other hand, I saw every movie I could in my youth. I once saw four movies in one day when I was fourteen. That was the happiest day of my life.

Int: Have you ever thought of acting, as Norman Mailer does?
GV: Is *that* what he does? I have always been curious. Well, I appeared briefly in my own *The Best Man*. I also appeared in *Fellini Roma*, as myself. I made no sense, due to the cutting, but the movie was splendid anyway. I have been offered the lead in Ustinov's new play for New York. To play an American president. What else? I said no. For one thing, I cannot learn dialogue.

Int: Has your writing been influenced by films?
GV: Every writer of my generation has been influenced by films. I think I've written that somewhere. Find out the movies a man saw between ten and fifteen, which ones he liked, disliked, and you would have a pretty good idea of what sort of mind and temperament he has. If he happened to be a writer, you would be able to find a good many influences, though not perhaps as many as Professor B. F. Dick comes up with in his recent study of me*—a brilliant job, all in all. Myra would've liked it.

Int: What did you see between ten and fifteen?
GV: I saw everything. But I was most affected by George Arliss. Particularly his Disraeli. I liked all those historical fictions that were done in the thirties. Recently I saw my favorite, *Cardinal Richelieu*, for the first time in thirty years on the late show. Absolute chloroform.

Int: Well, you seem to have had an enormous knowledge of movies for *Myra*. Did you have to go back and research any of that?
GV: I saw all those movies of the forties—in the forties. At school and in the army. They're seared on my memory. There wasn't anything in the book that I did not see first time around. Also—to help the Ph.D. thesis writers—almost every picture I mentioned can be found in Parker Tyler's *Magic and Myth of the Movies*. A work which has to be read to be believed.

Int: Have you ever had any trouble with writer's block?
GV: No.

*The Apostate Angel: A Critical Study of Gore Vidal, by Bernard F. Dick (Random House, 1974).

Int: When you get up in the morning to write, do you just sit down and start out with your pen? You don't have any devices you use to . . .?
GV: First coffee. Then a bowel movement. Then the muse joins me.

Int: You don't sharpen pencils or anything like that?
GV: No. But I often read for an hour or two. Clearing the mind. I'm always reluctant to start work, and reluctant to stop. The most interesting thing about writing is the way that it obliterates time. Three hours seem like three minutes. Then there is the business of surprise. I never know what is coming next. The phrase that sounds in the head changes when it appears on the page. Then I start probing it with a pen, finding new meanings. Sometimes I burst out laughing at what is happening as I twist and turn sentences. Strange business, all in all. One never gets to the end of it. That's why I go on, I suppose. To see what the next sentences I write will be.

Dialogue on Film: Gore Vidal

Hollis Alpert with Jan Kadar / 1977

From *American Film*, April 1977. Published by the American Film Institute.
© 1977 American Film Institute. Reprinted by permission.

In 1947 *Life* magazine published an article on the young, postwar novelists, pointing to Gore Vidal as one of the bright hopes. He was twenty years old and had already published two novels, both well received. But Vidal told *Life* he was unsatisfied; he dismissed his first novel, *Williwaw*, because it was "about a group of rather uninteresting men at the mercy of external forces." In the future, he promised, he would deal with more significant themes.

In the thirty years since, Vidal has spectacularly kept his promise—and novels have been only one of the ways. He has turned out plays, television dramas, screenplays, essays, and poetry. The subjects have varied widely—from a fourth-century emperor to presidential candidates to the extraordinary Myra Breckinridge—but one interest has been overriding: the state of American society. With a razor-sharp wit and wide learning, Vidal has become the man of letters as social gadfly; no sacred cow is safe, no institution immune.

In his latest novel, *1876*, he finds the country corrupt a century before Watergate. In an essay last fall, he lambasted revered novelists like John Barth and Thomas Pynchon as pretentious and impenetrable. Most recently, he has taken aim at Hollywood, terming the typical director a "hustler-plagiarist" and calling for writers to take over the movies as they have taken over the theater. The howls of protest have yet to die down.

Vidal's bluntness has earned him his critics, but no one has complained that he is dull. He grew up in decidedly un-dull surroundings. His grandfather was Thomas P. Gore, the first senator from Oklahoma. His father served under Franklin Roosevelt. The family was a prominent fixture of Washington, D.C. Vidal, educated at Phillips Exeter, startled expectations by skipping college and turning to writing and travel.

By 1953, with nine novels behind him, Vidal was writing television dramas. Other talented writers like Paddy Chayefsky, Reginald Rose, and

Rod Serling were also turning to television. The pace was fast, and much dross can be found among the Golden Days of fifties' television, but some of Vidal's work has the luster of quality. For example, *Visit to a Small Planet*, a delightful fantasy presented on "The Philco Television Playhouse" in 1953, opened two years later on Broadway.

In the wake of best-sellers and long-running plays, Vidal turned to Hollywood in the late fifties. Working as a staff writer for MGM, he wrote *The Catered Affair* and *I Accuse!* He collaborated with Tennessee Williams on *Suddenly Last Summer*. He also wrote the first half of William Wyler's *Ben-Hur*, though his name does not appear on the screen credits. In a recent essay, Vidal disclosed the explanation he offered Wyler for the extraordinary hostility between Messala and Ben-Hur: They had been lovers; Messala was rejected. Wyler, Vidal said, was startled by the suggestion but agreed to let the merest hint into the script.

Vidal's latest screenplay is for *Caligula*, a project shot in Rome and plagued by dissension. In the dialogue, Vidal offers choice observations on its director and the Italian movie scene in general, including the work of Fellini. He also discusses his Hollywood and television days and the state of television.

Vidal, who makes his home in Rome, took part in the dialogue during a recent visit. He was joined by Hollis Alpert, the editor of *American Film*, and Jan Kadar, AFI's filmmaker-in-residence.

Hollis Alpert: Gore, you're first and foremost a novelist, but you've mysteriously managed to function with enormous success in a variety of fields. You've written plays that have run forever on Broadway, you've written films, you've written some of the best programs on television. Lately, you've been turning out some provocative essays on Hollywood and the movies for *The New York Review of Books*. Let me quote the last few lines of a recent one—your definition of the director: "that hustler-plagiarist who has for twenty years dominated and exploited and (occasionally) enhanced an art form still in search of its true authors." Would you explain that?

Gore Vidal: My characteristic understatement has obviously led to ambiguity. I wrote a very long piece, and my thesis was that ever since the movies started to talk—that dread moment when Al Jolson said, "You ain't heard nothin' yet," certainly the most sinister line in all of world drama—it's been a writer's medium. But nobody ever knew this, except the writers—and the directors. I saw an interview with Henry Wilcoxon about Cecil B. DeMille, that gorgeous egomaniac, and he said, "You know, it's all in the script." Akira Kurosawa said, "It's the script." I think even Delmer Daves would say it's the script. The script is all-important. But the director is obliged to get the script away from the writer in order to become an *auteur du cinéma.* My piece in *The New York Review* was really an attack on the French theory of the auteur—that the director alone creates the film.

I call the directors plagiarists because they, literally, steal the script. Now this is done in a very sly fashion. First, they go to a writer for a script, because very few of them can write themselves—very few of them can direct, either. Once the script is acquired, they bring in a second writer in order to confuse authorship, so, just to make it tidy, they say, "Well, I guess I'll take the credit." In my piece I described how the noble Jean Renoir did that with *The Southerner,* one of the few good movies that Renoir was associated with in the United States. Renoir was a man who had great trouble speaking English, much less writing it, and the script was written by William Faulkner. According to Zachary Scott, who acted in it, Faulkner really liked the script and would have been pleased to have had the credit. But Renoir so muddled the business that the credit finally read: "Screenplay by Jean Renoir." That was a great heist.

Somebody recently asked me, "What about René Clair?" Everybody is trying to save their favorite directors from my ax. I said, "All right, what about René Clair?" I got a collection of his screenplays, each introduced with an elegant, pretentious preface. He sounds like Marcel Proust on a very good day as he discusses his own greatness. There was a film he did called *The Grand Maneuver,* and he said, more or less, "This film began when I was a small boy in the Bois de Boulogne. As the cavalry would go by I would hear their trumpets sound. . . ." I was in tears by the time I got through the preface. Then I looked at the credits: "From a story by Courteline, screenplay by Jérôme Géronimi and Jean Marson." So who the hell heard that trumpet in the Bois de Boulogne? Was it the man who wrote the play? Was it the two other writers? What did Clair contribute? We will never know. What we will know is that he took credit for everything.

Enough of that. Let us talk of other things. Let's talk about Edward Doheny. As I entered this gracious palace, it suddenly all came back to me. My grandfather, T.P. Gore, was the first senator from Oklahoma—nothing to boast of. Anyway, when the Teapot Dome Scandal broke during the Harding administration, it was discovered that my grandfather had moonlighted a bit as an attorney for Mr. Doheny, a criminal of Nixonian proportions. So for many a long year after, T.P. Gore was known as "Tea Pot Gore." But at least something good has come out of Doheny's criminality—this house for the AFI.

Question: You've written that once production starts the director might as well go home. In your view, what is it the director does?

GV: It varies. Some do more than others. I give credit where it's due. Ingmar Bergman writes his own script, knows the actors well—he is, in every sense, the creator of his own films. But, in the old days they used to say that the director was the brother-in-law. The producer was the important person. He put the thing together. Then he picked the stars, who were usually under contract; he picked the cameraman, who was very important, and the editor, who was more important still. And at the last minute, he'd call in one of the studio's staff directors, give him the script, and say, "Do you want to do it or not? If you don't want to do it, you go on suspension." That's what it was like in the fifties at MGM when I was under contract, and the forties and the thirties.

Nobody bright or ambitious wanted to be down there on the set all day. It was boring. If the director changed the script—if I had written "Medium-close shot" in the script and he decided suddenly to do a long shot—all hell would break loose upstairs in the executive dining room. Each day, Bennie Thau would watch the rushes, and he would say, "What happened here? You changed the shot. Why?" So the laughter that went through this town when the French, who are always wrong, suddenly decided that all these hacks were truly great creators. Whenever the French invent a theory, *méfiez-vous*. France is a nation devoted to the false hypothesis on which it then builds marvelously logical structures. The idea that Nicholas Ray—a dear friend of mine—is a great director is something that never would have occurred to those of us who lived in the Chateau Marmont at the time he was down there in the bungalow "prepping," as *Variety* would say, *Rebel Without a Cause*, a pretty good movie but nothing more. Orson Welles, a very funny man, once said to me, "You know, the French ruin everything. They come up to you and say, 'You are one of the three great directors of the cinema.'" Orson said, "I nod, I nod." "'There is D.W. Griffith. There is Orson Welles. And there is Nicholas Ray.'" He said, "There is always that third name that crushes you."

Question: How did you land in Hollywood?

GV: I needed the money. I wrote my first novel when I was nineteen. *Williwaw* was published in 1946, a mere thirty-one years ago. Novels did fairly well in those days. But then television came along. In the fifties the sales of everybody's novels, except a few golden best-sellers, in which category I was not, declined dramatically. So I started writing for live television. Then I was offered a contract at MGM. By 1956 I didn't really need the money, but I was terribly curious to see how a big studio worked. After all, even then, somewhere in my head the dread Myra Breckinridge was lurking.

HA: When you call movies "an art form still in search of its true authors," you're looking to writers to take over the function of directors?

GV: Yes. What the French were saying was, essentially, you must get rid of the screenwriter. Then the director would make the movie himself—with his own script, or perhaps without a script, or improvising. In my piece I turned their theory around. I said, let's get rid of the director. We don't need him. We do need the cameraman, the editor. But above all we need the script. Movies are stories; only writers can tell stories. So the wrong people are making the movies.

You see, I don't think there is much of anything to directing. I've worked on about fifteen movies, I suppose. I've done perhaps a hundred live television plays. I've done five plays on Broadway. I've never seen a director yet who contributed much of anything. Some are better than others; some are nicer than others; some are brighter than others. It's very good to have a director to play off—to say, "You're too long," or "You're repeating yourself." As editors, they can be quite useful. When I got to Cannes for *The Best Man*—I got the critics' award for the best script—there was a banner with the title in French and "Un film de Franklin Schaffner." Well, I hit the ceiling. This was my play, my movie. I had helped put the thing together—we had hired Frank. "Un film de Franklin Schaffner." I said, "There's something going wrong here." Anyway, that's when I first confronted the auteur theory—in 1964.

Question: The new version of *The Last Tycoon* has a prominent writer, Harold Pinter, and a great director, Elia Kazan. Whose movie is it?

GV: And it also has a very great producer, Sam Spiegel, for whom I worked twice because I couldn't believe it the first time. I wouldn't think there was any strong desire for anyone to take credit for that film. It's one of those movies where Harold Pinter might say the film was really Gadge's, and Gadge claim it's really Sam's. I thought the film was as well done as you could do it, but the original story isn't any good. There's no way of licking it. Robert DeNiro is a lovely actor, but he couldn't do much with Stahr. And the two women were impossibly bad.

Question: Do you believe you could look after the directing chores?
GV: I had a chance to direct in the fifties, and I turned it down. In those days, nobody who was a serious novelist would have dreamt of directing. And a great many successful screenwriters felt the same. Directing was for the hustlers. Then along came the Europeans with their theories, and suddenly directors were ennobled. We novelists who had been central to the culture began to float out to the far perimeter where the poets live, and I now think that, perhaps, I missed a chance. The other night I asked Peter Falk how much those little movies he does with John Cassavetes cost. He said about $500,000. They don't take salaries up front, so the actual cost of making the picture is not a great deal. Well, a William Faulkner—at the peak of his powers, as indeed he was when he was out here—could have directed as well as written the script of *The Southerner* for his friend, Zachary Scott.

So you don't need the director. You can go right through him. The cameraman, after all, does a great deal for you. Unfortunately, most directors are sometimes slaves of their cameramen. In Italy you should see one of the cringing little directors at work, say, with a huge Giuseppe Rotunno. The Italian movie is a photographer's medium, which explains why most of them are so bad. Movies are stories. To tell a story, someone has to have the narrative gift. That someone ninety-five percent of the time is the writer. I spent most of my time as a movie writer trying to explain to directors what a story is: where you start it, where it goes, how to keep the audience interested for a hundred minutes. I never worked with one who had a clue to the mystery of narrative. They think about shots—usually of cars racing. As for working with actors, forget it. Never ask a movie actor about directors. You'll get an extremely dark stare. Actors are on their own. If the director remembers their names, they're lucky. They're moved around like furniture. That is why type is all-important. That is what you are cast for.

Fellini has solved the problem by not using actors at all. He likes types. He tends to use people from restaurants. He loves eating. That marvelous man who played Trimalchio in *Satyricon* was the owner of Il Moro restaurant in Rome. Fellini had had so many good dinners there that when it came to cast Trimalchio, the man who gives the great banquet, he said, "Ees good. Ees nice man. Makes me hungry. I take him." It was an effective performance, too. All the man had to do was *be* there, and occasionally count. Fellini literally has his performers count: "One, two, three, four, five, six." "I like what you do around thirty-two," he once said to a "performer."

Question: Do you regard the director as useless for the theater, too?
GV: The director is even more useless in the theater than in movies. The American theater is, thank God, controlled by the writer. The Dramatists Guild contract makes it possible for us to get rid of the director, to shut the play the night before it opens, to do almost anything one wants. The writer hires the director to manage the traffic. Obviously, some contribute more than others. They also serve a more human function than in the movies, where the work is largely mechanical, technical. Directors in the theater must be good with actors. For some reason, I've never known a writer who was ever much use to an actor in a play. I don't know why. I certainly can't do it. Whatever it is that an actor needs to build a performance writers don't seem able to supply, other than the play itself. You need to be a sort of lay analyst, and most of the best theater directors—like Elia Kazan—are gurus. They make the actor fall in love with them, and then they pull the performance out. Yes, that is a very useful function.

HA: Wouldn't you give a movie director his due in his work with actors?
GV: Not in the movies. You hire Jimmy Stewart to be Jimmy Stewart.

HA: In my long slavery as a film critic, I found the better directors seemed able to get consistently good performances.
GV: Didn't you find, though, that they always worked with the same people? With performers they were used to? I mean, if you employed Spencer Tracy, you had your performance. People were cast to type. If you wanted somebody to sneeze you got Billy Gilbert. If you wanted a drunk there was the guy who always played the drunk. The directors who really tried to work with actors the way a theater director does usually loused them up. George Cukor, I guess, was very good with the ladies, but the ladies were all pretty good. Greta Garbo would direct—or arrange—herself for the camera's frame.

I once got Garbo to talk about acting. She doesn't like to talk about it, but once she gets started she goes right on and tells you a lot. For her everything was the frame. She knew exactly how the camera was framing her, and she would always consciously compose her own picture. Odd figure in our culture. Tennessee Williams, right after *A Streetcar Named Desire*, met her and said, "Miss Garbo, they want me to write for the movies. I don't want to write for the movies. But I'll do anything for you. What would you like to play?" She said, "Don't make me a man, don't make me a woman." The great androgyny.

Question: Is there a director you think would *add* to your work, who would challenge and reinforce your contribution?
GV: I'm sure such a person exists. I just never worked with him. Anyway, a truly creative director is one who does his own movies—script and all—like Ingmar Bergman or Jean Cocteau, and they have no need of me.

Question: Would someone like Francis Ford Coppola come close? The novel *The Godfather* is a gangster story, but he turned it into a study of power.
GV: Yes, it was a junky novel that provided the basis for a good movie. Francis was my assistant writer on *Is Paris Burning?* which has got to be one of the most awful movies ever made. He used to write a script in about three days for his employer, Ray Stark. Stark would, let us say, pay Carson McCullers twenty-five dollars for a three-month option on *Reflections in a Golden Eye*. Then he would go to Francis in the back room, and say, "I want a script by Friday." This would be Monday, and on Friday there would be a 210-page screenplay. Then Ray would gallop across town and say to Elizabeth Taylor, "Here's a fine property. So the script is lousy. Forget the script. I'll get you Harold Pinter for the rewrite." And she'd say, "Well, I kind of like it, but what about the director?" Ray would then go to John Huston and say, "Forget the script, John. You can write it yourself. Have we got a deal?" And that's how a certain kind of movie got made, because Francis spent five days typing in a back room without credit. But he learned a lot about the movies working for Ray Stark.

Question: Are there any directors you like?
GV: Well, I like Fellini. I think he's becoming terribly—I won't say repetitive, but he's got so proud now that he won't have actors, he won't have scripts, he won't have a narrative. But I think people don't approach his films in the

right way. You must think of him as the last of the great painters. He is paint-ing on celluloid. He's doing the Sistine Chapel over and over again. You look at him, but you don't listen to him. God knows he has no narrative gift at all. When he did have good writers like Ennio Flaiano, his pictures were very different. *La Strada* was totally different from these fantasies he is now painting for us.

I seem to be running out of directors. I liked the first half of *Zabriskie Point* of Michelangelo Antonioni. I thought what he did was amazing—the first time an Italian had a clue as to how anybody outside of Italy sounds. The New Left meeting with Kathleen Cleaver was marvelous stuff, but then at the end of the picture he started to paint that damn Sistine Chapel all over again, with that interminable explosion, like a Joan Miró painting. They're so pretty, the Italians. *Last Tango in Paris*, you know, might have been a good movie had it not been so idiotically pretty. Paris, when autumn leaves are falling! There's not one cliché that Bernardo Bertolucci missed. He should have shot it in Stuttgart or Duluth, and taken Marlon Brando's pants off. One look—and you could have eliminated a lot of dialogue.

Question: What about some of the directors who have claimed to be story-tellers, like Alfred Hitchcock and John Ford?
GV: Hitchcock I exempt in my piece. He was always his own moviemaker; he creates his own pictures. He is a true auteur—of very amusing junk. I sup-pose John Ford, but I don't like Westerns. I don't think I've seen more than three of his pictures, and I don't remember liking them, either. I'll tell you a young director I do like, Marco Bellocchio. I think he's one of the most interesting to come along in years. He writes his own scripts—very excep-tional in Italy.

To watch an Italian director putting a film together is wildly funny. Usually, he has a brother-in-law in one part of town who writes a bit. Then he's got a newspaperman who's moonlighting. Perhaps an *au pair* from Finland to do the English version. He runs around town, getting a scene here, a scene there. Then he puts it all together and announces that he is the sole creator. In a sense, I suppose he is. The result is almost always terrible.

Question: As long as we're on the Italians, what about Lina Wertmüller?
GV: She's a very likable woman. I have seen only two of her movies. I didn't much like them. She is a peculiarly New York phenomenon. She is not well

regarded in Italy. She's unknown in France and England. She is really the invention of one John Simon. Beware of anybody he likes because he is consistent in his judgment. I didn't see *Seven Beauties*. I saw *Swept Away* and *Love and Anarchy*. But the two pictures I saw just seemed to me awfully cutesy-pie and very much what people think Italians are. You know, lots of fun, life enhancing. Kind of dumb, but lovable. Actually, Italians are not like that at all. They tend to be gloomy, nervous, hypochondriacal. They bite their fingernails. Their hands sweat. They're very nervous people. She doesn't get any of that. She just shows a bunch of Italian waiters being bravura.

HA: You've been involved in your own Italian movie, *Gore Vidal's Caligula*. I read in the papers out here—what constitutes papers out here—that production has finished.
GV: In every sense. One of the interesting things I have discovered as I proceed along the great road of life is that you make the same goddamned mistakes over and over and over again. I can tell you right now that every mistake you've made so far in your life you will continue to make. There's not a chance of getting out from under. Now I know quite a lot about movies. I know, how they're put together. Yet I go from disaster to disaster. Obviously, I'm getting stupider. This time I have to get my name out of the title. I fear that Hugh Briss was back in town, as W.C. Fields would say. I'll probably have to sue to change the title of a movie.

Penthouse Films picked an Italian director, Tinto Brass. I said, "All right, if we can use him as a pencil, take him." I'mean, he's a competent cameraman and editor. He's made about ten pictures, each failed. Failure is a habit people seldom break. That's another thing to remember when you're picking a director. Peter O'Toole, who played Tiberius in *Caligula*, referred to Tinto Brass as "Tinto Zinc." O'Toole has a nice sense of the way the world should be ordered. "In a well-run world," he said, "this man should be cleaning windows in Venice. Instead, here he is spending $8 million and destroying a script." Bob Guccione of *Penthouse*—the mag for the gynecological set—is actually quite visual-minded and not entirely stupid; I thought that if the two of us had control of the picture, it would work. The script was strong, which is why we got O'Toole and John Gielgud and Malcolm McDowell and so on. Well, another disaster.

In any case, I should never have accepted an Italian director. The film was supposed to be made in English with direct sound—something Italians hate.

The Italians make silent movies, then they add a lot of noise they take to be dialogue. As a result, few Italian directors know anything about dialogue or how to tell a story—*in Italian*, much less in English. This is true even of the master, Fellini. When it comes time to make the English version, he calls in that dread *au pair* girl from Finland who is supposed to know English very well. "Yez," she says. "I know verry well the Eenglish." Then ten bad actors in Rome do the dubbing.

Fred, as I call Fellini—he calls me Gorino—decided with *La Dolce Vita* that he was going to get some good actors for the English version. So Marcello Mastroianni, whose charm is a low-keyed sleepiness, was dubbed by Kenneth Haigh, then starring in *Look Back in Anger*. Suddenly, out of this half-asleep face comes an angry English working-class voice. It made no sense at all. Yet Fred was really pleased: "Ees a very good actor, no?" I said, "Yes, but the wrong actor."

Question: Do you think Fellini has turned Donald Sutherland into any different an actor in *Casanova*?

GV: I think he just made a stick out of him. He wanted him literally to be a cock that is moved around from set to set. Fellini had no interest at all in Casanova. He seems never to have read the *Memoirs*. Casanova was one of the most interesting men that ever lived, and his sex life was one of the least important things about him. I suppose Fellini wanted to do an all-out attack on machismo, Italian-style. A good idea, but why call it *Casanova*?

I did the English-language screenplay out of admiration. I worked from the Italian script he had done with Bernardino Zapponi. Universal insisted on direct sound in English, and an acceptable American or English writer. So Fred came to see me and asked me to help out. Then he threw away all the scripts, and worked as he always does. He, not the actors, talks on the original sound track. At one point before a long speech, Sutherland said, "Do you mind if I just think a minute?" Fred said, "Oh, I disturb you? Then I go. I take camera. We all go." Sutherland was not well served by Fellini. Have you seen *1900*? Beautiful to look at in places, but naive politically, and, again, Sutherland is badly used. I think he will probably not work for another Italian.

HA: I wonder if Jan Kadar, Gore, has any response to your views of directors?

Jan Kadar: I am just a pencil.

GV: I had hoped Jan Kadar would do my novel, *Julian*. The BBC is doing it now, as a series. *Julian* is about a fourth-century emperor, which I think is a hard-hitting theme for today. We must always be up-to-date and "with it." It's so important to be with it.

HA: I take it you're more than dissatisfied with the way *Caligula* has turned out.

GV: It's not just another bad movie. It's a joke movie like *Myra Breckinridge,* which was not just a bad movie, it was an awful joke. And I have you, Mr. Alpert, to thank for that. You once reviewed a film called *Joanna,* made by an English pop singer named Michael Sarne. This film was like fifty-two Salem commercials run back-to-back—people running in slow motion through Green Park, girls with long hair, and lots of plummy dialogue. Anyway, you must have suffered a sudden lapse, because your judgments are usually impeccable. Richard Zanuck and David Brown, who were then running Twentieth Century-Fox, suddenly asked me to see *Joanna,* and I knew something was up. I looked at what I thought was one of the ten worst films. The next thing I knew they said, "Well, he's directing *Myra Breckinridge,* and he will also write the script," I said, "What has he done to justify giving him a major film to direct, a movie about Hollywood, a town he has yet to visit?" They said, "*Joanna* is a great flick." I said, "It's a terrible picture." They said, "Just look what the critics say." And there was the Hollis Alpert review. Seared on my memory is that review. I said, "What about the other reviewers?" They said, "What difference do they make? He's the best." Anyway, Michael Sarne never worked in films after *Myra Breckinridge.* I believe he is working as a waiter in a pub in London where they put on shows in the afternoon. This is proof that there is a God and, in nature, perfect symmetry.

Question: Did you write *Myra Breckinridge* at the Chateau Marmont with that awful, revolving figure outside?

GV: No, I didn't write it there, but when I was at Metro I lived at the Chateau Marmont. Oh, God, to wake up in the morning with a hangover and look out and see that figure turning, turning, holding the sombrero—you knew what death would be like.

HA: Have any of the movies made from your screenplays satisfied you?

GV: I think *The Best Man* was the least awful, but I really don't like any of them much, as opposed to what I had in mind.

HA: And if you had directed?

GV: They would have been more satisfactory to me. They might still be bad, but I would be making my own mistakes. The tiring part of movies is having to explain yourself all the time. I had to explain jokes to the director of *The Best Man*, which was based on a play of mine that had run two years, so I knew where the laughs were.

Question: What would you like to direct?

GV: Looking back on it. I think I probably should have tried to direct *Caligula.*

Question: Would you have changed anything?

GV: As soon as you hire John Gielgud, which we did, you start thinking. You have for two weeks one of the most beautiful voices in the world. It's like being given a marvelous oboe. You want to give it some more notes—to write for the actor. I think I might like to direct my novel *Myron*, but it's complicated. It all takes place inside a Westinghouse television set. I don't completely visualize that.

Question: You once mentioned Woody Allen for *Myron*.

GV: Oh, I think Woody Allen would be great playing Myron. Or Paula Prentiss.

Question: Back in the early sixties you formed a company to produce films, Edgewater Productions, with Robert Alan Aurthur and Reginald Rose. What ever happened to it?

GV: I'm glad you brought that up because I've never known what happened to that company. We were the three hot television writers of that day. Well, Robert Alan Aurthur was a bit cooler than Reggie and I. Anyway, Columbia wanted to have a writers' company; Edgewater was the name of my house up the Hudson River. We had a marvelous press conference— I remember that part—very nice and agreeable. It was a very warm feeling, and then I never heard another word from Columbia or anybody. I think Bob Aurthur inherited the company, which was nothing but a name. I'm glad you asked that question. I must find out why we didn't make any movies.

HA: Norman Mailer has made a couple of movies that can hardly be called total successes. They were even worse than *Myra Breckinridge.*
GV: Norman is an odd person. But somebody like Graham Greene, who writes the sort of novel that translates beautifully to film, could direct with the greatest of ease. But, as I said, in those days we didn't want to be bothered with directing, and now it's too late. But the younger people coming along should know that almost anybody can do what a director usually does. On the other hand, very few people can write or tell a story. Those who have the gift should go straight into the movies. Write your own scripts. Become your own director.

Question: If even you have had difficulties with directors, how can an obscure writer assert himself?
GV: You're going to have a very rough time. But it's not impossible. And if you go into directing, you can then write directly onto the celluloid. I see quite a few directors around town, and what are they looking for? A script. They're busy hustling. For any writer with any success at all, it's very pleasant to have every director at a party come over to you, looking for a script or, as they say, property. Warren Beatty came to me about doing a movie—the actors are now getting into the act. I told him how much I liked *McCabe and Mrs. Miller*, and he said, yes, he liked it, too. "Did Robert Altman write it?" I asked. He said. "Well, actually, but I did most of it." So I said, "Warren, if you can write that well you don't need me." And he said, "Oh, well. . . ." If you can create a story, you are way ahead of anybody else in the business. In the fifties we got rid of the producers—they became extinct. As the last memo fell from the hand of D. O. Selznick, that was the end. Now we've got to get rid of the directors. This can be done by becoming a director if you are a writer, a storyteller. If you're not, then become a director and hustle.

Question: When you emphasize the writer, are you also emphasizing more dialogue instead of more of what's called visuals?
GV: I like a talky movie. I believe that an audience will sit still for a great deal of dialogue, if it's good. A director told me the other day that you couldn't have any scene that lasted more than three minutes. The audience wouldn't sit still for anything longer, which is nonsense. If the scene is interesting, the audience will listen for as long as necessary. But you have to be interesting. Most directors seem to have given up on dialogue in favor of moving the

images very quickly in order to create a spurious sense of motion, which is not the same thing as narrative. The director who gave me the advice had just finished creating *The Cassandra Crossing*.

Dialogue is not prose. I think that's the first thing to learn. I once adapted *A Farewell to Arms* for television, and it was awful because I was trying to be faithful to Hemingway. I used his dialogue, his famous dialogue, and though it looks all right on the page, it does not play. We were not helped by Guy Madison's performance.

Question: How do you feel about movie actors?
GV: Oh, I love actors. Movie actors are a very special breed. Gregory Peck and I were once talking about Ronald Reagan, and I said, "I wouldn't want a professional screen actor to be president of the United States, no matter how nice or bright he is, because he's spent his entire life being moved about like a piece of furniture. He's used to being used." That's why all the male actors, almost without exception, become alcoholics. Traditionally, it is not in the male nature—this is a sexist remark—to be totally passive. The actor feels unmanly. He gets drunk. The women take up needlepoint, and survive. A major female movie star will have created ten miles of tapestry by the time her career is over. I couldn't imagine an actor as president. I could imagine a director. After all, he's a hustler, a liar, a cheat—plainly presidential.

Question: You mentioned your failure in adapting Hemingway for television. What sort of literature is most adaptable to the movies?
GV: The best movie adaptations have not come from high literature. A great novel like *Madame Bovary* always fails. *From Here to Eternity*, a so-so novel, was a marvelous movie. It seems to be a kind of rule that secondary works often make extremely good films. A first-rate work is hard to adapt because you can't capture in a movie the writer's personal tone. At one point I was asked to write the screenplay for *The Great Gatsby*. I thought and thought about it and decided not to because the tone of Fitzgerald's prose is what makes the book work, a lyric tone that cannot be filmed. Also, you don't get an English director like Jack Clayton to direct something so peculiarly American. The whole tone was wrong. I did some adaptations for television and the movies. But obviously I preferred my own original work. *Visit to a Small Planet* started on television. Then it went to the theater. Someone else made a lousy movie of it. *The Death of Billy the Kid* was also done on television, and

another lousy movie called *The Left Handed Gun*, which began the career of Arthur Penn, for which we're all grateful.

Question: You've written about Christopher Isherwood and his work in the movies. What's his reaction to the movies—*I Am a Camera, Cabaret*—that were made from his writings?
GV: I will not speak for him, but I rather suspect that he's a little embarrassed by them. But he did support himself for years at MGM. His *Diane*, with Lana Turner, was one of the great films of all time. He also did a fascinating picture called *Rage in Heaven*, with Ingrid Bergman and George Sanders, in 1941. He's actually a good movie writer. I remember one day we were walking down a corridor in that iron lung of a building named for Thalberg at Metro, and he said, "They pay us well for our anonymity." Under no circumstances was the word going to get out that the writers created the movies. In those days the producers got the credit. It was "A Pandro S. Berman Film." It was not "A Film by Christopher Isherwood." And it certainly was not "A Film Directed by Richard Brooks."

Question: Do you think films are affecting the writing of novels?
GV: Yes. Mine is the first generation of writers brought up on talking films, and I think we were more affected by films than any of the other narrative forms. Tell me somebody's favorite actor when he was ten years old, and I'll tell you who he is. Could Norman Mailer have existed without John Garfield? He's been playing Garfield, and I've been doing George Arliss. You get hung up with an image. Now, today's generation is being brought up on ninety-second television commercials. That might make for a certain oddness. Twenty years from now a girl might break down and discover that she's an Oil of Olay commercial. Or a detergent. Today's models for the young are not as gorgeous as ours were.

Question: When you sell the rights to a novel or a play to the movies, do you keep any proprietary interest in it?
GV: No. You assume that the movies will do what they want with it and that it's pointless to complain. I would complain about something like *Caligula*, which I wrote directly for the screen, or about a play, which is pretty close to a movie. *Visit to a Small Planet* was originally done with Cyril Ritchard. Then the movies bought it and gave it to Jerry Lewis, another enthusiasm of the

French. Well, it's never in my contract that I have to see the results. I have never seen *Myra Breckinridge, Visit to a Small Planet,* or *The Left Handed Gun.* They do crop up on television, and sometimes I'll hear something familiar and realize, "Oh, my God, it's that!" And the blood pressure starts to go up, and I switch to another channel, to the commercials, where all the genius goes.

HA: You mentioned earlier the importance of story and narrative in film. Is there a method you prefer in telling stories?
GV: Godard once made a marvelous remark to Clouzot. Clouzot was criticizing Godard's work and his methods, and finally Clouzot said. "You've got to admit, Mr. Godard, that a movie has to have a beginning, a middle, and an end." And Godard said, "Yes, but not necessarily in that order." There are many different ways of skinning a cat. The secret is that you must be very interesting. I don't know how you translate that into action, but one way of being interesting is to be interested. I've found that writers I've known for a long time whose work starts to fall off have first lost interest in the world. My old and dear friend Tennessee Williams is a great playwright. But Tennessee's work has been fading for some years, which he puts down to drink and pills and so on, but that is only part of it. He's got a very strong talent and a very strong physical structure. Unfortunately, he's lost interest in people. He doesn't read a newspaper, doesn't read a book, doesn't know what country he's in. He's a romantic writer who is essentially working out of his own past, and that kind of writer has just so many cards. He has the sister, he has the mother, he has the father, he has the piece of trade. He keeps playing with this same deck of cards, and at his best he's the best around. But you cannot keep on using your own youth, particularly if you're going to have a career that lasts forty or fifty years. You wear out the deck.

Mailer is another case. Norman doesn't read much of anything. Yet when he does get outside of himself and look at something, he's marvelous. He got very interested in—and therefore he was interesting on—the moon shot. He suddenly started describing machinery. He was trained as an engineer, and he has a convergent as opposed to a divergent mind, which means he's always trying to connect one thing to another. I'm just the opposite—I see no connections. There's poor Bill Inge, who died out here. Absolutely nothing was going on in Bill's life or in his head after about the age of thirty-five. He couldn't take in anything new. So the object is to stay interested and to try and pick up new things. Certainly, it's very dull if you don't, and failure isn't much fun, though I am told that there's plenty of room at the bottom.

I'm sort of a compulsive reader and student, and I think I learned the trick because I didn't go to college, and so was able to get an education. Otherwise I would have had four years of paralysis. After three years of the army in the Second World War, I said. "No institution will ever hold me again," and none has—except, briefly, MGM.

HA: Gore is a very successful high school graduate. In fact, he may be the most successful high school graduate in history.

Question: One of the dangers you're pointing to for a writer is a kind of narcissism in which a whole world becomes a mirror.

GV: Solipsism, yes. I think it is very dangerous. Yet it's very difficult to realize that other people actually exist. I think most people go through their lives not taking in or trying not to take in the reality of others. I find I can go twenty or thirty minutes at a time without thinking about myself. I think that's pretty good. But I have to force myself to think of, let us say, Ravenna mosaics. I start looking at the mosaics, and for a time lose myself, but then, suddenly. I think: I'm looking at Ravenna mosaics, and I'm back to square one, the beloved self.

Question: In writing your historical novels, are you consciously attempting to throw light on today through the use of the past?

GV: I think there's not a great deal of difference from one period to another, but, yes. I think re-creating the past illuminates the present. We're a strange society in that we have no past. That's why I wrote my American trilogy, *Burr, 1876, Washington, D.C.* Partly, I wanted to tell myself the story of the history of the country because I found history as boring in school as everybody else did, and I knew the national story could not have been that dull, and it wasn't. But we're a society forever trying to erase yesterday. Because of this we got the Nixons. We live in a world where nobody is accountable for anything. It's quite astonishing. We Nixon-viewers knew he was a criminal years ago, but we couldn't tell anybody. They wouldn't listen, they weren't interested. A society without a recollected history is also peculiarly vulnerable to anyone who wants to take it over. I do see Caesars moving in upon the forum, and when they arrive there will not be much resistance. After all, the average person watches six hours of television a day. How can they defend their liberties when they're busy watching *The Gong Show*?

Question: When you sit down to write, how much of the story do you have in your mind, how much do you discover as you go along?
GV: You start with a shape in your head. Virginia Woolf said that *The Waves*, which was her own favorite novel, started for her this way: "I saw a dark sea and the fin of a shark turning." That was her beginning image. When I wrote *Washington, D.C.*, I saw a storm and the garden of the house in Virginia where I was brought up. You start very often with an image, and I generally don't know much more than where I think it's going, where it should end. Then I sit there roaring with laughter as the sentences appear on the page. Where is this coming from? I sometimes wonder. Oh, it is interesting, the creative process. Where was this story before I wrote it down? I don't know. It certainly wasn't in my head. You can't walk around with all that stuff on file, particularly when you've written a lot of books over the years. Arthur Schlesinger, Jr., once was looking at his three or four volumes on Roosevelt and said, "You know, there are times when I wonder how did I ever know all those things that are in those books." Writing also acts as a kind of an eraser. I know nothing about the fourth century now, but when I wrote *Julian* I did. A kind of mental erasure takes place. That's why writing is also therapeutic. You can get rid of a lot of things.

Question: One of your earliest novels was *The City and the Pillar*, a bold work for its time. What censure did you encounter?
GV: A lot. It was the first book to deal with homosexuality as a perfectly normal activity carried on by people who were not necessarily demented, child-molesting hairdressers. It was about two quite normal, middle-class Southern boys enjoying one another. Nothing like this had been published in the United States. Up to then I had been a war novelist, and suddenly the war novelist had written this wicked, wicked book. My friend Anaïs Nin said, "It will destroy you." She was very dark about it. The daily reviewer for the *New York Times*, then as now one of the world's worst newspapers, said that he would never review another book of mine. And I was not reviewed for sixteen years by the daily *Times*. The Sunday *New York Times* would not take advertising for *The City and the Pillar* or for *The Kinsey Report*, which came out shortly after my book. It's a free country! But if you outlive

everybody. . . . I believe you can buy the *Times* for $41 million—Hollis, do you want to buy it?

HA: We'd have to edit it.
GV: No, the point of the *Times* is that it's not edited. They just put it out.

Question: You are writing novels and screenplays. Does writing for television still appeal to you?
GV: There's nothing to do. It's all hour-long adventure-gangster things. We used to do plays for television which were performed live. But that's all ended. I *have* been asked to narrate about four, ninety-minute shows on the American presidents, and I might do that. If the shows were done the right way, it would be interesting.

Question: What would be the right way?
GV: Objectively. Not disguising what the country was like, what its past really was. The interesting thing about the United States has been its unremitting imperialism, from the very first moment we killed our first Indian right up to Vietnam. We have been almost continually at war and on the march. To show all this, as reflected in the presidents and their rhetoric, would be very interesting to do. But I'm not sure that Xerox would pick up the tab.

Question: But television otherwise doesn't interest you—no specials or movies of the week?
GV: No, thank you. I'm not what they want. They have enough trouble with me as a talking head on television, without having me write things that offend. About every few years they try to bring back the golden age of television. People like Mike Dann call me in for lunch. He has lunch with Paddy Chayefsky on Monday, me on Tuesday, Reggie Rose on Wednesday, and then announces we're going to do something, and it never gets done. I've stopped having those lunches.

Question: There are people who regard the fifties as indeed television's golden age. How golden was it?
GV: Most of our stuff was terrible in the golden age. We did so much, too much. There were seven, live, hour shows a week out of New York. I don't know how we did it. Someone would ring up suddenly and say, "Tad Mosel's

script hasn't come in. We've got the sets built: We've got a bar, a bedroom, and there's a kind of ballroom. We've got Kim Stanley, we've got Paul Newman, and Vinnie Donehue is going to direct. Can you think of a play?" In three or four days you'd write something to fit the sets and the cast. That really is Lope de Vega time. I don't know how we did it. Most of the time it was pretty bad, but every now and then it was very exciting. It was also wonderful for actors—you would be up there live, knowing one mistake and twenty million people will see it.

I remember the night that the girl vomited in Albert Salmi's lap because she was so nervous. They were in a two-shot. Albert was talking, and she just very quietly vomited in his lap. You didn't see much because they were cutting it very tight. But there was a strange look on Albert's face. Then the camera cut to her face, and there was a little saliva. God, it was wild. There was the night Cloris Leachman went up. She was playing a Southern belle with long hair. She was sitting beside a pond and she said, "I'm just going to sit here and trail my fingers in the water and trail my fingers in the water," and she did. She kept on trailing those fingers until they cut away from her.

Question: Have you seen Chayefsky's *Network*?
GV: Yes, I liked that. Mrs. Martin Scorsese said to me, rather sharply, "Well, I didn't like it." I said, "Why didn't you? I think it was marvelous." She said, "It was like listening to two hours of Gore Vidal on television." I said, "What's wrong with that?" Anyway, the movie is fun, if a little overdrawn.

Question: Do you ever wonder if society is creating television or if television is creating society?
GV: If I could answer that, I could walk on water. It's a good question. I think society and television are totally interrelated now. I remember seeing one of Andy Warhol's early movies. *Chelsea Girls*, and I told him, "It's kind of dull." He said, "Oh, yes, that's the point." I said, "What do you mean, that's the point?" He said, "Well, you know, people will always watch something rather than nothing." There's a great deal of wisdom in that. There is the screen with these rippling colors and bang-bang and a decibel level that keeps you moderately interested. To think that an average American sits there six hours a day looking at that junk. . . . What sort of society is going to evolve I don't know. But I'm glad I won't be around writing books. Nobody will be able to read them.

Question: You appeared on *Mary Hartman, Mary Hartman* recently. Had you acted before?

GV: No, I hadn't. But I had always said acting was very easy for most people to do, except for certain professional actors. The Europeans discovered a long time ago that if somebody was physically right for a part and if he was reasonably at ease with himself, acting was easy. I wound up coldly upstaging Louise Lasser in our farewell scene—I must say the grips wept. We were sitting in the loony bin at Fernwood, and Louise, who has normally quite a loud voice, turned to me and said, "Gore, I've got to tell you—I'm in love with you." I said, "Are you?" "Yes," she said softly, "I am." "Oh, really," I said more softly. I wasn't going to let her out tender me, so every time she dropped her voice I dropped mine under hers. Well, by the time we finished all you could see were lips moving. I believe we were totally lovable.

Question: What attracted you to *Mary Hartman*?

GV: I like Norman Lear. I think he's trying to do something a little different. He said, "We'll write you in." I said, fine. I thought I was going to come for one show. Instead I did eight of the damn things. I got interested in the technical end. After fifty you have to keep thinking of new things to do, to keep yourself interested. Obviously, being a soap-opera star is new for me. I now sit by the phone waiting for job offers. On *Welcome Back, Kotter* there's a chance I might play a friendly psychiatrist, if one of the kids goes really off the rails.

The difficult thing was learning the lines, because soap operas have no action. You just sit at the kitchen table with the coffee in front of you, and talk. There's never any reason for you to get up except when you run out of pages. Sometimes the camera shows you going to the door; sometimes you are discovered halfway to the door. I finally worked it out so that I kept the dialogue on my lap. While Louise was on camera doing one of her arias—her speeches would run six to eight pages, mine about five or six—I would be reading my next speech. As a result my dialogue sounded very fresh because it was quite new to me. But there's that awful moment when you know you're going to forget it. This happens to me on television. Whenever I say, "Now there are three things that you've got to remember," I've already lost "three," "two" is beginning to fade, and "one" is crumbling.

Question: You're referring to your talk show appearances?

GV: Yes, but it's interesting talking on television. I do it quite cold-bloodedly, to propagandize. I pick a general direction I want to go in. Now you can't get on the tube unless you're hustling something so I have to pretend to be selling a book or play. I get that over as quickly as possible. I've even stopped Johnny Carson in the middle of a conversation about the book to get on to the attorney general's crimes. In a funny way, television is the only way you can get to people. Certainly, you can't trust a journalist: you end up as his invention, for good or ill. But on television your voice is actually heard without an intermediary. I was told that when I go on the Carson show, the ratings go up in all the cities, and the entire Midwest and South turn off. The show has to sort of work it out—when they feel they need the cities and don't really need Tulsa.

Question: Is there any attempt by network powers to keep you off?

GV: They don't like me, and Dick Cavett told me that the blacklist still goes on. He said that, periodically, he would be given a list of people not to have on, and sometimes I would be on that list. Then, for no reason at all, I'd be off it. Nobody ever figured out the rationale for it. But there is indeed a blacklist, and it does continue.

Question: What do you think of the talk shows?

GV: Each show has a different feel to it. Merv Griffin has got terribly good. He used to be about the worst, and he's almost the best now. I don't know what happened. He became a conglomerate. I think that's it. I think enormous wealth has relaxed him. He's also got a very interesting studio audience out there to play off. I don't know where they get the audience on Carson's show. I find them slow. But Carson is still the best of the lot when he's interested. But I think he must go crazy, being on night after night. On *The David Susskind Show* I do my state of the union once a year. We do an hour or two together. I suppose we lose all the cities before the end.

Question: You're a frank critic of this country. Do you regard yourself as an expatriate because you live in Rome?

GV: With air travel, nothing is so dramatic as either-or. Anyway, I've been involved in every election in this country for over twenty years. Italy's just a place to live, and I think I get a clearer perspective on the United States there.

And then I come back every six months or so, and sometimes I see things other people don't see because they're living here day after day. For instance, everything in New York is bent. I don't know who does it. But, somebody gets up in the morning and goes out and twists every piece of metal until he's bent it. But nobody in New York seems aware that everything is bent. I keep pointing it out. I say, "Who's doing the bending?" They don't know. All the cars coming in from the airport are dented.

Question: That's because you spend your time in taxicabs.
GV: No, actually, I make it a point to walk in from the airport. That's how I get to know the northern reaches of Manhattan. The cars are too big—that strikes you right off—these huge tanks moving along with the drivers all talking to themselves.

Question: Is there a country that you think has a healthy society?
GV: I did a play called *An Evening with Richard Nixon*, which was ahead of its time. It was done in 1972, just when all the newspapers were getting ready to come out for him, so you can see my sense of timing was excellent. We had a marvelous actor, George Irving, and he now has a marvelous Nixon number, which he does on television: "I see a nation without poverty, a nation without violence, a nation that is clean, a nation that is prosperous. I see Switzerland." That's your answer—Switzerland. But I wouldn't live there.

Question: It's been said on more than one occasion that you should be president.
GV: I think you're quite right.

Question: Norman Mailer, in fact, said that once.
GV: That's only when Norman decided that he was aiming for Jehovah. I could have the United States while he was the big one in the sky.

Question: You have a well-earned reputation as an outspoken person. Are there limitations you place on yourself, areas you think it best to avoid?
GV: No. The inner censor works only when I'm hired by a studio or when I was writing live television where I couldn't mention suicide and this and that—there were so many taboos. I've had to conform at times. But when I write a novel, I'm completely on my own. Occasionally, I find that I draw

back from something because I think I'm not the person who can say it.
I figured out that George Washington was in love with Alexander
Hamilton—it's absolutely apparent—and I'm the one writer in the country
who couldn't write that. Norman Mailer could. So I'm limited, to a
degree—limited, perhaps, by preconceptions.

HA: Your essays often draw on your own life. Are you thinking about your
memoirs yet?
GV: Oh, I'm not into memoir-time. That's what you do when you're broke.
Or the waters of the mind have gone dry. I am in the glorious summer—well,
early September—of my days.

Question: In the absence of memoirs, can you give a thumbnail sketch of
how you see yourself?
GV: I'm not that self-regarding. Early in life I decided I was the judge. What I
thought of people was more important than what they thought of me. I have
no desire to be lovable. Wanting to be loved is a common malady. I would
like to be useful, a less common form of illness.

Gore Vidal

Charles Ruas / 1984

From *Conversations with American Writers*, New York: Random House, 1985, pp. 57–74. © Charles Ruas. Reprinted by permission of the author.

Gore Vidal, as man of letters, has taken the position of legitimate arbiter of contemporary American politics and culture. With rationalism and wit, he has been the scourge of know-nothing popular culture, as well as a vigilant critic of prejudices, misconceptions, and facile writing among his peers. His essays and literary criticism have been collected in four volumes which target the political and cultural issues of the country for the last three decades.

Born in 1925 at the Military Academy at West Point, New York, where his father was posted and teaching, Gore Vidal grew up in Washington, D.C., under the influence of his maternal grandfather, Senator Thomas Gore. From him Gore Vidal derives his intimate knowledge of American politics and history as well as his grounding in the classics and modern literature.

He enlisted in the army in 1943, upon graduating from Phillips Exeter Academy, and his war experiences were the subject of his first two novels, *Williwaw* (1946) and *In a Yellow Wood* (1947), which established his reputation as a postwar novelist. His third novel, *The City and the Pillar* (1948), was a *succès de scandale* for its depiction of homosexual life. This was followed by *The Season of Comfort* (1949), *A Search for the King* (1950), *Dark Green, Bright Red* (1951), *The Judgment of Paris* (1952), and *Messiah* (1954). The failure of his next six novels caused Gore Vidal to write the Edgar Box murder mysteries, and to try writing for television, films, and the stage—*Visit to a Small Planet* (1957), and *The Best Man* (1960). In the same year he ran in New York State for election to the House of Representatives. Again in 1982 he ran for the Senate as a Democrat from California.

With the publication of *Julian* in 1964, Gore Vidal triumphantly returned to the novel form, and has continued his historical and satirical depictions of contemporary mores, in *Washington D.C.* (1967). *Myra Breckinridge* (1968), *Two Sisters* (1970), *Burr* (1973), *Myron* (1974), *1876* (1976), *Kalki* (1978), *Creation* (1981), *Duluth* (1983), and *Lincoln* (1984).

Members of the press were leaving Gore Vidal's Plaza suite when I arrived for my appointment. His reluctance to speak about himself or his work notwithstanding, he is a favorite with the media and had been giving interviews all day. His suite has a view of Central Park, which from this height is sharply outlined as a green rectangle fenced in from every direction by irregular rows of concrete apartment blocks. The green surface is slashed across by dark roadways. From here, trees are puffs of foliage growing densely along the perimeter and thinning as they spread towards the center, the dusty yellows, browns and greens giving the impression of rampant growth in a neglected planter. I examined the view as Gore Vidal picked up the phone to tell the operator to take messages, so that we could speak undisturbed.

Gore Vidal is tall and, surprisingly, slightly heavier than he appears in photographs or on television, because the camera brings out his strong bone structure—wide brows, straight thin nose, and firm jawline. His eyes are pale, almost a yellow-brown, and quizzical in expression—he sometimes squints. His dark-brown hair, streaked gray, is parted and combed straight back. He appears athletic, and dresses with elegance. When he is not mimicking characters, his conversation is equally elegant, rapid, almost clipped, and has the bite and brilliance of his written style.

Charles Ruas: In your novel *Julian*, the Emperor of Byzantium becomes an apostate because he attempts to revive the pagan gods and the cult of philosophy in opposition to the state religion, Christianity. Again, in your novel *Creation*, an enlightened and skeptical narrator encounters the world's major religions. Whether you are writing about antiquity or American history, the subject is the nature of governments, politics, and the wielding of power. The position you take, as expressed by various narrators, is like Julian's, the opposition from within.

Gore Vidal: Unfortunately, I never achieved the high office that Julian did as Emperor of Rome, but I certainly was an apostate. A political family is an unusual background for a writer, a novelist. In the American context, a writer whom I think I resemble in some ways is Henry Adams. But there was no model for me when I began. I wanted to be a politician. I was constantly reading to my blind grandfather Senator Gore. We read everything—a great deal of history, particularly classical history. He was born in 1870. That means between his memories and my memories, we encompass half the history of the United States. The Reconstruction in the South—in Mississippi, where he came from—was as vivid to him as my race for Congress when Jack Kennedy was running for president is to me. So I know half the history of the country, as it were, first hand. In due course I got very interested in the half I didn't know—before his birth and mine.

CR: Is that the reason why artistically you turned to history as your subject?
GV: Inevitably, one brings to bear upon these reflections about the American past a knowledge of the political life of the present era. I know what politicians are like because I was around them; I know what presidents do and don't do; what the Congress is like. That's why I was always startled in school by textbooks that were neither interesting nor truthful. I was as bored taking history in school as everybody else was. Eventually, I decided that I would go back to the Revolutionary period to find out what the country's founders had in mind. And, as I suspected, American history was extremely interesting. Out of all this reading came the American trilogy—*Burr, 1876, Washington, D.C.* Now, God help us, a tetralogy—with *Lincoln.* What little the average thoughtful American—that is, the 5 percent of the country who read books—what little they know about American history, I taught them. [*Laughs.*] I never intended to do this. I certainly wasn't trained to do it—I was self-taught. Rather an awesome responsibility. Fortunately [*smiles*], someone else will come along in another generation or sooner and take my place. I was happy to have made a contribution. Simultaneously, I was curious about the invention of Christianity [*Julian*]. Most of it was done about the fourth century A.D., when the mystery cults and so forth were absorbed into Christianity. That, in a sense, was also the inspiration for *Creation,* which then goes back five or six hundred years before Julian, when suddenly the entire human race began to write and to ask such questions as: How was earth created? Every system, philosophic, ethical, religious, and scientific, was really all present in the fifth century B.C. in embryo form. I want to know everything—that is temperamental—and, combined with the accident of being born into an active political family, I had the sort of background that made it possible—inevitable—for me to write about men of power from first-hand knowledge, as Henry Adams could, and as the great Thucydides could.

CR: Did the development of your political sense as a child, listening and reading to your grandfather, cause you to start writing at an early age?

GV: I was taught to read by my grandmother at the age of five. By six I was reading tales from Livy, the first grown-up book I read. By seven or eight I was attempting to write novels and a great deal of poetry. Between the ages of fourteen and nineteen I had started five novels. The fifth was completed; that was my first book, *Williwaw*.

CR: Did reading create the impetus to become a writer?

GV: I never wanted to be a writer. I mean, that's the last thing *I* wanted. I expected to be a politician. My grandfather at one point thought he might have been president, and once you get that in the family, the family never gets over it. That was the unfinished business of his life. I was very close to him, and his son was a disappointment, and my mother, his daughter, equally a disappointment. I was the oldest grandchild, and I lived with him. I would be his political heir. That's what I wanted, too. Unfortunately—or fortunately, as the case may be—I was a writer. I simply could not *not* write. A writer is someone who writes, that's all. You can't stop it; you can't make yourself do anything else but that. I took ten years off, hoping I could kick the habit, turned to politics and to writing for the stage, movies, and television. I don't regard those things as proper writing; writing they are, in a way . . . but God!

CR: But that's just transferring your skills to another medium, so I don't understand why you did it.

GV: I did it partly for financial reasons. I inherited no money and I had to make money. Also, it amused me: Maybe I can finish with this thing; maybe I can go into politics. But by 1960 I found myself writing again, *Julian*.

CR: In 1960—that's when you ran unsuccessfully for the House of Representatives in New York State.

GV: But I did very well in that race, was the leader in five counties of the Mid-Hudson. I ran twenty thousand votes ahead of John F. Kennedy, who was the head of the ticket. I lost by about twenty-two thousand votes, which means that if Jack had done a little better, I would have won. In '62 I was offered the nomination for the Senate to run against Javits, and I turned that down. In '64, when I was in Rome finishing up *Julian*, I was offered the seat for the race upstate again, and I would have won. We had turned the district around. I said, "No, I don't want to be in the House of Representatives. I am now a writer again."

CR: The kind of mind that engages in writing and politics has a historical perspective. Even *Kalki*, with its scenes about the end of the human race, reveals a historical imagination, so that your fiction is always informed by a sense of history.

GV: I divide my novels between reflections and inventions. Reflections on Christianity and history, as in *Julian* and *Creation*; reflections on American politics in the tetralogy. In these books I'm doing the work of a historian or biographer, reflecting upon the past and making narratives out of it, in much the same way as the historians who interest me the most do . . . Thucydides, say, who was a proto-novelist. I enjoy the reflections. But I much prefer the inventions, because I make them up out of my head. If I'm remembered at all as a writer it will be for *Myra Breckinridge, Myron*, and *Kalki*. The reflections may be superseded by other reflectors, but my inventions are not going to be deinvented.

CR: Didn't the publication of *The City and the Pillar* affect your chances in running for office, since the subject of homosexuality was considered so scandalous at the time?

GV: No. If it did, it would have come up in 1960, when I ran. I got the most votes of any Democratic candidate for Congress in that district in fifty years. It didn't seem to cause any distress to the crowd. Mind you, the press's axes were constantly grinding. I have a great deal of problem with the print media. But as long as I have television, I can counteract what they do.

CR: It constantly occurs to me that as a man of letters, you are a political writer in your essays, always in the public eye, yet the media present you as a personality rather than as a political commentator or as a novelist.

GV: The media trivialize everything and everyone. What are they going to do with ideas they can't cope with? Nothing. So they just do personality. They create a fictional character called Gore Vidal, which bears no relationship to me. Also, I never try to present my work as a writer. That's for the critic to do, that's for the publisher to do, that's for the books themselves to do. I go on television to try to change people's minds.

CR: In your essays I can define your stance as that of arbiter; how do you see yourself when you address the public directly?

GV: What I do when I make an appearance is—well, be political. I am seen in political terms and newspapers tend not to like what I say. Why should they? I regard them as very much a part of the problem. I am attacking the ruling class of the country, and the economic interests that dominate the United States, and the fact that we have no politics, etc. But on those occasions when I am able to go on television and talk directly to the people, a fair proportion apparently like what they hear. What they like is that I am attacking something that they sense is all wrong, and I am trying to define a prospect which is obscured, to say the least. But then it is meant to be obscured because the great interests in the country do not want to illuminate the darkness.

CR: Your early work was highly praised. How do you explain this conflict with the print media?
GV: *The City and the Pillar*—it started then and it was relentless. Orville Prescott, a reviewer of enormous power in the daily *New York Times*, wrote a marvelous review of *Williwaw*. But then he read *The City and the Pillar*, and he said to my publisher, "I will not only never review another novel by this disgusting writer, but I will never read one." So my next five books were not reviewed by the *Times*—or by *Time* or *Newsweek*. I was excluded, when the previous year *Life* had pictured me as *the* young war novelist.

CR: Are you saying the issue was homophobia?
GV: Oh, nothing but fag bashing, going on all the time. They never let up.

CR: How do you think that Truman Capote's early novels escaped that?
GV: Fairly obvious. He played the part. He was entirely what you would expect a person of that sort to be.

CR: The whole persona he created then?
GV: Exactly. They don't mind hairdressers. They are not threatened by someone who is effeminate and freakish and amusing; he's good copy. I was a six-foot soldier with a much-admired war novel who had suddenly written a book of the sort that nobody else had ever done [in this country], showing the normality of a certain sort of relationship. This was unbearable to the media. From then on it was trouble. The other writer who had the same problem was Norman Mailer. They really turned on him for radical

politics [*Barbary Shore*], for radical statements about life, and sex, and so on. But he set to work, doggedly, to get them to accept him and they did.

CR: You believe the media try to control artistic careers?

GV: Take Tennessee Williams—he commanded Broadway for ten years, which is a long time in that business. Brooks Atkinson at the *Times* was quite autonomous. Although the people who ran the *Times* did not like Tennessee or degeneracy, Atkinson was just too big, they couldn't handle him. But the literary reviews of Tennessee were poisonous. *Time* magazine's Louis Kronenberger never gave him a good review; he attacked everything from *Glass Menagerie* on. But then it was house policy, because I asked Henry Luce.

My stepfather was his roommate at Yale and put up about a fourth of the money to start *Time*. So, Uncle Harry, as we were taught to call him, and I were on a shuttle from Washington to New York. I said, "You know, I think it is disgusting, what you do in your magazine in the theatre reviews"—they were unsigned in those days. "We have only one great playwright in the United States, who is Tennessee Williams, and he has never had a good review in *Time* magazine. This makes *Time* magazine look silly, because he is read around the world and everybody is doing his plays, and they pick this up." And Luce said, "Well, I don't like him." And I said, "Yes, but other people do." And he said, "Well, it's *my* magazine." That is right from—as they say—the horse's mouth.

Finally, Tennessee was put on the cover of *Time* for *Night of the Iguana*. Kronenberger was gone by then and Luce was dead or withdrawn. So I did a piece for *Esquire*, unsigned. On one side, I quoted every *Time* review of Tennessee's work, each one a blast. Beside it, I put all the words of praise from the cover story. The article was illustrated with a painting of Tennessee emerging out of the swamp, busy typing away. The heading was from Ecclesiastes, "In *time* all things shall come to pass." Tennessee was annoyed. He said [*imitating voice*], "Why did you remind them about my bad reviews, why did you do it? You did it deliberately!"

CR: You've often said that your work is not autobiographical, but your first two novels are about the war. I was wondering how *The City and the Pillar* affected your family.

GV: My father quite liked it. But then we always got on well. For one thing, I have supported myself since I was seventeen. I enlisted in the army. When I was twenty my first book was published. I have supported myself ever since, which is probably the rarest story in American literature—all by writing. Fathers tend to like that. I have never been a teacher. I did not marry money, as some of my wise confreres have done.

CR: Was it right after the war that you met Anaïs Nin?
GV: I was still in the army when I met Anaïs. A friend was giving a lecture at the YMHA and I sat next to her. This must have been in '45, when I was stationed at Mitchel Field, just back from overseas. And thus began our relationship, capital R, and that went on and on, and then on and off. Then she came down to Guatemala and stayed with me, and I went to Acapulco and stayed with her, and nearly died of hepatitis, which she nursed me through. We had a great row over *The City and the Pillar*. She thought I depicted her badly; she gave it much thought and read a position paper on it.

CR: If anything, I thought the character of Maria Verlaine was idealized.
GV: Anaïs said the character was sordid. What bothered her, I think, was the fact that the woman was twenty-two years older than the young man. But Anaïs wasn't really the character, and God knows I wasn't the character. I know when Tennessee read it—he almost never read a book of any kind by anybody—but he sat down and read that one straight through—and he hated the ending. He said [*mimicking voice*], "You didn't know what a good book you had. Why did you tack on such a melodramatic ending? Of course, I liked particularly your family." I said, "What?" "You know, that Virginia family, exactly like my own background." I said I had made it all up, I got it all out of James T. Farrell. I would have liked to be the tennis player that Jim Willard was, but not the hustler. He was quite startled. Most people think that you can't write a book like that at such a young age, that you can't invent. But it's all an invention. Closest to life was the character of Anaïs, someone *like* her, but not her.

CR: But that didn't cause the final break between you.
GV: That was the first break. She was forever denouncing people. She'd write out a position paper, why she could no longer see you, you had betrayed her. She wrote one to Maya Deren. She fell out with Jane Bowles when Jane published *Two Serious Ladies*, of a brilliance beyond anything Anaïs could

achieve. It had the *succès d'estime* Anaïs lusted after. Paul Bowles described in his memoirs walking down a street in the Village. A funny little woman darts out of a doorway, grabs Jane, and pulls her to the corner. He sees them talking very intensely, gesticulating, and Jane looking bewildered and finally breaking away. "What on earth is that?" Jane says, "That was Anaïs Nin." "What on earth was she carrying on about? You don't know her, do you?" She says, "No. She was just telling me what a bad writer I was." Anaïs took it personally that Jane could have had such a success.

CR: Anaïs Nin was very frustrated at having such a hard time bringing out her work and meeting with so little understanding.
GV: There's a lot to be said on Anaïs's side. What she did wasn't really very good unless you managed to fall in love with her. She just didn't fit into any category. She wasn't a novelist; she wasn't a short-story writer; she wasn't an American. These were all things which mattered in *those* days in *this* world, particularly in the New York publishing world. To get her published by E. P. Dutton, I forced them to take her, and no reference is made to this in the diaries. She did dedicate *Ladders to Fire* to me, but the dedication was removed from later editions.

CR: You satirize these traits in your novel *Two Sisters*. But was Maya Deren your introduction to filmmaking at that time?
GV: My mother had spent the war years in Bungalow No. 1 at the Beverly Hills Hotel, and that put me right in the center of the stage. She was surrounded by film people, and they liked the idea of a great Eastern lady living among them. She was an alcoholic, the life style of many people then. Later she worked for Alcoholics Anonymous. I'd been frozen—got arthritis in the Aleutians—and I was in Birmingham General Hospital in Van Nuys. So I used to hitchhike every now and then over to Hollywood and hang around the studios. I was there about three months, until I was restored to active duty. Later, after the war, with Maya, I saw experimental filming. Anaïs and I acted in one of Maya's films. We stood around and made symbolic gestures. I never saw the movie. I'd like to see what we all looked like then.

CR: That was your first encounter with the surrealist movement?
GV: Anaïs was on the fringe of the surrealist movement, and I remember she took me to a party at Peggy Guggenheim's where I met André Breton,

Charles Henri Ford, Parker Tyler, and Jim Agee. Ford and Tyler used to put out *View Magazine*, and I was charmed and intrigued. After all, I was a war novelist in the tradition of Stephen Crane, and it was miles different from what I thought literature to be. Later, I was to absorb some of the paradoxes of surrealism—which you can find in Myra/Myron.

CR: Do you see your first eight novels, before you left off with the genre, as having a direct line of development?

GV: Only *Williwaw* works aesthetically, because I knew what I couldn't do. There wasn't much that I *could* do, but I knew how to deploy it. It's a small book, but it works. *In a Yellow Wood* is small and terrible. *The City and the Pillar* is a kind of innocent book, rather flawed. With *The Season of Comfort* I attempted a major breakthrough. By then I was a modernist, reading Joyce and so on; and the result was a mess. I have never allowed it to be reprinted. Then came *A Search for the King*, my first historical novel, twelfth-century, which has a certain charm, like an E. B. White kind of legend. *Dark Green, Bright Red* is about the revolution in Guatemala, and very good on action. It generally bores me to read battle scenes, but they are interesting to write because they are so difficult. Then I was trying out different voices in the short stories, *A Thirsty Evil*. At the age of twenty-five, I settled down in the Hudson Valley and wrote *The Judgment of Paris*, my first good book. I found my voice, and the style is what it has been ever since. Next came *Messiah*, which became an underground favorite for many years. Then came my oblivion, because without *The New York Times*, *Time*, and *Newsweek* my books were vanishing. So I quit for ten years.

CR: Seriously, was it mixed reviews or lack of attention that forced you into this decision?

GV: It was financial. I couldn't live. I had a best seller in *The City and the Pillar*, but the others were, literally, unnoticed. I had a marvelous reputation in England and certain European countries, but I couldn't live on my royalties, so I had to do something else. I went into television.

CR: Is that also the reason you started writing those wonderful Edgar Box detective novels?

GV: Well, because I was broke, I really had only two choices: one was to write under a pseudonym, and the other was to quit and go off and do something

else for a while till the troubles blew over. So I did both. I went off to television, and I published three mystery stories, all written in one year. I wrote
each one in eight days. Each has seven chapters of ten thousand words. I
would do ten thousand words a day, and on the eighth day I would revise.
They were published under the pseudonym Edgar Box and received glowing
reviews. I did it because my editor had said, "We have Spillane. Now we need
an up-to-date S. S. Van Dyne." They are still in print around the world, and
certainly more translated than most of my novels.

CR: How do you think writing for television, the theatre, and films affected
your style when you returned to the novel?
GV: You learn a great deal. What you learn is something you ought to
know anyway but you don't. The novel in English has always tended to be
discursive, and if you add that to the tendentiousness that is so natural to
Americans, the result is often windy and garrulous. A detail is there just
because the writer put it there, and there's no selection. What you learn in the
theatre is that every line must mean something, must have a purpose. This is
extraordinary news to most novelists, because most of them just go on and
on until they finally stop. Occasionally you get a perfectionist like Flaubert
who desperately tries to remove double genitives and so on, but that is very
rare. You can see in James an immediate difference from his early books and
What Maisie Knew, The Awkward Age, and *Turn of the Screw,* which came
right after his long period of trying to break into the theatre. My career was
the reverse of his. I went into the theatre and made the money that James
dreamt of making. Then I went back to the novel having learned better how
to make scenes work—and how *not* to write.

CR: During this early phase of your career, having grown up in Washington
with your grandfather who was from Mississippi, you never identified with
the Southern writers.
GV: I didn't really like them. Maybe I got too much of it at home. Anyway,
I was drawn to European writers. Earlier, when I was a kid, it was Somerset
Maugham—and James T. Farrell: *Studs Lonigan* was my first sexy book.
Then, as I started to read seriously, D. H. Lawrence immediately captured me.
Now, of course, I wonder what it was I saw in *Women in Love.* With great
admiration I read and reread Thomas Mann. *Dr. Faustus* may be the best
novel of our period. Then Balzac. Then, Stendhal, who is a young man's

writer. I couldn't read Proust then; you have to be over thirty to enjoy Proust. These were the writers I looked to, in what you call my "early phase."

CR: Which of the great Americans did you read?
GV: I couldn't take Hawthorne; I still can't. I don't like anything he wrote except *The Blithedale Romance*, which is almost a novel. The others are romances. I do detest *Moby Dick*, and I never finished *Pierre; or the Ambiguities*. But then, I don't like Melville's writing. It is windy and pretentious, it is bogus Shakespeare.

CR: Some of the very best American writers were working in the South then.
GV: At that time Faulkner had done his best work, but he wasn't very popular. I admired *All the King's Men*, Huey Long and politics, but I can't think of any of the other Southerners. Faulkner came from not far from my family's place in Mississippi. Mary Gore Wyatt, my great-aunt, had been his Latin teacher. We only met three or four times, but when we got together, we would talk kin. We would review what had happened to Cousin Addie and what happened after the fire. Southerners make such good novelists; they have so many stories because they have so much family. I adapted "Barn Burning" for television and I saw him after that. He said [*mimicking voice*], "I myself did not see it, I do not have the television"—as he called it—"but members of the family in town told me it was very good." I said I was going out to Hollywood. I had a contract with MGM. He had one with Warner Brothers. He was a cold little man, very impersonal. He said [*mimicking voice*], "If I may give you some advice, never make the mistake of taking films seriously. Fitzgerald did, and I think that was a mistake. You do it, you get your money, and then you go and do your own work." What he would say about the *auteur* theory would be wildly funny, because he knew what actors and directors were.

CR: But aren't you passionate about films?
GV: Yes, I was brought up on films. I am the generation of sound, which came in when I was four years old. I barely remember the silents, and I certainly remembered the heyday of MGM, the greatest studios, and all the great stars of the thirties and forties. By the fifties, I was writing movies. The curious thing is that as a child I saw *A Midsummer Night's Dream*, and by the time I was fourteen I had read all of Shakespeare with pleasure because I had

seen this "great" movie. Now, I don't think that happens when a child today watches television.

CR: I see what you mean. Films stirred people to read more, whereas television refers only to itself. Except for the tie-ins, it positively discourages people from reading. Was the culture less materialistic, less blatantly commercial, when you began publishing your novels?
GV: No. It was somewhat different, but it was the same. The same commercialism, the same dullness prevailed, duller in some ways. The one exception is that the novel was at the center of the culture, and now the novel is off on the periphery. I never thought that would happen.

CR: In the writing of your novels, is the awareness that they might be turned into films a consideration?
GV: I always regarded it as two different sets of muscles. You use one set to make a movie and another set to make a novel. The better the novel is, the more untranslatable the tone of the author's voice is. That's why *Myra* doesn't work. *Portnoy's Complaint, The Great Gatsby, Madame Bovary* don't work, because there was a tone to them that doesn't translate.

CR: My next question, then, would be, Is your imagination verbal or visual?
GV: When you imagine, you *image-in*. I hear things much more than I see them, but I can start seeing after a time when I am writing. I hear voices, I am a mimic. I have just so many actors in my repertoire, and I know what they can do, and I make the scenes for them. As a novel, *Kalki* was like a movie. I even adapted it.

   It may well be that the cinema has affected the novel, but, on the other hand, there were cinematic novels long before there were films. I was reading *Jude the Obscure* the other day, and, God, Hardy writes absolute movie scenes. There is a scene in *Jude* where the boy is being slung around by his father and as he goes around he sees the towers of Christ Church and Oxford in the distance. That's cinematic.

CR: In the second phase, with your return to fiction, people start describing your work as novels of ideas, beginning with *Messiah* and *Julian*. The point of view is one of wit and skepticism. And the central characters are adversaries from within. Is that the perspective that brought you back to fiction?

GV: After my ten years of "commercialism" I returned to fiction with *Julian*, which, of course, by the ultimate irony, proved to be more successful than any of my commercialism. It was followed by *Washington, D.C.*, *Myra Breckinridge*, *Two Sisters*, *Burr*, and *1876*. I try out different voices which is why I do all those first-person narratives. I like impersonation. I like going into another character. I really believe *mimesis* is one of the highest aspects of art. So the "I" is mimetic. When you are in the first person, you have to have some connection with the character though I come back to the mystery of Myra/Myron, which I think must be unique. I have nothing in common with Myra Breckinridge except total admiration. She is magnificent, she is mad as a hatter, and yet that is one of my voices. It just came to me one day. People are now talking about the "urbane, familiar tone" of my narrator; now, that really irritates me. In *Julian* I have four voices: Julian as emperor, trying to sound like Marcus Aurelius; the private Julian, who is frantic; Priscus, who is dry, cold, and sardonic; Libanius, who is feathery and oratorical. These four voices go all the way through the book and provide the variations.

CR: What of the Proustian idea that the novelist has one book to write, so that all of a writer's future development will be found in a germinal state in his very first work? Are your novels part of a larger structure?
GV: A unified-field theory? Well, if it is there, it is still inside of me. I have no master plan that I am conscious of. It may be that I am doing something instinctively, a bit the way a coral reef gets made. The little corals do not know, as they cling to the debris of their predecessors, exactly what kind of a creation they are going to make—a barrier reef. It may be that in the accretion of all these books and themes and characters I am constructing some whole, but I don't know what it is.

CR: You said that *Creation* came out of your work on *Julian*. Is there a continuum through the historical novels?
GV: I'm sure the lines converge. There is only so much a writer does.
I use somewhere the idea that every writer has a given theatre in his head, a repertory company. Shakespeare has fifty characters, I have ten, Tennessee has five, Hemingway has one, Beckett is busy trying to be none. You are stuck with your repertory company and you can only put on plays for them.

CR: At some point have you considered bringing all these aspects of yourself together in one work?

GV: No, because it would be necessary for me then to sit down and consider what it is that I have been doing for thirty-five years, and I'm not about to do it. I'm not very personal, as I keep saying, and I am not even personal about the books. "It is not wise to investigate these things," as Tennessee would say. "There should always be an air of mystery in the work." To which my answer was, when I was having a little trouble in adapting one of his plays [*Suddenly Last Summer*], "Yes, but there should not be an area of confusion. Mystery is one thing, confusion is another."

CR: Would you consider doing a document such as Tennessee has done, an autobiography?

GV: After I read *Les Mots* by Sartre, I realized I would have to find a form as unique as he found. He created a small masterpiece. Between *Les Mots* and *The Education of Henry Adams* I am abashed. Unless I could find an arresting form, I wouldn't do it. But to remember personalities is probably worth doing, and now that I have lived so long and known so many people, I think I'll do more and more essays of the sort I did on Tennessee and Isherwood, in which I'm able to bring myself in as a sort of counter-memoirist, to show them from another angle—mine not theirs.

The Scholar Squirrels and the National Security Scare: An Interview with Gore Vidal

Jon Wiener / 1988

From *Radical History Review* 44 (July 1988), pp. 109–37. © 1988 MARHO: The Radical Historians Organization, Inc. All Rights Reserved. Used by permission of the publisher.

This interview was conducted on July 12, 1988, in Ravello, Italy.

Jon Wiener: In 1984 you told the *Washington Post*, "The American people have a passion to know about their past, but the TV networks won't show it because they've made up their minds that if Americans had a clear view of their past they might not like the present, might change it." Your critics call you a compulsive cynic, but this sounds very optimistic.

Gore Vidal: Well, I can say from personal experience that the popularity of these reflections of mine on American history in the form of novels proves that there is something going on out there. Apparently, the minority that reads books is very interested in the American past, and it beats me why the television networks, which are nothing if not greedy, don't plug into that. But they don't. I think the thing is much more complex. Partly it's that the educational system is now so bad. History is taught very badly.

JW: History is not a popular subject.

GV: No. It comes in number 50, I think, out of 50 subjects in one of those "Purdue Polls" of high school students. But it's taught so badly. Is there any design to that? I'm not a conspiracy-type person, but I do think that there's probably some motive for making our history lethally dull. If you want, let's say, to deny the people certain rights, keep them ignorant of the Bill of Rights. If nobody understands who we were, he won't question why we are what we are. After all, if you had an educated electorate, you couldn't get away with 40 years of a national security state, and you couldn't elect people like Reagan. So it's to the interest of the oligarchs—the national security states-persons—to keep the people ignorant.

JW: Then you don't think that people are hopelessly hypnotized by the media or they're helpless in the face of advertising?

GV: There are people and there are people. The people who see a Spielberg movie are still not a majority of the American people. People who read books are an even smaller minority. A book like *Lincoln* in hard cover was the number two bestseller of 1984. Number one is Ludlum. So I'm in competition with pop writing. There's nothing wrong with pop writing. I'd rather have people read a bad book than no book—at least there's hope they will go on to literature of some kind.

JW: The project of your book *Empire* is an unlikely one. If anyone else had gone to a publisher and said that he wanted to write a novel about the origins of American imperialism during the McKinley administration, he wouldn't have been given very much of an advance.

GV: Perhaps not quite seven figures.

JW: Yet you were confident that this would be a bestseller.

GV: No. It doesn't quite work like that. There is an audience for my books on American history; that audience is determined by their past performance. 70 percent of all books are sold by these great chains. It's all done on computers. You press my name in connection with an American historical novel and the computer estimates its probable sale—two, three hundred thousand hard cover, and then the Book-of-the-Month Club will take it. So best-seller status is sort of built in, even if I am doing "The Niece of Chester A. Arthur." The subject of the American empire was a rather good one for that time, which could not have been calculated by me or anybody.

JW: The book tells about the origins of the American empire in the Philippines and comes in the year that Marcos is in the headlines.

GV: Yes, Marcos was in the headlines. But more important, the book came out right after we became a debtor nation. Thirty years ago I was the first person to bring into the discourse of journalism the phrase "the American Empire." In a review of one of my early books of essays, *Time* magazine did a raging attack on me—saying that one of the things that made me such an evil figure was that I used that phrase, "the American Empire." We cannot be an empire, of course. I remember Jack Javits years ago saying "Gore, how on earth can you say 'American Empire?' We don't have an empire. We're a republic. We believe in freedom and democracy." Now, I hope "national security state," which I'm currently explicating, will catch on.

JW: In your book *1876* your characters discuss the place of truth in fiction and historical writing. "What we think to be history is nothing but fiction," one character says. Another disagrees: "I want to know, I always want to know what is true, if anyone knows it." Therefore, he concludes, history is better than fiction. His questioner says "But how can we know what is true? Isn't everything that is recorded just one person's effort to make himself look best?" Clearly, this is a discussion about your own writing.
GV: I don't have a name for my books on American history. I don't like the phrase "historical novel" because it seems to cancel itself out even as one says it. I usually refer to them as just reflections on American history or narratives.

I use the phrase "agreed upon facts." That is all a historian can use, and this is why the pretensions of the history departments sometimes set my teeth on edge. They really think there is such a thing as "historical truth," if enough of them agree. Well, they agree on many absurd things and I brought up the subject in my second go-round on Lincoln. During the '60s, many blacks decided that Lincoln was a honky. Obviously he did not want the two races living side-by-side. His desire for separatism led him to advocate the colonization of freed slaves outside the U.S. That was not a practical solution, but he clung to the notion of colonization as late as July, 1864.

In the age of Martin Luther King scholar squirrels were obliged to make Abraham Lincoln a generous, wonderful, loving man, a man without a racist bone in his body, who knew that the two races would be divinely happy together. The truth? He comes out very strongly for colonizing blacks in his State of the Union address in December, 1862. He asks for money to buy land, for a piece of what was then called New Granada, which is now Nicaragua.

LaWanda Cox has made the case that he could never have been serious about it. Other scholar squirrels decided he dropped the notion because he had a vision of Martin Luther King, standing in the saint's own temple with this dream. Abraham Lincoln changed, they argue. Well, he didn't change, though the logistics of removing several million mostly unwilling people was, finally, beyond him.

Now the squirrels are trying to eliminate the evidence that he never really gave up the idea. Ben Butler said that a few weeks before Lincoln died, Butler talked to him and Lincoln was still talking about colonization. One squirrel has determined that Ben Butler was not in town at the time, and that that eliminates Ben Butler as a witness. So they all agree that this conversation never took place. But it could have taken place a bit earlier. And Butler is writing many years later. They tend to overlook John Hay's letter of July 1, 1864. Hay said, he's "sloughed off that idea of colonization." This sentence is acknowledged. Hay's next sentence is ignored: because of political thievery involving shipping, Lincoln has been "about converted" to the barbarousness of colonization. The "about converted" doesn't sound to me like a sprint to Damascus. Anyway, the history department revisionists are eliminating a witness to the Lincoln administration who is neither more nor less reliable than anybody else. Ben Butler's a liar. Hay is sloughed off. Now they can say Lincoln had given up on the idea of colonization two years before indeed he did.

I have the same problem with the *New York Times*. They have consistently lied about me, misinterpreted things that I have said in interviews, changed the wording around, right down to the preemptory strike they made against the dramatization of *Lincoln*. A week before it appeared on TV they got this hack to come in and say it isn't accurate. He gives a garbled report, to say the least. Now the *New York Times* is a primary source for any historian.

If you go through the clips, and there's a clip that says Abraham Lincoln gave an interview this morning and he said "I love the blacks and I want them to stay here forever, preferably in my wife's bedroom." There it is. In the *Times*. So what is history? As Tolstoy said, "History would be a very good thing if it were true."

JW: Could you talk a little bit about how you work? When you sit down to do *Lincoln* or *Empire*, do you take notecards like the rest of us?
GV: Well, I'm not very good at notes. Oh yes, I'm indebted to scholar squirrels. Were it not for them I couldn't do my work. I don't do very much primary source stuff, but neither do they unless they're focusing on some small area. I've got several thousand books downstairs, which is sort of a basic library. When I start on a book I just go around and get as many "texts" as I can find. I use different libraries when I'm back in the states. At the moment I'm doing 1917 to 1923. All those books over there in the corner, on those

tables, there are about a hundred that I have to have at hand, biographies of Wilson, Theodore Roosevelt, Hearst. I'm also going to do a lot about the origins of Hollywood. It seemed to me that the real theme of *Empire* was the invention of "news" by Hearst. Now I'm going to show the invention of the world by the movies, a far greater theme than Warren Harding's administration and in a way rather more interesting than Wilson, though the Wilson era was a climacteric in our lives.

JW: Could you tell us about your formative political experiences? What was the process by which you became a radical?

GV: I don't know how I did. I was brought up in an extremely conservative family. The British always want to know what class you belong to. I was asked that on the BBC. I said "I belong to the highest class there is: I'm a third generation celebrity. My grandfather, father, and I have all been on the cover of *Time*. That's all there is. You can't go any higher in America." The greatest influence on me was my grandfather, Senator Thomas Pryor Gore.

JW: The Populist from Oklahoma.

GV: Yes. That's his chair. Not from the Senate. From his office. He was blind from the age of ten. He would plot in that chair. He made Wilson president twice rocking away in that thing.

JW: He's denounced by Teddy Roosevelt in *Empire*.

GV: Yes. T.R. didn't like anything about him. But T.P.G. was only 36, I think, when he came to the Senate. He was a Populist who finally joined the Democratic Party. They all did. He helped write the constitution of the state of Oklahoma, which is the only socialist state constitution. He was school of Bryan: anti-bank, anti-Eastern, anti-railroads, anti-war. Also anti-black and anti-Jew—what they now call nativist. But he was not a crude figure like Tom Watson or the sainted Huey. He was a very literary man. So his prejudices were all low-keyed, except the hatred of the rich and the banks—because farmers suffered at the hands of capital that was in the East. They had no capital; only land and lousy crops. He was a tribune of those people. As he got older he got more and more conservative; later he wrote the oil depletion allowance. But he was honest personally. When he died, he was far from being a millionaire, which most Oklahoma senators are—with the exception of the sainted Fred Harris.

JW: I gather you were not on the Left as a young man.

GV: No. I was very much on the Right. I was a practical politician. This is very hard to describe, particularly in a journal like yours, where ideology and political thought matter. They don't care if you are brought up in a political family, with every intention of being a politician, which I had. There's no such thing as ideology. You have, as the Marxists would say, a structural response to things. You have class responses, which, as a kid, I was not about to start analyzing. But I thought of the world in practical terms. I knew how politics worked, which the theoreticians and the people who learn about politics in school never quite grasp. I knew that it didn't make any difference what your *positions* were, the game was power. I was, to use the boring word, pragmatic. That's how you get elected.

My first political activity: I was America First at Exeter when I was 14. My guru in Washington was Alice Roosevelt Longworth, who was a maniac on the subject. I knew a lot of the leading America Firsters. I did not see why we should go into a European war because I saw it in terms of the First World War, and I still believe we should never have gone into that war, which my grandfather nobly opposed. Of course we didn't know anything about Hitler at the time—I'm speaking now of 1939 and 1940. In 1941 it all changed. The Japanese attacked us and I enlisted in the army at the age of 17 as a private.

JW: What happened between your America First days at Exeter and your work on the national security state and the American empire in the '70s?

GV: I suppose it was an evolution. In 1948 I wanted to go into politics and I was all set to establish residency in New Mexico, whose governor was a good friend of my grandfather's; I would have been put on the ballot as a presidential elector in the 1948 election, and, as I have an Hispanic name (although my family is from the Alps), plus help of the governor and his machine, I was all set to start out and have a conventional political career. But I'd written *The City and the Pillar*.

JW: —which described the life of a young man who was gay.

GV: Now I must make a decision: am I going to publish this book and get into a lot of trouble, or, shall I suppress the book and go out to New Mexico and settle in Santa Fe and, in due course, go to the House and the Senate and whatever might happen. I made a decision. Well, I think that is what we call a radicalizing decision.

JW: Then you would say sexual politics played a part in your radicalization?

GV: It played a crucial part. You see, my first two books had been greatly admired; the *New York Times* thought I was wonderful.

JW: So you were not prepared for the response to *The City and the Pillar*.

GV: Well, I knew it was going to be rough. Luckily, being brought up in a public family I could handle that rather more easily, I think, than somebody who is shy.

JW: What do you mean, it was "rough?"

GV: Well, you must remember I was highly praised at 19 and 20 for the first two books, particularly the first one [*Williwaw*]. That was one of the first war novels. There were four or five of us young war lions, and we were the toast of the country. Then I published *The City and the Pillar* and I hardly get a good review in the United States. I'm totally blacked out for my next five books by the *New York Times*. The daily reviewer said he would never read, much less review me again, and five books went unnoticed by him, by *Time*, by *Newsweek*. I had been demonized. Once you're a demon in our society you are ignored until you, somehow, become unavoidable. Then you are trivialized.

I had taken on the whole establishment of a pretty—rustic?—country and said, "Fuck you, you've got sex all wrong." Thus, I found my role. I exist to say, "No, that isn't the way it is," or "What you believe to be true is not true for the following reasons." I am a master of the obvious. I mean, if there's a hole in the road, I will, viciously, outrageously, say there's a hole in the road and if you don't fill it in you'll break the axle of your car. One is not loved for being helpful. So my radicalization begins with *The City and the Pillar*.

When I was blacked out, I saw the powers of censorship in a free land and that made me a little cynical about freedom. I was told by Harvey Breit of the *New York Times*, a good friend of mine—he was number two at the book section—that "anything you publish will not be reviewed in the daily and you'll get a bad review on Sunday. Why don't you do something else or write under a pseudonym." So I did both. I wrote Edgar Box books in '52, published them over the next years.

JW: What is this?

GV: Edgar Box—three mystery stories that were very successful, published in every language. One of them is out again in Italy this month. Rave reviews in

the *New York Times*. Twenty years later I brought them out under my own
name and the *Times* slammed them.

But that wasn't enough to live on. Then in 1954 *Messiah*, the best of
my early books, came out; it was barely reviewed here. I was getting a fine
press in England, and other countries, but nothing in freedom's land.
So I went into television. Although the *New York Times* still didn't like me,
they didn't take television very seriously and it doesn't make much
difference whether you got a good review or not. From '54 to '64, I wrote
television; I wrote movies; I had two hit plays back-to-back on Broadway,
which is fairly rare. Lester Markel, who ran the Sunday section at the
Times, was so affronted by the success of my play *The Best Man* that he
called up four different writers to write an ax job. One of them was
Richard Rovere; Murray Kempton was another, and finally, Douglass Cater
wrote a tepid piece. From '54 to '64 I made enough money for the rest of
my life, which gave me an independence that the John Updike Chair of
Quality Lit at Rutgers would not. In my busy decade I wrote, I think, 100
television plays, about 12 movies, three Broadway plays, and started writing
essays.

In my long, roundabout way, I'm answering your question. After *The City
and the Pillar*, the next radicalizing thing was Joe McCarthy—watching the
blacklist in operation. I wasn't directly affected because I almost never joined
anything. I was also the wrong age to have been a Communist, and probably
the wrong class as well. If I had been ten years older I might have been a
Communist, but I wasn't. But I was horrified to see friends in television—
writers, actors—not be allowed to work. With every play, the producer would
have to submit every name of those involved to the network for approval.
The process was inscrutable, more suitable to an Eastern Paradise than
bravery's home.

I was deeply pissed off. So I decided that I would do an anti-McCarthy
play on Philco-Goodyear Playhouse: something called "A Sense of Justice."
The plot concerned a boss of a state played by E.G. Marshall. A young man
decides to kill him out of a sense of justice. He's never met him, has nothing
personal against him, but the young man sees him as a figure of great evil. He
comes to kill him; and so on. It was very effective television. It caused quite a
stir. Everyone got the McCarthy analogy. NBC was going to redo it the next
summer; then—what else?—it was cancelled. So now we have two steps
towards radicalization.

In 1960, I ran for Congress in upstate New York. By then I didn't have to worry about money anymore and it was partly a lark. A friend of mine, Kennedy, was running for President.

JW: You did a lot better than JFK in your district.
GV: I ran 20,000 votes ahead of him, yes. And I carried every town. I carried Poughkeepsie, Kingston, Catskill, and Hudson. But the countryside made the difference in those days. But the problem was Jack at the head of the ticket. If he hadn't been running, I would have been elected. That was old-fashioned politics. I quite enjoyed myself, but then I went back to novel-writing with *Julian*.

JW: You ran as a liberal Democrat?
GV: I was the nominee of the Democratic and Liberal parties, yes. But there was no such thing as a real liberal-democrat. Jack was a very conservative politician, and I was much the same, as Al Lowenstein discovered. I think my campaign was the first he worked on. The 29th was the biggest district in the state. I had been working at it for five years before I ran. Judge Hawkins, the Democratic chairman of Dutchess County, and I had put together a little organization. We had a hand in picking candidates here and there. There was not much in the way of liberal politics then. I wanted to clean up the Hudson River. I was premature with that. I also wanted recognition of Red China. Eleanor Roosevelt said, "For God's sake don't say that because there will be nothing but trouble from the China Lobby." I said "I don't think anybody will mind," and she said "At least say 'If they conform to the United Nations rules,'" so I used that dim formula.

I came up with the idea of the Peace Corps instead of military service. Of course it never occurred to me to ask what in the name of God we're doing with universal military conscription in peacetime. I hadn't thought that through. But I did think there should be alternatives to military service. So I came up with that idea and it was passed on to Jack by Harrison Williams, Senator from New Jersey. Jack then put it in a speech at San Francisco and that's how it got started. That was about all I did.

JW: Was there any gay-baiting in this campaign?
GV: Even then it was considered bad karma to fuck around with old Gore. But just to be safe I had something on every politician and publisher in the

district. There was one old newspaper publisher up in Columbia County, the most conservative of the five counties. He was making some giggly hints about me, and he was also having an affair with his son's wife. So after he took one particular swipe at me, I went on the radio in Hudson, the county seat, and I was asked, "Are you getting any ideas for any novels while you're doing this?" I said "Well, every now and then I do get an idea. I thought of a funny one the other day. A father and a son. The son marries this woman who's very good looking and the father has an affair with her." The whole county burst into laughter, and I never heard another word from the *Chatham Bee*, I think it was called. Do that sort of thing once or twice and you don't have to worry. In fact, the only real trouble I had was the *New York Times*. They ordinarily don't handle campaigns that far north. But they sent a special guy up to do an ax job on me for the Sunday section. It was too badly written to hurt, but it was the thought that touched me. Like the attack on *Lincoln*, the *Times* never sees a well that it doesn't want to poison.

In terms of radicalizing experiences, nothing much happened in that campaign except that I understood how the country worked politically. Also, by then favoring the recognition of Red China means I'm moving out of the pragmatic zone of politics. But I turned down a sure-thing election in '64 to go back to novel writing, with *Julian*, on the origins of Christianity. I've always been anti-Christian, but I wanted to know why. So I investigated the cult, a radicalizing thing to do since I come from that tradition. Then, from there to here, I don't know what happened.

JW: Your book *Washington, D.C.* ends up with a portrayal of a Kennedy-type figure as a ruthless and dishonest person.
GV: Kennedy was just an operator. I was pro-Jack because he was a great charmer.

JW: What is the joke that you heard Kennedy telling about James Baldwin?
GV: He called Jimmy Baldwin "Martin Luther Queen." He thought that was wildly funny. That's very Kennedy. The worst epithet that the Kennedys had for a man was that he's a "woman." Adlai Stevenson was worse—"an old woman." Except for Jack, I would say that that family, of that generation, anyway, had all the charm of two tons of condemned veal. You may use that.

JW: 1968 is the year of the New Left. It's also the year of *Myra Breckinridge*. The world is turned upside down briefly in 1968 and *Myra* is part of that.
GV: Was. Now erased. Walter Clemons, my biographer, is going through that now, showing how carefully I'm erased from establishment versions of history. In the United States of America what ought not to exist does not exist. I am invisible.

JW: *Myra* in a way has the spirit of '68. She is wild, she breaks all the rules.
GV: *Time* magazine wrote, "has literary decency fallen so low?" The book was also the number one bestseller. So it's not as though it was obscure at the time. Of course it was also one of the greatest disasters ever made in the movies. It had more advance publicity than any movie since *Gone with the Wind*. *Myra* was on the cover of *Time*, of *Look*, of *Collier's*, all those magazines then. I've never seen such publicity. And then they made the world's worst movie, and the book was erased.

In '68, I connect up with the mainstream of the radical movement. I do three things in '68. One is *Myra*, which is sort of sending everybody up, including the sexual revolution, and I'm sending up the '60s types, too, because I'm not taking them too seriously. Then my debates with Buckley during the Democratic National Convention, which, of course, the whole country watches. Though I thought Mayor Daley and Abe Ribicoff more exciting. Then I was caught in the Chicago police riot. The night Humphrey was nominated was the night that I was obliged to discipline Buckley.

The next day, Marcus Raskin and Jules Feiffer and a bunch of us founded the New Party as a vehicle for Gene McCarthy. After we had gone to all the trouble to get the party's names on a couple of dozen state ballots, he torpedoed it. I just saw Marcus in Washington last March and he said, "You should have been our candidate." I said, "I thought so too, but I was waiting for you to ask." He said, "Well, we didn't," and I said, "No, you didn't." We could have launched a real party at that moment.

With that I actually came out, as it were, into radical politics. Later I became co-chairman, with Ben Spock, of what later turned into the People's Party. I was involved '68 to '72. I quit when McGovern, in the primaries, was saying everything we were, and rather better. That's when he wanted a law that $500,000 was the most you could inherit. Poor guy didn't know he was living in the wrong country. So there's the history of my becoming a radical.

JW: Your books of historical reflections are all about the unspoken fact that there's a ruling class in America.
GV: Yep.

JW: How do you explain the ignorance of Americans about this elementary fact?
GV: The Depression. Before that the ruling class was into conspicuous consumption; they built their palaces at Newport and they went with their diamond tiaras to the opening of the Met. Suddenly a lot of people are poor. But *they* aren't poor. On the other hand, they're jittery. So they completely withdrew from the public gaze. A few went into politics, but it was frowned on. Of course they're all in politics, but they don't run for president; they buy the president. Nelson Rockefeller was considered a dangerous idiot by his class for turning the spotlight on them. By and large, since '33, they operate in the shadows.

JW: Your critics say these books are cynical.
GV: They don't mean cynical, they mean realistic. But they have no way of knowing what the reality is. They are inoculated against the truth by the school system. They have been taught about all these saints—Washington, Lincoln, Jefferson—by the hagiographers who keep the saints polished and beautifully lit in the schools. And that's that. There are not now and never were any issues to agree or disagree upon. 1988. Why does nobody talk about the defense budget? Because the consensus requires that the money be wasted as it is being wasted. To point this out is to be—cynical.

JW: Would it be fair to say that you're cynical about ordinary people in American history? The radical historians who came out of the '60s were very much interested in history "from the bottom up," portraying popular consciousness and popular experience; your radical history is very different. Some people have said what you find in Vidal is the portrayal of the masses as manipulated and deluded..
GV: I don't characterize the masses because I have no conception of the masses. I don't know what the word means. I can understand administrative numbers, but that's something else. I write about the rulers because they leave records. The only members of the lower orders that keep diaries that I am aware of are lone, crazed killers of presidents. They *always* keep diaries.

I don't know of any novelist of rank who does, but from Sirhan Sirhan to the guy who shot George Wallace, they all keep diaries.

JW: In *Empire,* you have Teddy Roosevelt worrying about the possibility of revolution if reforms are not made in the way that the new rich conduct their business. Ordinary people are a presence in the background of your central characters.

GV: Madison's "iron law of oligarchy" is eternally true. From Shay's Rebellion on, the people have had the potentiality to disturb the reigning oligarchs. But nothing more. The American oligarchy have never not been in full control.

JW: Richard Poirer reviewed *Empire* in the *New York Review;* he said that while Vidal writes about the ruling groups in his historical reflections, you find out what Vidal thinks about ordinary people in his wild novels *Myra, Myron,* and *Duluth.* There, ordinary people are portrayed as—

GV: Off the wall. I think that's well observed.

JW: So you have put these two together to get a complete portrayal of American consciousness.

GV: There was a very good critic in England in the '60s and '70s called Peter Conrad. He had a wonderful line. He was reviewing *Myron* and said people have been writing about how *Myron* is the sequel to *Myra* and they don't like it because of that, or they do, or whatever. He said it's not the sequel to *Myra,* it's the sequel to *Burr.* That's pretty shrewd. What I had done straight in *Burr,* I'm now doing fantastically in *Myron.* After all, there is Richard Nixon wondering back in 1948 if they have extradition to his own period, whether he can stay there in the past or not, whether he will be pardoned. All of that is not unlike Burr on the lam.

JW: What Poirer seemed to be saying was that in your writing the ruling elites are extremely articulate and historically conscious, but the ordinary people like Myra live in a world of media images and are therefore totally deluded. That seems wrong. Myra is an extremely sharp person. Myra knows what's going on. Myra tells the truth.

GV: I'll say. She certainly was onto overpopulation. Holy Myra Malthus, as I used to call her. On the other hand, if you want a version of the American as TV-watcher/consumer, *Duluth* tells it all.

JW: Your portrayal of Lincoln is different from your portrayal of everybody else in your historical books.

GV: Well, I don't go inside of his mind for one thing. He's only observed by others. That's a necessary cop-out. Shakespeare could have gone inside his mind, but I'm not Shakespeare. I wouldn't dare try.

JW: You leave readers in the same position as the people around Lincoln, trying to figure him out.

GV: You can add him up any way you like in the book.

JW: At one level your critique of Lincoln is devastating. Basically you trace the national security state back to him: the suspension of habeas corpus, universal military service, high military budgets.

GV: Certainly he left us with a centralized "blood and steel" state. And he had absolutely no right to hold the South in the Union. The South had every moral and constitutional right to leave. If Lincoln had taken his stand on the high moral ground of abolition of slavery, then he could at least have said, "There is a higher moral good than the Constitution." But he didn't. He took his stand on the Constitution and he fell right through the fabric.

JW: This is somewhat more interesting than the date on which Lincoln ceased to advocate the colonization of slaves.

GV: Of course. This is the essence of Lincoln. I repeat all the arguments that he gave for the Union, and I have all the arguments that were made against him; his answers don't add up.

JW: It's a devastating portrait. You said subsequently that Lincoln demonstrated how, if you had sufficient will, you could manipulate the Constitution any way you wanted.

GV: Sufficient will and a "military necessity."

JW: You said Lincoln provides a blueprint on how to subvert the country, how to rule by decree.

GV: Exactly. Why do you think all the right-wingers have been reading the book and studying it?

JW: Yet your Lincoln is not an evil figure. He's a hero, a person with real authority. That kind of figure doesn't exist anywhere else in these books.

GV: No. I think that maybe Washington was a bit like him, but Washington was always tangential to what I was doing. I was more interested in Jefferson and Hamilton. No, Lincoln was an autocrat. He was dictator. He was more benign than not, but God knows what he set in train.

JW: Yet you make him an admirable person.

GV: Well, dictators can be admirable people, it's the fact of the dictatorship we don't like. We might like the man.

JW: Is there any explanation of Lincoln's motivation in your book?

GV: Sure. It's all in that speech about ambition that he gave at the Young Men's Lyceum in 1837. In my first *Lincoln* exchange in the *New York Review*, I quote from the speech at great length. He predicts himself, he predicts Abraham Lincoln. He says that the ambitious man can not follow in another's footsteps. He must always be first. He cannot succeed to the office of the presidency that's been invented. He must reinvent it. He warns you against himself and then he goes right out and does what he says this man of the race of the eagle and the lion would do.

JW: In his review of the book, Harold Bloom wrote, "Lincoln's obsessive drive to preserve and restore the union was a grand restitution or compensation for what could never be healed in his own personal and familial life."

GV: I'm surprised Bloom would have latched onto that because I'm not a very personal writer. I don't put personal things at the center of people's characters. I'm convinced Lincoln did have syphilis and I'm convinced that Mary Todd died of paresis, contracted from him. I don't make much of it in the book because there isn't that much evidence. I don't think that anything he did was ruled by anything in his private life. Long before he had syphilis or was married, he had this urge to be great. It came from reading Shakespeare, it came from reading the King James Bible. That famous style of his also came from Blackstone. His favorite book was Parson Weems' *Life of Washington*. But, by and large, he didn't read history, he didn't read biographies, but he certainly had an idea of what greatness was: greatness was to be a founder.

JW: Lincoln is fascinating also because he is not a part of the ruling circles; he's a westerner.

GV: Yes. He's quite innocent of all that, although as a smooth railroad lawyer he could have become a Clark Clifford.

JW: In the book you don't let us forget that.

GV: Never for one minute. He had moved out of his class and by marrying Mary Todd he was announcing to the world that he was going to move into the aristocracy. Which, indeed, she was.

JW: One thing is missing from *Lincoln*: the Union under Lincoln undertook the most radical of all slave emancipations. Nowhere else was there such a massive war to destroy slavery, nowhere else were slave owners denied compensation, nowhere else were ex-slaves armed and enlisted in a war to abolish slavery. This doesn't seem to add up with the picture of Lincoln that you give us.

GV: No. Because I don't believe it. A lot of things happen. A politician must do many, many things simultaneously and many of them are contradictory and this drives history professors crazy. But in the real world of politics you say one thing to John, you say another thing to George; they're perfectly contradictory, but it all comes out your way if you're lucky. The principal reason for an Emancipation Proclamation was that England was getting close to recognizing the South. If they did that they would be buying southern cotton and the South would be economically viable. That had to be stopped. Pressure was being brought on Lincoln to emancipate because there were a lot of powerful abolitionists in England. That's really what it was for.

Then he comes up with a proclamation emancipating not the slaves in the border states, that were still with the Union, but only the slaves in the South over whom he had no power. A horselaugh went up in Parliament. American historians like to ignore that: emancipation was treated as a great joke.

The arming of black troops? Of course. They would try anything. But by and large he wanted to colonize the freed slaves and I don't think he ever let go of the idea. He finally gave it up because it was simply impractical. Nobody had the money, nobody had the ships, and the blacks didn't want to go. So that was the end of that plan. And that is the real Lincoln. The fact that at the end of the war slavery was over—well, slavery was going to be over anyway, and he was in no hurry about it.

JW: In all of your historical books you tell the story of what happened through conversation. You portray our rulers as highly articulate, historically conscious people.

GV: They used to be.

JW: Does this require that you distort the way things really happen? Do you portray them as more conscious and more articulate than they really were?

GV: Let me say between "distort" and "distill" there can be a certain leap. Of course, I have to distill. Professional politicians never tell you anything and they certainly don't tell each other anything. They talk in code. I remember Jack Kennedy when he saw *The Best Man*. It was the first play he saw after he was elected. He loved it. I watched him from back stage just to see what was holding his attention. "The only overall flaw," he said—this is Jack Kennedy, drama critic—"is that politicians never, in my experience, philosophize about what they are doing." I said, "I've been around politics, yes, it's all in code." And he said "Yes, you send signals." You can have a conversation which will swing a whole state and you haven't said more than four words. You just mention George, and you mention Tom; well, you know, the judgeship; yes, I know. That's all you have to say and somebody's going to get a judgeship and you're going to get the state. So I have to play Corneille or Racine to my native folk. Obviously I have to heighten it and distill it.

But whenever I have Theodore Roosevelt say something, other than "good morning," I've taken it from a letter or from a conversation. I'm not making up. The same thing with Lincoln. It's all stuff he's been known to have said or something very like it. It's just that you don't do as much of it in real life as you have to do in fiction, where you have to concentrate it.

JW: Tom Carson wrote in the *Village Voice*, "Vidal turns history into something made by enormously well spoken people." This sort of personifying of historical forces, he argues, leaves out a sense of a system which has its own requirements, its own dynamics. He says, "Who, reading his version of Teddy Roosevelt, could believe that Teddy was acting on behalf of any interest more abstract than his own crackling energy?"

GV: I think that's the only principle that he was acting upon. He had political debts to pay. He belonged to a political faction which he manipulated and sold out whenever it served him. With *Empire* I think that Mr. Carson is on fragile ground. They were extremely literary, this group. Teddy Roosevelt must have written 20 books. Henry James did say the things I have him say, Henry Adams said the things I have him say. You are talking about the most articulate generation that we've ever had. And Washington was, as Henry James says, the city of conversation. It was that way right up through my own youth. Everybody talked, and talked quite well.

JW: You write about history in different genres. You write essays as well as novels. Before *Empire*, you wrote a long essay in the *New York Review* on Teddy Roosevelt where you dealt with the same issues as the book. And you have the wild books like *Myra*. How do you decide which genre is appropriate to which issues? Why not a wild sex farce about Teddy Roosevelt and a sober and scrupulously accurate assessment of gender in twentieth-century America?
GV: I would have to have the genius of Doctorow.

JW: On the Jewish question, your article "The Empire Lovers Strike Back" in *The Nation* offended many people. Podhoretz says to Vidal, "To me the Civil War is as remote and as irrelevant as the War of the Roses." Vidal writes, "I realized then that he was not planning to become an 'assimilated American,' rather, his first loyalty would always be to Israel."
GV: Let's look it up. What I wrote is always shaded this way and that way in order to change the meaning. It's been so shaded now that I am supposed to have said that all Jews are Fifth Columnists. Now here's the exact sentence: " 'Well, to me,' said Poddy, 'the Civil War is as remote and irrelevant as the War of the Roses.' I realized then that he was not planning to become an 'assimilated American,' to use the old fashioned terminology, but, rather, his first loyalty would always be to Israel. Yet he admits that they ought to remain among us in order to make propaganda to raise money for Israel, a country they don't seem eager to live in. Jewish joke circa 1900: a Zionist is a someone who wants to ship other people off to Palestine."

I had this out with my old friend Norman Lear, who said, "You can't say assimilated." I said, "Come on, you started People for the American Way. Well, which are you? If you're not going to be an 'assimilated' American, then what are you? Are you an Israeli who happens to be living here?"

My argument is only weak at one point: what on earth does Vidal care about nationality? I hate the nation-state. What am I doing saying you've got to be either a good American or a good Israeli, but you can't be both? Why not to hell with both of them? That would demolish my argument.

But no Jew can do that, at least none who likes Israel, because they have to protect this peculiar little state. So, instead of hitting me where I am really weak, they get hung up and try to talk about anti-Semitism. Which has nothing to do with it.

JW: But you're also talking here about a historical consciousness of the American past, which is increasingly rare.
GV: That may have to do with my age and class and background, but you can't expect me not to be.

JW: American historians understand why the Civil War is the key to our history, but I suspect that most twentieth-century immigrants—Italians or Poles, or more recently, Asian or Mexican immigrants—have the same feeling that the Civil War is as remote for them as the Wars of the Roses.
GV: You're absolutely right. But look at the context of my essay: the Podhoretzes are giving out marks for Americanism. They write about me, "He doesn't like his country." That's the standard neocon line about all liberals. "Well, one thing is clear in all this muddle," writes Midge [Decter], adrift in her tautological sea, "Mr. Vidal does not like his country." They talk about me not liking my country, but they have no interest in the Civil War—or, I suspect, in the United States except as Israel's financier.

JW: When I read this I had a different complaint: I'm not sure that their first loyalty is to Israel. I think they are more ideologically consistent than that. If there was some change in Israeli politics, if Peace Now gained power, do you really think that Podhoretz and Decter would be out on the hustings campaigning for a treaty recognizing the Palestinians?
GV: Murray Kempton said to me, "No, their first loyalty is not to Israel, you exaggerate, it's to making it." This was the only game in town that they could play.

JW: Do you accept Kempton's view?
GV: I think there may be something in it, yes.

JW: Let's talk more about the '60s. Some historians have argued that if Kennedy had not been shot he would have ended the war in Vietnam and saved us from our terrible fate.

GV: I don't believe it. Too many people have told me that he was all for going on. A few weeks before he died, he said to old Mr. Canham, the managing editor of the *Christian Science Monitor*, "After Cuba, I've got to go all the way with this one." Somebody, I think it was Frank Church, said that Albert Gore—the father—was also talking to him about how they were going to "stand tall," or however he would have put that in his own style.

He loved war and he had this sort of schoolboy attitude toward it. He loved counterinsurgency. I teased him once. He was sketching insignia for the Green Berets.

JW: You saw him sketching insignia for the Green Berets?

GV: Yes. I said, "The last chief of state that I know of who designed military uniforms was Frederick the Great of Prussia." He didn't find that very funny. He liked war. I think he would have gone on and on. I think he probably would have got out before the other bums did, but for most of his second term we would have been fighting in Asia.

When he gave that inaugural address I was thrilled because I was as stupid as everybody else. I remember it was old Max Ascoli, whom we used to laugh at—he was married to a Rockefeller, Italian-Jewish intellectual, ex-liberal, and put out something called *Reporter* magazine. Arthur Schlesinger and I were praising this wonderful speech, and Max Ascoli said, "I haven't heard anything so dreadful since Mussolini." We thought, "sour old Max." I remember Arthur said, "and now we hear from Eisenhower's widow." Well, when you read that speech today you realize that we're declaring war on the entire world. The national security state's voice had spoken.

I asked Jack once about the Defense Department. I didn't know anything about the national security state then, but I certainly knew that they took up a lot of money and I knew that I was paying 90 percent income tax in those days. This is what Ronald Reagan and I had in common, we were both paying 90 percent tax. And if you're a writer—or even an actor—who knows if you're going to go on making money? But we were getting to keep an agent's commission on what we made. This is the late '50s. And it was all going for this military budget and we couldn't understand what it was all about. It was "The Russians are coming! The Russians are coming!"

I remember I was up at Hyannis Port with just Jack and Jackie and Chuck Spaulding. Jack said, "Oh, the Pentagon, there's no way of controlling it." He said, "A president, if he wanted to devote four years and do nothing else, he might penetrate it." He said "I think McNamara's the best man for it and he understands that kind of thing," et cetera, et cetera. This is 1961–62. He just accepted it as something that was uncontrollable. Now it's even further institutionalized, with bigger and bigger budgets, and untouchable.

JW: Those who defend the national security state say "the Russians are coming," but now we have Glasnost. If it continues, it's going to make it harder and harder to convince people that the Russians are indeed coming. Does this mean we are in for a change?

GV: The change in the works won't be due to anything so intelligent. It's going to come from the complete collapse of the economic system when the Japanese stop financing our deficits through their quarterly buying of treasury bonds. When that happens, we'll fold the empire fast. The next president will probably be in charge of that sad task.

It is my impression from the Moscow meeting, and I've been back a couple of times, that Gorbachev is unilaterally disarming. He hasn't got the money and that's that. He knows we don't dare attempt a first strike against him. He isn't going to do one against us. When we challenged him on Afghanistan, he said, "Okay, I'll get out." And he gets out. Eventually they'll abandon the Eastern buffer states. Too expensive. Too much trouble. Too much minority trouble at home.

That leaves the United States with a very large omelet on its not-so-innocent face, because we've demonized Russia since 1917 and seriously since '47 with the national security state. We have nothing else to hold the country together but "The Russians are coming!" It is my theory that every treaty that we will make with them now will be made in total bad faith. I bet that the CIA is going to report within the next year that the Russians are developing Star Wars in Nicaragua and we must immediately invade because we are now at terrible risk. The oligarchs lie constantly because that's the only way we know how to hold together the United States. I'm praying for a large economic collapse so that we then put our house in order. That's my Henry Clay solution.

JW: In your 1986 essay in *The Nation*, "A Requiem for the American Empire," you write about intellectuals: "At the dawn of the empire for a brief instant our professional writers tried to make a difference. Upton Sinclair and company attacked the excesses of the ruling class." But no longer because "most of our writers are paid by universities, and it is not wise to be thought critical of a garrison state which spends so much money on so many campuses." Do you really think that intellectuals had more of an adversary stance in the early twentieth century than they do today? Midge Decter would say no, it's today that the intellectuals are the most anti-American.

GV: Well, Midge's idea of intellectuals and mine are not quite the same. When I said "intellectual" I had in mind something rather larger than paid publicists. Russian writers, for instance, set the tone for their country and defined its prospects. American writers did that even down to Mark Twain, who generally was too frightened to speak out and lose popularity, but by God he spoke out on the acquisition of the Philippines. Those voices were heard. Henry James: he didn't do it publicly because he wasn't that kind of person, but his private letters on the Spanish-American War are violently anti-imperialist. Howells was superb at the Haymarket Riot. His *J'Accuse* at that time was one of the most powerful statements ever made by an American writer. "In the first republic of its kind in the world four men have been executed for their political opinions." That was a powerful piece. And Howells was the smoothest of our professional literary men. Yes, their voices were heard and were to a degree heeded.

Today I don't notice anybody with a voluntary audience saying anything. I think that the general flatness of intellectual discourse comes from the academization of not just literature but of everything. History, politics, everything is academic, and academic is government, and government is ruling class. It's circular.

JW: Yet the neocons are constantly sounding the alarm that the universities have been taken over by the Left.

GV: I don't know what they mean by that. Anybody who says there's a hole in road is a communist? That's about their range. I don't find any Left in America. But, mind you, I don't find much of a Left anywhere. On the one hand you have nervous pragmatists like Gorbachev who are not ruled by ideology and superstition, who are trying to salvage something; on the other hand you have the mad, who are fighting some specter, whether it be Islam, or communism, or Jesus.

JW: Before the 1980 election you urged people not to vote for Carter. You said that Reagan's administration would not be any different from Carter's. After eight years of Reagan, do you still think that was the right argument? It seems to me that Carter would have been a lesser evil on Central America, on the Sandinistas, on the Supreme Court, on the balance between social programs and military spending.

GV: I had not put it together then, but I knew instinctively that there was no difference between the presidential candidates. Now I realize that each represents the national security state. You might have gotten some different Supreme Court justices, but so what? Whizzer White was Jack Kennedy's invention. That is his eternal demerit. Are you so sure that Carter wouldn't have sent the helicopters into Managua, to be shot down like the ones he sent to Iran? I think he was a hopeless selection of the Trilaterals, the short-lived phrase we used in those days—which is all a piece of the national security state. I don't think that there's essentially any difference. He was over-attentive to detail and couldn't make anything work. Reagan has no interest in detail and can't make anything work.

JW: The national security state is a concept that historians have not put in the textbooks yet. How would you sketch out its history?

GV: As you pointed out, you can even find roots of it in Lincoln. But officially it began in 1947. Really it began as a determination at the end of World War II not to disarm and to continue high government spending. There were legitimate reasons for that—a fear of going back into the Depression. Nobody was afraid of the Russians. Their omnipotence is one of the great myths. I knew Washington in those days; nobody took them seriously. They were a bunch of clowns. Everybody knew that they had lost 20 million people, they had no technology to speak of, what industrial capacity they had had been knocked out, we had the atom bomb. And yet this scare campaign was put on.

For the purposes of teaching I would start with '47, when the National Security Council, CIA, etc. were invented. Then in 1950 the NSC was set in motion with NSC order #68, a blueprint for the state in which we still live, where 86 percent of the federal revenue goes for war, and the rest supports the largely irrelevant cosmetic government of Congress and Judiciary and the never-ending issues-less presidential elections. Ollie North gave the game away on TV. In effect, he told the Senate, the Chorus, "We are the government of the United States and what are you clowns doing getting in our way? Don't

you know that you are nobody? We *are* the government. We're saving freedom. We're saving mankind. And here you are screwing us up." Ollie was my
road to Damascus. I gazed into those tiny little dishonest eyes and saw
America, with a "k" that the NSCers had inserted in place of our "c."

JW: At one point in your not-too-distant past you spoke of the period
1945–50 as a "Golden Age" in America.
GV: That was also the age of the national security state that ate them up, but
we didn't know it. That's my final volume if I survive—when I sum up all
these books in my own life. I'm going to zero in on what an extraordinary
period that was in the arts and in the life of the country. But now, with later
knowledge—I'll be writing about it from the point of view of today—little
did we know as we danced on the rim of Vesuvius that deep below us infernal
forces were at work and we butterflies would all be turned to stone.

JW: So the sense that this was a golden age now is tarnished?
GV: No, it's not tarnished. It *was* a golden age, but the blighting was going on
in secret. You know, the first thing the CIA did when they got their first
funds, around 1949 or '50, was to infiltrate the trade union movements of
Italy, Germany, and France to keep them from going left—not communist,
just left. Then we established a military and imperial apparatus all around the
world which did not—and does not—conform to the constitution of the
United States and its agreed-upon republic. This was done by Harry Truman
and Acheson, working with senatorial geese like Arthur Vandenburg.

JW: Many things in 1947–1948 were not kept secret. The Loyalty Security act,
the beginning of the purges of reds. 1948 is the turning point, with the
smashing of the Wallace campaign.
GV: Yes, but we didn't—I didn't, anyway—understand it at the time. But
Henry Wallace understood it all. Particularly, when he was smeared as a
communist in the 1948 campaign because he was anti-imperial.

JW: What then makes '45 to '50 a "golden age?"
GV: The arts. *A Streetcar Named Desire, Death of a Salesman*, the best of
Lenny Bernstein, *On the Town, West Side Story*, all the arts took off. Broadway
was very exciting. Every night there was something worth seeing. By 1950
television suddenly got serious and interesting things were being done there.

No, it was a blazing time. The fact that it was secretly going wrong politically makes it a fascinating story to tell. What I want to do is portray two stories, the golden age and then the demons at work beneath the floor.

JW: You've written a lot recently about the decline of American empire. You told *Interview* magazine that you "hate to fall into a Braudelian Marxist determinism, but I do think that nations just run out of energy." You suggest there is some structural dynamic that no ruling class could alter. Could you explain a bit more about the dynamics of empires as you see them?
GV: Other countries come along and they're not all in sync, each goes through phases. Look at what is probably the greatest society the world has ever created—China, the Middle Kingdom, which had a good 1500 years and a rather lousy 400 years. Well, China will come back, as Confucius himself is coming back there.

JW: But this is sort of a way of letting our rulers off the hook. It isn't that our ruling class is completely inept and incompetent, it's just that they are part of a historical dynamic.
GV: I would be a perfectly good Marxist on that: what they do won't make any difference. If the thing is expanding and the energy is burning along merrily, you can't do badly. You can be Abraham Lincoln and Thomas Jefferson rolled into one. If you're on a losing streak, then the country's gone. Jack Kennedy knew that. He was talking about great presidents once and he said, "The more I read and the more I think about this job, everything is contingent upon what you're faced with while you're in it." That's really why I think he liked war, because he knew perfectly well that war presidents got better press, more space in the history books. I'm afraid it's as crude as that.

JW: You never attended college. How did that happen?
GV: I graduated from Exeter and you really don't need any more education after that unless you're going to be a brain surgeon. I had read Plato and I had read Milton. I had read Shakespeare. I had had fair American history. And a lot of Latin. That's all you need. And very good English.

JW: Did you know Reagan in Hollywood?
GV: Yes and no. I've been at functions with him a dozen times. Hollywood is a very small place; he was active in television and I was active in television.

In '59, I was casting *The Best Man* and MCA offered us Reagan to play the good guy, an Adlai Stevenson sort of presidential candidate. I said I just didn't think that Reagan would be very convincing as a presidential candidate. Instead we hired Melvyn Douglas. As a result Douglas' career was totally revived, he won every prize in sight and was a star from then on to his death. Reagan by then had nothing, he was by that time a host on that TV program.

JW: So if Reagan had been cast in the lead of *The Best Man*—
GV: Melvyn Douglas would have been President—a very good President. And Ron today would probably be touring in *Paint Your Wagon*.

JW: Do you have any thoughts on how history ought to be taught?
GV: Yes. I'll tell you exactly how to do it. You start in the first grade and you teach every creation theory there is, from Big Bang to Garden of Eden, give 'em all. Kids love that. With as many audio-visual things as you want to, since they're television children. In the next 11, 12 years you make history the spine to every thing you teach. Everybody takes it. You give them simultaneously what's happening in China, what's happening in Europe, what's happening to the Incas, and so on. It's riveting stuff and kids will like it. There are audio-visual aids—I'm trying my best to be up to date here.

As you go along you will naturally teach science, as science starts to evolve. Those who are going to specialize in it will start drifting in that direction, but they will never lose base with the spine that runs straight up from the first grade to the twelfth. The famous difficulties over teaching sex: by the time they get into puberty, sex is part of history. You can teach that along with everything else. Everything is ancillary to history, history is the spine.

By the time they get to the present, or as close as you dare get to it without being partisan, they have had a good notion of what happened to the whole human race between the Big Bang and the moment that they're leaving school. At the end of it? I don't think anybody 17 should leave school without knowing about the Roman Empire, knowing about Confucius. They've got to know these things. Foreign languages should be woven through. I'd prefer them to learn Japanese or Russian, or Chinese. Anyway, this kind of pan-history, or whatever word you want to use, is not that difficult to set up. It's just that there are not that many people capable of doing it. But once you do set it up, it should be a dream to teach and boring to no one.

JW: And what about American history? What should our students today know about the history of their own country? Radical historians have argued that they should know more than the acts of the great white men.

GV: Well, we're talking about up to 17. You're talking now about universities, I would think. What I hate is good citizenship history. That has wrecked every history book. Now we're getting "The Hispanics are warm and joyous and have brought such wonder into our lives," you know, and before them the Jews, and before them the blacks. And the women. I mean, cut it out! Teach the history of the place; what were the problems? You'll certainly have enough spare to explain black and Indian problems, and why women were not enfranchised, and how they got enfranchised. All these subjects should come up in a normal way, and I think it can be done without loading any dice, you just follow the track. Finally, you wouldn't get to American history until you're about 14 or 15 anyway because America is quite recent.

JW: The last chapter is the rise of the American Empire, the national security state and a very quick coda.

GV: I don't think they'd let you teach that, but even if you stop with the Civil War, or the First World War, you've done all that you need to do. I'd rather have them know the history of China and Japan, because they're going to have to live with the Chinese and the Japanese.

An Interview with Gore Vidal

Jay Parini / 1990

From *Gore Vidal: Writer Against the Grain* by Jay Parini, pp. 278–90. © Columbia University Press. Reprinted with the permission of the publisher.

This interview with Gore Vidal took place at his villa in Ravello, Italy, in the summer of 1990. The villa, called "La Rondinaia," is a five-storied house that clings like a swallow's nest to a steep cliff overlooking the Mediterranean. It has a dizzying view of the Amalfi Coast, looking southward to Salerno. On a clear day one sees the faint outline of Calabria in the distance. Directly below, the little town of Amalfi—once a major port of call and commercial center—hugs the shore.

Vidal has been living in this part of Italy since 1972, and he obviously adores the situation he has created for himself: the writer in voluntary exile. And it's a splendid exile. One approaches the state grounds of "La Rondinaia" by following a long and winding path that proceeds through a grove of cyprus trees, past a deep-blue swimming pool (its color is meant to imitate the legendary "blue grotto" of Capri) through an old-fashioned loggia, down and up many stairs, to the villa itself. Above the door is a statue of Cybele with her wheel.

Inside "La Rondinaia," high ceilings and sweeping marble stairwells add to the spatial sense. Vidal lives much like a Roman emperor in exile, enjoying the fruits of his craft. Having written numerous best-selling novels, countless television and movie scripts, and several Broadway hits, he does not have to worry about money. What separates him from almost all other writers of commercially successful projects, of course, is the quality of his work. Vidal is a major writer, an intense and witty man who has thought deeply about many of the most difficult issues of our time.

We talked over a drink in his large study, surrounded by editions of Henry James, Turgenev, and dozens of other writers who have an important place in Vidal's continuously expanding universe. The shelves also boast a leather-bound set of Vidal—itself an amazing sight, and a wall of framed magazine covers featuring Vidal. On a table, one sees photographs of Vidal's father with Franklin Roosevelt, of Vidal grandfather, Senator Thomas P. Gore, and other celebrities, including Italo Calvino, whom Vidal considered a friend.

We talked about his craft, mostly, and about the reception of his work in academe. Critics—especially academic critics—have not always been kind to Gore Vidal, for many reasons. This is Mr. Vidal's own version of what has happened to him in four decades of creative work, with assorted comments on the nature of his own achievement and some thoughts on his contemporaries.

Jay Parini: Your writing career seems to have elicited such a wide range of responses from critics, ranging from enthusiastic to downright mean. What's going on here?

Gore Vidal: For a start, there's just so much of it. I've had one of the longest careers in American literary history. Very few writers who began publishing in the forties are still at it in the nineties. I don't think a lot of critics now working really know much about the war years, about my generation. Everything is so quickly forgotten, especially in the U.S., which I often call the United States of Amnesia. There is also the fact that I write in so many different genres: novels, screenplays, essays, stage plays, and so on. That seems to puzzle everyone. The general pattern isn't easy to work out, so I don't blame anyone for not trying.

JP: Are you talking about changes that have occurred in the critical aesthetic?

GV: No, just a lack of knowledge. The critics don't know an awful lot. They think that American literature began when, in 1969 they first happened to read *The Great Gatsby*.

JP: Is there some basic pattern in your own work that you'd want to point out?

GV: The novels fall into two categories: meditations on history and politics— book such as *Burr* and *Julian*—and what I call my "inventions"—such as *Myra Breckinridge* and *Duluth*. The second category of books are rather like satirical arias; nobody else seems to write that kind of thing.

JP: Quite a few writers, on the other hand, write historical novels, don't they?
GV: Yes, but my "meditations" deal with matters that most of the others
ignore. The Good Novelists—as opposed to the trashy bestseller types—
usually avoid topics such as the nature of society, the fate of the republic,
or the origins of Christianity. Elizabeth Hardwick once said to me, after the
publication of *Julian,* "Only you could have written that, Gore." I said, "Yes,
and I'm the only American writer who would have *wanted* to write it. I may
be the only American writer who would even *read* such a book!"

JP: It often strikes me that you're not really a writer in the American
tradition. Your work harks back to the British satirists: Swift, Peacock,
Evelyn Waugh. Is that fair?
GV: Yes, and P. G. Wodehouse, whom I adore. He was a very great influence
on me, as he was on Umberto Eco. But my early novels were influenced by
Mark Twain, Stephen Crane, and Theodore Dreiser—all Americans.

JP: At a certain point your work changed quite dramatically, didn't it?
GV: *The Judgment of Paris* was my turning point. After that, I no longer
echoed the ancestral voices, I suppose. I found something like my "real voice."

JP: Let's talk about your early education. What authors did you read as a
young man—before you started writing?
GV: As you know, I never went to college, so my reading was idiosyncratic.
Unlike most American writers, I was never afflicted by The Tradition. The
American canon, you know, doesn't compare to the English, French, or
Russian. But American educators, desperate to have a literature equal to
their empire, have tried hard to make Herman Melville into a major writer;
the work, however, just isn't good enough. It won't bear that kind of
examination.

JP: So who did you read?
GV: I worked my way through a shelf of Scott. I read all of Meredith and
Henry James. When I was a bit older I read Flaubert, Proust, and George
Eliot. And, of course, I loved Peacock, Huxley, Wodehouse—the satirists.
I read Swift, I admired him, but he was not a very important influence. I'm
not conscious of that, in any case. Mario Praz once pointed out that Voltaire
had influenced my work, and he was right.

JP: I can't get Swift out of my head. The similarities are too great.

GV: As a polemical essayist, yes. I took Swift as a model. A better place to look is to the American pamphleteers of the Southwest. My grandfather loved them, and so do I.

JP: One senses that Mark Twain lurks in the background somewhere, not only in the essays throughout but in some of the novels, too.

GV: That was all pointed out by Leslie Fiedler in his famous essay "Come Back to the Raft Again, Huck Honey." He noticed that in *The City and the Pillar* I'd taken *Huckleberry Finn* a step further.

JP: Did the later Twain, which is so very dark, influence novels like *Kalki* and *Duluth*?

GV: Maybe so. What you mustn't forget is that Twain was always a great entertainer.

JP: And a public figure, like you.

GV: But unlike me, he was afraid of losing the favor of his audience. He would never have said, as I have, that he was an atheist. He was an atheist, of course, as the posthumously published work shows, but he was too frightened during his lifetime to admit it.

JP: What was he afraid of?

GV: His wife, certainly. And his public. They wouldn't have stood for Mark Twain the Atheist.

JP: Can we talk about your work as a scriptwriter? You've written endless television scripts and screenplays. Why?

GV: Contrary to legend, I did not inherit a great deal of money. I have supported myself from the age of seventeen. Perhaps I should say that the U.S. Army supported me between the ages of seventeen and twenty-one. After that, I supported myself as a writer. I've gone where I had to go to make a living. When I was blacked out by *Time* and *Newsweek* and the *New York Times*—back in the late forties and early fifties, in response to *The City and the Pillar*—I had no way to continue as a writer of novels. So I turned to television. Within a year or so, I was doing extremely well for myself. I went on to write for the theater, for the movies. I turned to politics for a while, and to writing essays and reviews. Then I returned to the novel, with *Julian*. Necessity is what drove me. The fact that I was versatile was simply good luck.

JP: If you had it to do over, what would you have done?
GV: Stayed with the drama, in whatever form it took—stage plays, movies. I understood the theater in the fifties and sixties, but Broadway is, of course, dead now.

JP: You've had at least two major hits on Broadway and a string of huge bestsellers. What accounts for your popularity?
GV: I have no idea. Perhaps it's because history is so badly taught in the schools, which means there's a real hunger for information of a certain kind. Americans want to find out about their past. There's also the fact that I deal with interesting subjects. Most writers today are not interesting because they're not interested. What concerns them is something called The Novel. But The Novel doesn't exist. There are only novels. And most of these are disguised autobiographies. Writers tell us about their marriages and mental problems. But who cares? If nothing else, by reading *War and Peace* you'll get a wonderful recipe for strawberry jam. Great books teach you lots of things. And then there's the delicate matter of class—a taboo subject in America. Most writers come from the middle classes, and they never venture outside their little realm. They don't even know that there *is* a class system in America. The myth is put forward that we have no ruling class. Anyone can become president of IBM, they argue. Sure they can. But who owns the majority of IBM's stock? The small number of families who actually own America are unknown to most people, especially writers. Nevertheless, they do exist.

JP: Does this lack of awareness of the class system lead to a certain naïveté in American fiction?
GV: Yes. Novelists ought to explore the issue of class and write for the society at large. But novelists today prefer to write for each other. They know very little about the way the country is governed or how society works. They imagine that if they sign a petition against South Africa that they've made a great political gesture. They have no idea about how the mayor of their city was elected, however. Or what that process says about their world.

JP: Have none of our writers dealt with class in a way that strikes you as mature?

GV: Louis Auchincloss has. He understands about the old families, and he knows how their interlocking trusts actually work. Only junk novels commonly deal with these subjects.

JP: You've been extremely hard on academics and university life. What's going on here?

GV: I don't take most academics as seriously as they take themselves. If I had known that the academics would absorb the novel in such a total way, I'd probably have been more polite. That took me by surprise. The academic novelists are the worst, however: Barth, Gass, Barthelme, and so on. For them, nothing exists but what is happening on campus. They're obsessed with theories of the novel, and they write to mirror those theories. It's all a vicious little circle, and it doesn't result in something anyone would like to read. These books exist to be put on a college syllabus or dissected by an academic critic. There is no sense of a genuine audience.

JP: What about reviewers? Has much changed in the four decades that you've been on the scene?

GV: The reviewers are all professors now. That wasn't the case in, say, 1950. I have nothing against professors as such. But the influence of the academy has been unfortunate for American fiction. Again, what gets left out of the equation is the "real" world.

JP: You've often said that Hollywood has taken over where literature left off, and that future generations will have lost all interest in books. All they'll want to do is watch movies. Isn't that partly true of your generation, too?

GV: Of course. I grew up in the Golden Age of talking pictures. The language of film is as natural to my generation as the language of fiction. When I turned to writing for Hollywood, I was already well prepared. I knew how the thing was done because I'd seen so many films. If you grew up in the thirties and forties, the movies were your world. It's one of the great things people of my age have in common: we've all seen the same pictures.

JP: Your novels seem consciously constructed along cinematic lines, which is to say they proceed by scenes. Reading them is like watching a film.

GV: I don't work so consciously. I prefer writing dialogue to description, I suppose. Description is usually boring. On the other hand, if you have a gift for pursuing narrative through dialogue, you can end up taking too many shortcuts. Your novel will look, in the end, like a movie script that was thinly adapted to the conventions of fiction. Ideally, the making of sentences creates a sense of kinetic energy that's different from the dialogue of scripts.

JP: Do you work from an outline?

GV: If I'm working on an historical novel, then history itself provides the outline. When I was working on *Lincoln*, for instance, it seemed quite natural to end with the assassination. There would have been no point in continuing with Mary Todd's story. That didn't interest me anyway. Historical novels seem to follow their own designs, their own self-limits.

JP: What about the fictional aspects of the historical novels? *Lincoln* is, after all, described as "a novel."

GV: I like to invent characters—fictional persons—who will then observe the "real" people. In *Lincoln*, I tell the story from about five different view-points—though I never pretend to get inside Lincoln's head, as such. I've always found first-person narrative the easiest, I suppose. Once you get the tone of voice, the book writes itself. That was certainly true of *Myra Breckinridge*, *Messiah*, and *Julian*—each of those novels is a form of acting. I just invent a character and let him or her talk. Dickens, you know, was marvelous that way. He conjured such a wide range of voice. He could act them all. That's pretty much what I'm trying to do.

JP: Did you discover a good deal about each character or "voice" as you went along?

GV: Myra didn't even know she'd been a *man* until halfway through her narrative. How's that for a little surprise? *Myra*, for me, was simply a case where the voice took over, took possession of me. The same thing happened with *Duluth*, which is my favorite of these books. "*Duluth! Love it or loathe it, you can never leave it or lose it.*" That sentence just came thundering into my head one day as I was walking down the street in Rome. What on earth is *that*, I thought. I sat down at the desk, and there it was: the whole novel just opened itself before me. It might interest you to know that this novel has been one of my most quietly popular books. I got a list recently from the

British Public Library of my most popular books, and *Duluth* and *Creation* were the ones most frequently taken out.

JP: What about *Kalki*, which has a lot in common with *Duluth*? It's essentially what Anthony Burgess would call a "dystopian" novel. Did the voice come easily?
GV: That voice was much harder to get at. It betrayed me several times. The whole thing needed recasting.

JP: You wrote more than half a dozen novels in your twenties, including *Williwaw, The City and the Pillar, In a Yellow Wood, The Season of Comfort, A Search for the King,* and *Dark Green, Bright Red.* That's quite an array of books, though they seem so very different from the work of your later years. How do you think about those books now? Are they something of a lost continent? Or do you go back to them occasionally?
GV: I don't think about them. I never reread them. Oddly enough, they stay in print, especially in translation. *Dark Green, Bright Red*—a novel about CIA activity in Guatemala and other such things—is very popular in Brazil and Latin America. *The City and the Pillar* seems to have a life of its own. *Messiah,* written at the end of this "early" period, has always had a following.

JP: Going back to the novels about American history: Did you think of them as a sequence?
GV: Not at the outset. I suppose it was during the composition of *Burr* that I realized that a sequence could be made of that material. I had several references to Aaron Burr in *Washington, D.C.,* and of course my stepfather's family was related to Burr. Somewhere along the way I realized I was involved in a family history, that it could all be expanded from there. In *Burr,* I focused on the first thirty years of the Republic. I wanted to keep going, to see what would happen to these people and their descendents. Eventually, the story spanned two centuries. I suspect that few critics have really read the novels in sequence and understand what I was trying to do.

JP: Those novels are so full of data—historical information, period detail, the minutiae of politics from each era. Do you employ researchers or anything?
GV: I've simply got to do all of the research myself in order to *discover* what I want to know. The process occurs like this: I order boxes full of books from

American booksellers. I may buy two or three hundred books for each novel. I read the books here, in Ravello, taking notes. After I've written the novel, I always get a professional historian to check the novels to see that I've not made any great gaffs. Writing these books has been my education. *Creation* was, for me, a crash course in comparative religion.

JP: *Creation* seems an odd book for you to have written, though it's full of fascinating material. I found the voice rather flat—at least compared to *Myra Breckinridge* or *Duluth.*
GV: Flat! I found the voice of Cyrus very interesting, full of biases of one kind or another. He's anti-Greek, pro-Persian by temperament. He thinks he knows the truth about things. But he gets hung up on the notion of creation—how it all began. As he goes farther and farther East, he sees that it's a non-question. It didn't ever begin. And it won't end. Finally, with the Buddha, he realizes it's not here at all. The world doesn't exist, as such. Life is a dream. What he comes to see is that he was asking the wrong questions. Western culture is always asking the wrong questions. It's our fatal flaw.

JP: How would you describe the goal of life as Cyrus—and perhaps Gore Vidal—have finally come to see it?
GV: To be free of desire is true knowledge, to break the repetitive cycles of birth and death and rebirth. That's the goal.

JP: Is the Buddha your philosopher of choice?
GV: No, I prefer Confucius. Confucianism isn't a religion at all; it's a system of education, of administration. It's the sanest approach to life that I know about.

JP: Your narrator in *Creation*—Cyrus—is certainly a type of philosopher and teacher. His blindness reminds me of your grandfather, Senator Thomas P. Gore, who was blind. Is there anything autobiographical about this novel?
GV: No, it's an objective book—if there can be such a thing. I'm tired of Romantic modernism and those autobiographical books like Joyce's *Portrait of the Artist,* a novel that gets written over and over. Many critics seem to believe it's the only novel worth writing, that it's The Novel. It is *not.*

JP: One critic, Frederick R. Karl, has complained that you have not taken modernism seriously. He seems to believe that you never really took on the modernist revolution, which means that you're stuck back in some premodernist limbo. You and George Meredith.

GV: Modernism was finished by the time I was born. All sorts of mediocre writers enjoyed playing at being "modern." They still do. But there's nothing in it.

JP: Italo Calvino once described you as a postmodern writer, like himself. I can see that, with your interest in "doubleness," the wittily self-conscious nature of your inventions. This label—and I detest labels as much as you do—would seem to work best with the satirical novels—*Myra*, *Duluth*, and so on.

GV: Yes. Calvino said that in a review of *Duluth* that appeared in an Italian newspaper. But it was Peter Conrad who, in the *TLS*, called me a "duplicitous" writer. I liked that, largely because it seemed to describe my work in a way that made sense to me. Fortunately, I don't have to teach literature, I only write it. So I don't need those categories.

JP: You've spent a great deal of time in Italy in the past three decades. Have any of the Italian writers—Calvino, Umberto Eco, Moravia—influenced you in any way? I suppose this is a roundabout way of getting at the subject of living abroad generally. There must have been, must be, an effect.

GV: Living out of the country concentrates your mind wonderfully. You see your own country more clearly. I really can't say that I have ever been much influenced by Italian or European writers, at least not consciously, though of course I've read them all. Calvino I considered a friend, and I admired his books.

JP: And, of course, you introduced Calvino to the American public.

GV: A fact conveniently forgotten by many.

JP: What attracted you to Calvino's work?

GV: He was essentially a scientist, with a scientist's eye for detail. *Mr. Palomar* is the ideal example of this, the last novel published before he died. I admire any writer who has gifts that I don't have.

JP: How would you describe your own particular gifts?

GV: I can invent worlds that were not there before. That's the supreme task of a writer, isn't it? Swift did that, of course, but he was very different from me.

We create such different kinds of worlds. *Duluth* is my best work in this regard.

JP: Critics often comment on your language, which is remarkably fluent and clear.
GV: It varies, depending on the voice of the novel. My essays are closest to my own actual voice, though I couldn't imagine doing *Duluth* in the tone of my essay on William Dean Howells. I do suppose that an ear for language is one of my strengths—and it's something unusual for an American writer. The language of the American novel is now a much diminished thing. The general vocabulary of fiction has shrunk visibly in my lifetime. The average educated person in my father's day had access to many more words than people do now. Even Tennessee Williams used to tell me that my novels were full of so many strange words that he couldn't read them. I once asked him for an example. "Solipsism," he said. "I had to look it up." I said, "Look, Tennessee. If there's any word you *need* in your vocabulary, it's solipsism!" Of course, Tennessee never read anything.

JP: What does a writer need to succeed—not only in the commercial or critical sense, but aesthetically?
GV: A writer needs energy most of all. Physical energy and imaginative energy.

JP: What are your weaknesses as a writer?
GV: If I could see them, I'd avoid them. What I do see is that nothing I've written has ever satisfied me. You can't really succeed with a novel anyway; they're too big. It's like city planning. You can't plan a perfect city because there's too much going on that you can't take into account. You can, however, write a perfect sentence now and then. I have.

JP: That reminds me of Randall Jarrell's famous definition of a novel as "a book that has something wrong with it."
GV: Exactly. Nobody can command it all. The minimalists have gotten onto something here. They half suspected there was no way they could write a good novel: they lacked the gift for language, and they had little in the way of knowledge of the world. You have to have those things to write a good novel. So they worked backward, eliminating things. The instinct was sound.

Raymond Carver kept as safely as he could to the little he knew, though he knew that little bit of the world very well. Some of his writing is very good indeed—so well observed.

JP: What other writers do you admire—among current writers?
GV: William Golding is very fine. Saul Bellow I've known for years—we used to live near each other on the Hudson, near Bard College—and I admire his intelligence. His novels, however, don't interest me very much. I find them difficult to finish. I tried recently to read *Humbolt's Gift*, but my energy ran out after about a hundred pages. Or perhaps *his* energy ran out. I've had the same experience with most of his other novels, including *Herzog*. Nabokov I admire, except the later work. *Ada* is unreadable. Self-love on that level is difficult to respond to. I adore some of the early books, though, such as *Laughter in the Dark*. He was, as V. S. Pritchett once said, a grammarian of genius. I also like reading what I call "the girls"—Joan Didion, Diane Johnson, Alison Lurie. They operate so well in the diurnal world of marriage, teaching, jobs, children. They have such malicious eyes. And I love Jeanette Winterson, a young English writer who is extremely funny. She's absolutely wonderful— the best thing to come out of England in the last twenty years.

JP: Would you say you're hopeful about the future of literary writing in America or, for that matter, anywhere?
GV: There will always be a certain amount of good writing, but what I have to wonder is who will read it? There was a time when only the poets read other poets. That's true of novelists now—serious novelists, as they're called. I notice myself much less interested in reading other writers—in fact. I've got an endless supply of old movies to watch on video. They're heavenly. On the other hand, I keep writing—novels, essays, screenplays. Again, it's simply what I do. I'm a writer.

An Interview with Gore Vidal

Harry Kloman / 1991

From *The Gore Vidal Index*, a website maintained by Harry Kloman. Reprinted by permission of the author.

In November 1991, Gore Vidal came to Pittsburgh to shoot his scenes for the movie *Bob Roberts: The Times Are Changing Back Again*, a mock documentary about a right-wing businessman-cum-folk-singer who runs for a U.S. Senate seat in Pennsylvania.

The movie's writer/director/star, Tim Robbins, was the husband of the actress Susan Sarandon, with whom Vidal has been friends since Sarandon appeared in Vidal's 1973 Broadway play, *An Evening with Richard Nixon*. But even without the Sarandon connection, the role of Sen. Brickley Paiste—an old-fashioned liberal with supreme self-confidence—was perfect for Vidal, who has always called himself something resembling a liberal, but who is no less critical of liberalism than he is of any other political philosophy.

Vidal maintains that The System has failed the American ideal of democracy and freedom, and that the Democrats and the Republicans are merely different branches of one big political party, which he calls the Property Party (a borrowed term), with self-interest at their collective heart.

Vidal also claims that the art of the novel has withered in the past several decades. And he offers a most startling theory of what has gone wrong with the study of the novel in 20th Century America.

We had our conversation on the afternoon of Nov. 15, 1991, seated in the back of the auditorium of Soldiers and Sailors Memorial Hall in Pittsburgh. Vidal wore a three-piece suit and a bow tie, his costume for the movie. He had just finished filming a short scene and was waiting for a call to film his biggest scene—a debate between his character and the right-wing upstart. The debate would take place on the stage of the auditorium, where a production crew was busy setting up as we talked.

Harry Kloman: In 1956, you wrote about what the novel should be. You wrote that "it seeks the exploration of the inner world's distinctions and visions

139

where no camera may follow, the private, the necessary pursuit of the whole, which makes the novel at its highest the humane art that Lawrence called the one bright book of life." What American novelists now do you think achieve what you spoke of a number of years ago as being the ideal for the novel?
Gore Vidal: Well, that piece went on to make the case that the novel was pretty much finished—not as a form, but the audience had gone. There are more novelists in England than there are novel readers. I was commenting then that film had taken over and was the preferred artform of this period, and that the novel has now joined poetry as something well worth doing for its own sake, but it no longer has a great public, it's no longer essential. The film director has taken the place of the novelist.

I said to an interviewer not long ago, "You know, I used to be a famous novelist." He said, "Oh, well, you're still well-known. People read you." I said, "I'm not talking about me specifically. My category has vanished." Saying you're a very famous novelist is like saying you're a famous ceramicist— maybe a good ceramicist or a successful ceramicist, but famous? That was lost on our watch, Norman [Mailer] and I. So is the whole notion of the great writer who sort of spoke for his time.

HK: You say on "your watch . . ."
GV: Well, during the period which Norman and I were principal players over the last 40 years—the war novelists, of which we were about the last. What good writing do I see? I don't see much of anything that I find terribly interesting. Like everybody else, I'd rather see a movie usually.

HK: Two of the best-selling literary novelists in America—that is, people who sell well but who also are considered to be literary figures—are Updike and Doctorow. Would you comment on them?
GV: I don't really read them very much. I've read a book or two by each one. I think they write very well. There are obviously many different publics in the land. Updike has a sort of exurban New Yorker reading public, Doctorow more a city college intellectual. But I've never been very interested in either of them. The writers that interest me are a little bit more adventurous perhaps than they are. A woman in England now called Jeanette Winterston, a marvelous writer. I find someone like Golding interesting. I introduced Calvino to the American public about 15 years ago. That's what interests me. I don't care so much about naturalistic novel writing. It's had its day.

HK: Do you believe that your novels achieve what the novel should be?
GV: Well, some do and some don't. It depends on what I'm doing. I do two kinds of books: I reflect upon history and religion; and I have my total inventions, like *Duluth* and *Myra Breckinridge*, and those alternative worlds, comic and satiric, whatever word you want to use, the reverse of realism. Actually, I've been what they call an experimental novelist, probably the most varied of the lot. But as nobody knows what anybody has written—nobody knows. [Chuckles]

HK: Is there one or two of those books you're most fond of?
GV: I like *Duluth*, and certainly *Myra* and *Myron*.

HK: *Messiah*?
GV: *Messiah*, yes. It's an interesting book. Certain of them have become cults. *Messiah* is a cult book, *Kalki* is. *Duluth* never really caught on because nobody knows about it. Perhaps they'll find out. There's no longer a grapevine for books. In the old days somebody would read a book and tell somebody else about it. It would be word of mouth. That's just sort of stopped. We don't really have any critics that people pay attention to. In the old days, someone like Orville Prescott in the daily *New York Times* could make or break a book.

HK: Why has this happened?
GV: Lack of interest.

HK: What creates that lack of interest?
GV: Two generations have now grown up on television. They don't learn to read very well, if at all. If you don't enjoy reading by the time you're 13 or 14, you're not going to pick it up. And they watch television from babyhood, as a sort of pacifier. I think that a mind shaped by flashing images works differently than a mind that has been shaped by linear type. Don't ask me what the difference is because I haven't a clue, because I belong to one side and they're on another side.

HK: Is there any irony that you do films?
GV: No, no. I do everything, whatever amuses me. Narration is all the same. The big question: Are the movies an artform? That's a hard one. The result

sometimes looks like it, but it's such a collective enterprise, you can't really say where the authorship is, which is where the *Cahiers du Cinema* people lept right off the edge, particularly with those cornball Hollywood directors of the '30 and '40s whom they began to call masters. They were just sausage-makers turning out what the studio told them to do.

HK: You wrote in 1966 that "in a civilized society, law should not function at all in the area of sex, except to protect people from being interfered with against their will." You included prostitution on the list. In 1991, we feel we're more enlightend about prostitution, we know what leads so many women to prostitution. Any thoughts on that?
GV: Well, men too. Prostitution is a great necessity, and should. . . .

HK: But sociology points to the fact that so many prostitutes were abused or sexually molested . . .
GV: . . . So many wives, too. Prostitution is a natural thing, and in a world made more dangerous with AIDS, [we need] legalized prostitution with medical examinations, which is pretty much what they did in the 19th century. 1948 was the terrible year. A French Communist senator—a lady—and an Italian communist senator—a lady—each of them in '48 passed laws banning prostitution. They had houses and they were legally and medically inspected at regular intervals. Then of course all the women ended up on the street, and they had a huge epidemic of venereal disease, which was a disaster. Misplaced morality.

HK: Politics. When the Kennedy presidency began, you said that "civilizations are seldom granted a second chance," and you somewhat looked fondly upon the Kennedy administration as a second chance. But in '67 you said, "something mysteriously went wrong" with the presidency. Might he have become a great president in a second term with more experience? What was it that went wrong?
GV: That's what he told me. [Chuckles] He didn't have it. He had no plan. He was playing a game. He enjoyed the game of politics, like most of them do. There was no real substance to him. He was quite intelligent, very shrewd about people, but he liked the glamour of it all. He loved war, he had a very gung-ho attitude. I began to part company with him about the Bay of Pigs.

Then we all forgave him, and he started the invasion and started to beef up the troops in Vietnam.

HK: Was the Bay of Pigs naivete?
GV: Well, it was pretty dumb. He could easily have said no. The intelligence was so dreadful. Of course he was then blamed by the CIA for not using aerial backup, but then it was pretty clear that we'd made an error. They convinced themselves that the Cubans were going to rise up against Castro.

HK: How much of your assessment of him do you think he would agree with himself? Was he aware of his lack of substance or depth? Did he think he was a great man?
GV: He thought himself a pretty good man. He wasn't at all vain, I mean no more than the average man. His line to me was that a so-called great president is entirely happenstance, the period you happen to be living in, and all the great presidents have always been living in disastrous times, like Reagan. In other words you have to have war. It's the war presidents that people remember, not the ones in between. And I think he designed the uniform for the Green Berets himself. I saw him drawing it, and I said to him, "Do you know the last Chief of State who designed a military uniform was Frederick the Great of Prussia?" [Chuckles] He was not terribly amused by the comparison. [Laughs]

HK: Vietnam would not have been different had Kennedy lived until 1968?
GV: Nah. I think he might have just played right along. They got themselves into so much false thinking—the "Dominos," if Vietnam falls, Thailand falls. But it doesn't fall. [Chuckles] But they get these mindsets, then nothing they do makes any sense. "We fought the war to contain China." I mean, what's he talking about? If you want to contain China—I knew enough history and geography, which he didn't, and nobody in the administration did—the Vietnamese had been for thousands of years dedicated enemies of the Chinese. If you want to contain China, you help Ho Chi Minh—you don't drop bombs on him. I used to go on television and argue with the administration people—this is after Jack was dead.

HK: What kind of president would Bobby Kennedy have been?
GV: Pretty sinister. A little Machiavellian. Not Machiavellian, he was Savonarola, he was highly moral, obsessed, vengeance. Jack had a funny story

about him. Nobody could stand him, they put up with him because of John. And somebody came up to Jack and was complaining about Bobby's behavior. And Jack says [slipping into a hauntingly good Kennedy impersonation]: "Look, you've got to remember, Bobby's a policeman, he's gotta arrest somebody. If he hasn't arrested somebody, he'll go home at night and he'll arrest Rose." [Laughs]

HK: In 1968, you wrote about liberalism: "Trying to make things better, trying to compromise extremes, trying to keep what he has from falling apart, the liberal goes about his dogged task." Who are the great liberals today, who can we look to to make things better? Who can the Democrats look to next year?

GV: Well, I think since I wrote that, the system has collapsed. What is wrong is systemic. A change in personnel is not going to make the slightest difference. No matter who's going to be elected president, the situation is going to get worse. The Constitution has ceased to function. It's totally corrupt. The elections now cost the world. Whoever's elected president will not represent the people of the country, he'll represent the interests who gave him the money to run. Why do you think Bush can run on cutting the capital gains tax? That's the price of having the office bought for him.

HK: There's no chance for a true populist?

GV: None. None. Even if he could find the money, which is quite doubtful, billions of dollars would be dedicated to destroying him. They wouldn't allow such a thing to happen. The two parties are the same, and some people pay for both. The decisions are made in the corporate boardrooms, not only in the U.S., but in Tokyo as well. We don't have representative government. Congress has given up. The only two powers it has—one is to declare war, the other is the power of the purse, the budget—it has given up both. So the Congress has ceased. Watching Clarence Thomas being coached by the White House, one realized that this Supreme Court has nine mediocre lawyers acting as a legal council to the executive. They're there to scream "hosanna," right on, at any executive decree. So where are the checks and balances, where's the government? We have a national security state, and the country's run by the national security council and is not accountable to anybody. Ollie North is still at large.

HK: How do they get away with it? Surely the people must be somewhat complicitous in this?

GV: The people don't know anything about it. Only about 10 percent are interested in politics at any time. In bad times, people get interested because they want to know why they don't have any money.

HK: But if only 10 percent are interested, then the other 90 percent are complicitous for not being interested.

GV: They have no control. People aren't stupid. They're ignorant—we have the least well-educated population of any First World country. We're at the bottom of every single list for reading skills and mathematics. We have no public education, so you start right off—they don't have much information. Half of them never read a newspaper—just as well, looking at them—half of them don't vote for president. But they understand the system. They know it's corrupt. Every poll you take, Congress is way down there among people you admire. They're not admired. Everybody knows it's a corrupt game. What we need, a way out, is a constitutional convention. We can start this thing over again. Liberals immediately start screaming, "They'll take the Bill of Rights away." Well, the point is, they're taking it away anyway, the Supreme Court. If they're really going to do that, the famous "they," why not do it in an open convention, see where you stand. Jefferson wanted to have a constitutional convention every 30 years. "Nobody should expect a man to wear a boy's jacket," he said. Nobody dreamed this document would still be sitting around 200 years later with all its patches.

HK: You open *Messiah* with the words, "I envy those chroniclers who assert with reckless but sincere abandon: I was there, I saw it happen, it happened thus." It goes on to say that "we are all betrayed by those eyes of memory, the vision altering, as it so often does, from near in youth to far in age." You were not yet 30 when you wrote that. You're, well, older than that now. I wonder, is that true of you? How has your vision altered from youth to advanced youth.

GV: Hmmm, to old age. I remain the same. The wisdom in that passage is that what alters is memory, that the way you remember things changes as you get older. Some things you remember more clearly, and some things you start to forget.

HK: Some of your memories, as you're talking now, seem very vivid. Gene Luther in the book says, "Something has happened to my memory." What do you find yourself forgetting, or wondering if you can trust to memory?
GV: Well, I'm now at the point where I'm the subject of a number of biographies.

HK: Authorized?
GV: There's one that is, Walter Clemons at *Newsweek* is writing it, he's been at it five years now. So I am obliged to think about the past. My memory of almost anything is not the other person's memory, it's totally different. And you get really to the point: What do you trust? I'm supposed to have invented something called "historicity," and I'm going up to Dartmouth for a Gore Vidal week starting Monday. They've got about six professors from around the country, and there's a whole theory which they call "historicity," which I represent, which is the intersection between fact and fancy exemplified by my books about the American republic. I'll know more about what it is when I get there. I'm not a literary theoretician. It really is a relativeness, it's Heisenberg's law applied to history. Heisenberg's principle is that nothing "is," but it only "is" in relation to where you're standing to see. There is no actual thing there, there's just a variant view of it one has.

HK: You're standing farther away from the things you once saw. How do you find your vision of the things you know you've seen alter?
GV: Well, the mind is always kind of a machine. The mind doesn't remember anything, it remembers what it last remembered. It's like an onion, there's just layer after layer. If you've had a long life, you remember quite a lot.

HK: Do you ever read the books you wrote in the '40s and '50s? I wonder how you see them or think of them now.
GV: No. I read about them because they do these Ph.D. things and sometimes I look at them, I don't really read them. It comes back to me, the books, when I read what they're writing about.

HK: Do you find there's a lot of scholarly interest in your work now?
GV: Oh, yes.

HK: Why?
GV: Well, I was blacked out for 40 years by the American universities and by the press.

HK: Why?
GV: Oh, too numerous, the reasons. And they suddenly realized that they had been putting on *Hamlet* without the Prince, and you can't go on doing *Rosencrantz and Guildenstern* forever. And it just suddenly hit them. And I didn't much care for the universities. I don't like the bureaucratization of literature which goes on there, or history. So I've been sharply critical of them. Now they realize the game is over, there are no longer voluntary readers, very few of them, dying out. And the universities want to at least keep some part of literary culture alive—usually the wrong parts, since they have no ability in telling what's what. So I went to Harvard this spring and gave the Massey lectures. Now I do the week at Dartmouth, they'll show two films of mine, do a play. And then the seminar in historicity and so on. Papers will be read, it should be interesting.

HK: Some people might say—but I would never ever say this—that to hear you say they've been doing *Hamlet* without the Prince—that sounds as little, what's the word, egotistical?
GV: Sure it is. But it's pretty clear to me that there's a big hole in the middle, and if it isn't me, what is it? Why is there a hole there? What they do is they want people who celebrate received opinion. And this is a very, very conservative country intellectually, very meager, to be blunt. So they want very safe, everyday sort of writers. They have experimental writing, but it has to look like somebody has studied *Finnegans Wake* very carefully and is going to try to recreate another sacred masterpiece. I think [Joyce] wrote to be read, not as much to be taught. You have two generations now that are writing books within the universities to be taught within the universities.

HK: It seems that if there are no voluntary readers, then you must write to be taught.
GV: I wouldn't know how to do that, and I wouldn't do it if I could do it. But that seems to be the canon.

HK: Your story "A Moment of Green Laurel" is about an adult who essentially encounters himself as a child. It's nostalgic, melancholic . . .
GV: It's also ripped off by Rod Serling.

HK: For a *Twilight Zone*?
GV: Yes.

HK: Did you know him?
GV: Yes. I told him, too. [Chuckles]

HK: Did he admit it?
GV: No.

HK: I wonder how often you look back, consider the past, relive the past, as that protagonist does in the story?
GV: There's flashes occasionally—of memory.

HK: What sort of things do you flash on when you have flashes like that of the past? Perhaps mystical, melancholy flashes?
GV: Oh, I don't do much memory lane. It's just that a place, perhaps, will trigger the imagination and memory. I don't traffic much in the past. But as I said, it's on my mind now because I have to answer all these questions.

HK: A theme that has run through your work is the final line of *Washington, D.C.*, where you write: "Change is the nature of life, and its hope." Can you tell me some of the changes you've seen yourself go through in your public and private life?
GV: I seem to be a rather monotonous figure. I don't think I change much at all. Change is going on all the time. We can't control change.

HK: But individual change, personal change? Does that statement not apply to the individual as well?
GV: That line applies to the human race, the species actually, species and adaptation. That's what I had in mind there, not the individual changing. People do—from what to what, since you don't know what you started out as? Where's the measuring stick?

HK: What was the impetus to write *Messiah*? It's almost 40 years old, and it seems more relevant today than ever. *Bob Roberts* is about, in part, what *Messiah* is about.
GV: It's the same story, in a sense.

HK: Did others see the media-ization of public figures at that time like you did?
GV: It did so badly. Nothing of mine would be reviewed in the daily *Times*, or *Time* or *Newsweek*. Five books were just blacked out, so I had to go to television.

HK: Not reviewed at all? Why?
GV: After *The City and the Pillar*, Orville Prescott of the *New York Times* told Nicholas Wreden of E. P. Dutton that he would never read, much less review a book of mine. So that meant the daily *New York Times*—he did all the daily reviews. *Time* magazine and *Newsweek* followed suit. So I was blacked out by the *Times*, my least favorite newspaper. Oh, they poisoned a lot of wells. Just as recently, when my *Lincoln* was being done on NBC, the "dreaded" William Safire, author of *Freedom*, a book about *Lincoln* which did quite badly, got them to write a piece about the mini-series, trying to kill it before it was shown: It was full of errors, the historians didn't like it, and so forth and so on. It was pure *New York Times* poison. They do it all time. They just did it to poor Norman, getting John Simon to review him, knowing that John Simon would give him a venomous review, which is what John Simon exists for.

HK: When you say poor Norman, are you being ironic, or do you really feel bad for him?
GV: Oh, I feel for him, I do. I have a certain fellow feeling for Norman.

HK: The idea that you put forth in *Messiah* is what *Bob Roberts* is about, and now we're beginning to realize it. We certainly began to realize it with the 1960 presidential elections . . .
GV: . . . As they say, "ahead of its time." A lot of people have tried to make movies of it over the years. A lot of scripts were written.

HK: Seriously? Anybody of note or significance?
GV: Well, the guy, what's his name, the guy who produced *Hair*, Michael Butler. He tried five, six years ago for a film or a play.

HK: I always wondered who would play John Cave in the film. I've also had some wonderful casting in mind for a film of *Washington, D.C.* I've always imagined Paul Newman as Blaise Sanford and Burt Lancaster as Burden Day.
GV: That would be nice. Someone just bought *Empire*. We're trying to get him to do the whole lot.

HK: How common, in the early '50s, was the idea of people being sold by the camera, what *Messiah* and *Bob Roberts* are all about.
GV: It hadn't started really. Television was very new. The first sort of TV campaign was '52, Eisenhower vs. Adlai Stevenson.

HK: Was that in any way an impetus for *Messiah*.
GV: It might have been. Adlai Stevenson was an unknown governor of Illinois but had been picked by Harry Truman to be the nominee. And Stevenson, unknown, got up and made a speech at the convention welcoming the delegates, and he was famous for a night, the whole country knew him. And I thought, "This is new." That was about the time I turned my attention to *Messiah*.

HK: When you wrote *The City and the Pillar*, what consequences did you expect to face after its publication? I believe I read once that you said it ended your chance for a political career.
GV: Well, it did at that time. But I picked it up again in 1960 and then in '64. I had the election to the House but turned it down because I wanted to go back to novel writing. I knew it [*The City and the Pillar*] was going to cause a lot of distress . . .

HK: What sort of distress?
GV: Well, for the press and so on.

HK: For friends and family?
GV: Oh, that's their business. Some interviewer for a magazine asked my father—very clever interviewer, they usually aren't that enterprising—she said to him, he was a charming man: "Don't you find Gore terribly courageous for the positions he takes?" He said, "Well, what's courageous when you don't care what people think about you?" [chuckles] It was a rather good take on it.

HK: Were there any personal consequences among friends and family?
GV: None.

HK: Peers? Other writers?
GV: No, no. I think they were delighted. I was the leading war novelist, and suddenly I was eliminated. I was no longer competition to any of them. [Chuckles]

HK: The book is not very sexually explicit, whereas of course *Myra* makes up for lost time. Was that because of the times? Did you feel restricted from writing explicit sex in the book? Certainly in '68 you didn't.
GV: No, in '48 it was pretty explicit.

HK: By today's standards . . .
GV: . . . oh, it's mild, yeah . . .

HK: But by the standards of the time . . .
GV: . . . oh, it was pretty far out, yeah.

HK: Did you want to go farther? Did you want to describe more?
GV: No, I'd done quite enough.

HK: Did you ever consider a sequel to the character in the book?
GV: He crops up again, Jim Willard, in *The Judgment of Paris*. It was all invented you know. I wanted to make this thing look like a very all-American, middle-class, Norman Rockwell boy to give it its force. Some brilliant type wouldn't have worked.

HK: In the '90s, one of the big issues of the gay rights movement is outing. Any thoughts on that?
GV: Well, the theory is okay. But you have to go back to what my positions are, which is that there's no such thing as a "homosexual" person and no such thing as a "heterosexual" person. These are adjectives which describe actions. They never describe a person. So I start out by denying that these two categories exist. Well, to say that to the average American, they just can't get that through their heads, no matter what their interest might be. So once you take that, then of course I'm all for changing laws and removing persecution and

so on, but not ever in admitting that there is such a thing. I mean, only a society as sick as the United States would come up with these categories.

Behind it is this really very, very primitive society—you asked about the reaction to *The City and the Pillar*—I hadn't realized to this extent that there really was no civilization here at all. We have brilliant people every now and then, but there is no intellectual world, for instance. The nearest thing was the sort of Jewish group in New York to which I belonged—*The Partisan Review*, now *The New York Review of Books*—but it's so small. It's basically rather incoherent.

HK: So the responses of intellectuals to some of these issues . . .
GV: . . . Well, they were just as bad as my Baptist cousins in Mississippi. From intellectuals I would have expected more intelligence, but then you realize there isn't much intelligence. I always thought I would live long enough to see some sort of civilization take root in the U.S. I did my bit, but it's rather worse than it was.

HK: The women's movement has made some progress, the civil rights movement has made progress. The gay rights movement seems not to be making as much progress . . .
GV: . . . Well, AIDS put a big cramp into that, of course. It's helped demonize it all over again.

HK: Will it ever happen that the gay rights movement will make the advances that women's rights and civil rights have made?
GV: Oh, sure.

HK: How long will it take?
GV: Who knows, who knows. I'm all for militant action and changing the laws.

HK: How militant? Some see outing as militant. Revealing people in positions of influence?
GV: Yeah, but you know, a man is married, he has four children, and occasionally he goes out with a Boy Scout. But what is he? He's a married man, he's a father, he's bisexual like everybody else. What's the big deal? It's of no interest at all what anybody does, nor should it be of any interest. It carries no moral weight.

HK: But it does for so many people.

GV: Well, it does because they don't understand morality and they haven't got anything else going on in their head. I would say that certainly I would be in favor of outing a judge coming down hard on the rights of quote-homosexuals-unquote if he were discovered in a compromising position—why, yes, he should certainly be exposed.

HK: Actors and actresses?

GV: Why bother with them? They're not doing any harm. Rock Hudson was very funny about that. He was in some faggot bar in San Francisco—I knew him slightly for years, a nice guy—and a journalist said to him, "Aren't you worried about appearing at a place like this?" This was 20 years ago. And he said, "No, why should I be?" The guy said, "Yeah, but they'll write about you—you're queer." He said, "Try. The American people will not face the fact that I'm queer." And the journalist said, "Okay, may I write a story and try to sell it to *Confidential* or something?" He said, "Go ahead. They won't take it." And the guy went ahead and did it, I read about it somewhere. But it was out of bounds, it was just not going to be considered, it couldn't be considered.

HK: When you were writing *Myra Breckinridge*, did you realize—I don't know, "shock" is such a hard word, but it was certainly different from anything you'd written before it. Did you realize people would raise a few eyebrows at it? Were you laughing while you were writing it?

GV: Oh, I thought it very funny, extremely good for the folks.

HK: "The folks?"

GV [wryly]: The folks.

HK: The ones who liked *Washington, D.C.* so much?

GV: And *Julian*, yes. They may not have liked [*Myra*] all that much, [chuckles] but I thought it was funny.

HK: What was the impetus for that book?

GV: I just heard a voice.

HK: What did the voice say?

GV: "I am Myra Breckinridge, whom no man will possess." I didn't even know she'd had a sex change until I was almost half way through.

HK: Seriously?

GV: Yeah. I had no idea. It came out of the ba-loo.

HK: The British edition of the paperback says this: "Wanting in every way to adapt to the high moral climate that currently envelopes the British Isles, the author has allowed certain excisions to be made in the American text." Was that true? Did you participate in the excising. Or did you just allow them to be made?

GV: Yeah. Then about 10 years later, I put it out again with all that had been removed.

HK: I once compared Chapter 29 to see what they took out. Just a few details and references to anal penetration and stuff like that, literally just three or four words. What's this "high moral climate" that enveloped the British Isles in the 1970s?

GV: [Chuckles] I forget what that was.

HK: What happened to *Myra*? What went wrong with the film?

GV: One of the worst directors probably in the world was assigned to it.

HK: When it began, did you have hopes of it turning out?

GV: Yes! Mike Nichols wanted to do it. All we had to do was wait for him to finish *Catch-22*, and he would have gone on to do that. He wanted Anne Bancroft as Myra.

HK: Anne Bancroft was interested in Myra! And they wouldn't wait? Imagine how film history would have been changed—or something like that.

I'd like to do a few quick takes on some people you've known over the years. Just say a few things about them. Norman Mailer.

GV: Mmmm. No, we don't do that.

HK: Truman Capote?

GV: No quick takes.

HK: No quick takes? Paul Newman?

GV: Old friend.

HK: Guccione?
GV: Nothing to say.

HK: Richard Nixon? Surely you have something to say about Richard Nixon.
GV: (yawning, stretching) I did, in *An Evening with Richard Nixon*, in
which appeared in 1972 an actress called Susan Sarandon, which is why I'm
here now.

HK: You live mostly, where, in Italy?
GV: In L.A.

HK: How much of the year in Italy?
GV: Every year is different.

HK: What will your next novel be.
GV: *Live from Golgotha.*

HK: What's it about?
GV: Well, NBC is trying to restore its ratings. They get a team back to
Golgotha to make a special about the Crucifixion. Now, who's going to be on
that cross? Everybody thinks that Shirley MacLaine is channeling in and a
cyberpunk is at work and the memory banks of Christianity are being
eliminated. Only one person can tell the story, that's Timothy, a friend of
St. Paul, and he'll act also as anchor at the Crucifixion. That gives you a little
idea. A story of worn faith.

The Sadness of Gore Vidal

Larry Kramer / 1992

Larry Kramer is a writer and AIDS activist. The Larry Kramer Initiative for Lesbian and Gay Studies at Yale was founded in his honor. Gore Vidal attended a major symposium about his work there in 2003.

He sits across from me at a comfortable, quiet table in the Edwardian Room at the Plaza Hotel. The staff knows him and is attentive. The woman at the next table leans over to inquire what he thinks of the upcoming Presidential election. He is very fat. His face is lined. His hair, all of which he still has, looks like it's at the end stages of a coloring job. He says he has to worry about his health, but he orders a steak.

He is one of my heroes and, like me, he's obviously very tired. Of fighting and seeing so little progress. Of raising a voice no one hears with any sufficiency. His voice rises almost automatically to sound angry—to sound the anger that he knows we expect from him. His list of wrongs that provoke this anger because they are wrong is by now too familiar to him. He goes on automatic anger. His conversation is sprinkled with the buzzwords of a lifetime; they no longer seem to convince even him. I identify with him completely. Who has listened to him? What has his wrath made right? The world is further away than ever from his dream.

He calls *me* the romantic.

I protest. He is as romantic as I am.

He denies it.

I tell him that anyone as angry as he is *must* be a romantic because otherwise life would be unbearable.

He has fought and created and never stopped trying for as long as we have known him. At the end of our meal, which was excellent, and our conversation, which was great fun, and my being with him, which was, for me, exceedingly moving, he pulls his huge self up and lumbers out of the room and into the lobby and into the street. He has many people to speak to while he is still in our city. He is still trying. He may be exhausted and despondent and cynical (no, the romantic never becomes cynical), but he is still trying.

Oh, that I can go on, still trying.

Larry Kramer: I should like to start by saying that you are one of my all-time heroes and role models, for more years than either of us wants to count. I pulled out my copy of *The City and the Pillar* and I looked at it in terror to see what year I read it—I was thirteen years old. Can I tell you that it is probably one of the seminal books of my development? Good heavens, and you were twenty-one when you wrote it, which was extraordinary.
Gore Vidal: 1948, yes, I was twenty-two.

LK: Twenty-two. Well, I guess what I want to talk about today mostly is homosexuality.
GV: *Startling* subject to bring up.

LK: At the Edwardian Room of the Plaza. Well, it was enormously courageous of you to write this book in 1948 but you've said that afterwards you didn't write anymore about homosexuality because you thought you would hurt your career in a literary way.
GV: Oh, no. I never take back anything. It certainly did me great damage, yes. And you know the story which I repeatedly tell: Orville Prescott of the *New York Times* said he would never read, much less review, a book of mine again, and didn't for five books, a couple of which were among my better efforts. *Time* and *Newsweek* also refused to review me. I was so dead-broke I went into television, movies, theater, politics. And in ten years I made enough money so I didn't have to bother about doing work I didn't want to do. I came back to novel-writing with *Julian,* and I've never let go of the subject when I felt I had something to say about it. I'm sometimes put out at how little that I've written on the subject is known. Nobody seems to know my essays at all in all these quote gay unquote—"gay" is a word that I hate— periodicals. I mean there is so much that they can mine from what I've written about sex as politics. I've done a lot of work in that field, trying to analyze the situation, rationalize . . .

LK: Maybe some of it has got to do with the feeling—whether it's only perceived or accurate, I don't know—that for many years you didn't announce your homosexuality or that you maintained that you were bisexual and that sort of put you on the outs with a certain political correctness.

GV: Yeah, well, that's bad luck for them because I have a lot to say on the subject. I don't categorize—that's the first position I take. There is no such thing as a homosexual person. There are homosexual *acts*—

LK: Well, let's talk about that.

GV: We all know about *heterosexual* acts. Is anybody 100 percent one thing or the other? I rather doubt it. Is anybody fifty-fifty? I rather doubt that too. I haven't seen many examples.

LK: But isn't that just a safe kind of definition? (*A waiter interrupts.*) No, no, I'm interviewing Mr. Vidal, and he's more important than the chicken soup.

GV: Look, what I'm preaching is: don't be ghettoized, don't be categorized. Every state tries to categorize its citizens in order to assert control of them.

LK: But you're living in a time when many of us *want* to be ghettoized and categorized.

GV: Well, I disapprove.

LK: Because there's safety in numbers and perhaps we feel that's a way of exerting—

GV: Well, I'm on a double-track. It never occurred to anybody before St. Augustine that there even *was* such a category. I've never applied [these labels] to myself nor have I applied them to anybody else, even when they have invited me to. Simultaneously, the other track: If the categorization is going on in a vicious way, as it does on the part of our monotheistic, near-totalitarian state, then one *does* organize, and one does fight back. I have two things in my mind. One, that there is no such category, and two, that if the category is invented by the powers that be—largely Christianity, although the Jews are not much better on the subject—then, indeed, it must be fought. I'm all for organization, politicization. I'm even for violence.

LK: Oh, we must talk about *that!* So you approve of ACT UP?

GV: I approve of ACT UP very much—but I approve of successful violence, not unsuccessful. You have to pick the way to do it. You *have* to have a strategy.

LK: Well, we've tried many strategies, all unsuccessful, I'm afraid.

GV: I'm completely in agreement with the spirit of it, that the only thing Americans really respect is a kick in the teeth. And if the police need it or the courts or the Congress or the President needs it, let the kick in the teeth come. It's intolerable to allow this situation to go on. AIDS has been a "Spaniard in the works," as John Lennon would say. It's helped the demonization all over again of the category that *I* say does not exist, but *they say does* exist and therefore I would certainly protect those who have been stigmatized.

LK: You've not spoken too much about AIDS.

GV: I'm not a virologist.

LK: No, but surely you must have lost a lot of friends or people that you've known or whatever. And, certainly, aside from everything else, it's a phenomenon.

GV: Well it's an ever-present phenomenon, certainly. I'm not a handwringer. If I don't have anything useful to say, what am I to say? It's a terrible thing. Of course it is. AIDS hasn't come to me closely except in my own family. I have a twenty-nine-year-old nephew—my sister's son—who is, of his generation of my family, the only talented member. Hugh Steers, you probably know his paintings. He paints about people with AIDS.

LK: Oh, indeed, yes.

GV: Becoming quite famous.

LK: I didn't know he was your nephew.

GV: Yes. I think he's been diagnosed for eight years and he's twenty-nine, and that obviously brought it home dramatically to me.

LK: Is this not cause for you to write an essay of great strength and anger about what this country has not done to save this young man's life?

GV: Well, yes. But don't you think it's better that I attack the national security state which has given us a kind of police state? Isn't it better I attack the Supreme Court that takes away our rights? And isn't it better I attack Jesus Christ and Moses who have brought on the mentality that has done this? I'm radical—which means I go to the root of it.

LK: Let me say no in answer to all those questions because you have *done* all of this and we know how you feel on all these issues but we *don't* know how you feel on this new one, which is perhaps closer to home and much more personal.

GV: That is wrong in my view. Why get upset only when it touches you personally?

LK: Oh my goodness!

GV: Shouldn't you be, in the abstract, for *justice*?

LK: Now you're getting too existential for me.

GV: I really believe—

LK: I never became political *until* it touched me personally.

GV: I've been political my entire life and politics need not ever have touched me.

LK: Well, I don't know if that's an answer.

GV: Isn't there something in you that makes you feel an obligation to see that justice is done?

LK: Indeed, but—

GV: I believe in going deeper and deeper into the roots of *why* it exists.

LK: But back to this "categorization" business. I wonder if it isn't more of a generational thing than a philosophical thing. What I find, and I'm certainly closer in age to you than I am to the "Young Turks" of today, but I think that, for some time, there's been a very strong desire to be categorized as homosexual, to he proud of being gay and to almost *resent* the notion that people consider gay people bisexual. I think most gay people today don't *want* to be bisexual whether it's in their purview or their skills to be so.

GV: You know, I haven't been *plugging* bisexuality. All I say to interviewers who bring up the subject of my private life—which I was brought up not to discuss, and I *don't* discuss—I just say, "Everyone is bisexual," and I quote Freud, his standard textbook definition. The next thing, I read "Gore Vidal Proudly Claims to Be Bisexual." Well, I never *said* it. I always give the same answer the same way. So that goes, as you know, into the computer, and every time they press that button, they come up with "Gore Vidal Proudly Claims to Be Bisexual."

LK: I don't think I've ever seen "Gore Vidal Says He's Homosexual."
GV: Because I don't believe in it.

LK: But, Gore, you *are* gay. You've lived with a man for forty years or something, and everyone who knows you personally knows you're gay. And I think *you* think of yourself as gay.
GV: I promise you I don't think of myself in these categories. It's like saying, "I'm a carnivore." Well, yes, I *am* a carnivore, but I'm very fond of the movie *Airplane.*

LK: Which is very carnivorous.
GV: I regard it as more vegetarian.

LK: As someone who made a film for Ross Hunter, I can assure you it's carnivorous.
GV: You poor thing! I didn't realize that.

LK: It's nothing I brag about. But I made more money than I made on anything in my life . . . I guess we desperately want to claim you.
GV: Well, *everybody* has. I don't mind that.

LK: Again, this is something that AIDS has brought about—this desperate need for role models, for people we can call our own . . . We want to somehow tip you over the edge so we can have, I don't know, *The City and the Pillar*—the Nineties. So you can write about your life as it applies to our lives now, in a personal way.
GV: You have to take into account our temperaments. You're a subjective and romantic writer. I'm an objective and classical writer. The two are totally at odds. I've had the same conversation with Norman Mailer. He is in your situation and I am in mine. We see the world entirely differently.

LK: But I bet there is a big romantic streak in you. Perhaps that's why you're so angry. It takes a romantic to be so angry.

GV: Well, perhaps when Bette Davis in *Dark Victory* is planting her plants. That is universal! No, that is Warner Brothers!

LK: My brother would not know who Bette Davis was in *Dark Victory*. It takes a romantic to be as caring and as angry and as put-out and . . .
GV: Raging!

LK: Raging—as you are. So, don't give me, "I am not a romantic."
GV: I was brought up with a very over-developed sense of justice—and not only about myself. I have a general view that this is *my* country. My family helped start it, and we've been in political life of one kind or another since the 1690s, and I have a very possessive sense about this country, an ecumenical sense. I don't divide people into men and women, blue eyes and brown eyes. Obviously I do on some levels—we are all filled with wild prejudices and madnesses that strike from time to time. But it's this sense of justice that keeps me going and fuels my rage. It isn't just that I feel upset that I've been discriminated against, as indeed I was. I was blacked-out as a novelist. I was practically destroyed. My friend John Horne Burns *was* destroyed.

LK: But what difference does it make what fuels the rage?
GV: The difference is in the tactics you use.

LK: I use the same tactics as you use.
GV: Except a lady stopped by here before and wanted to know what I thought about the election this year and the Constitution—

LK: Well, we can walk down the street and someone will stop and ask me a question.
GV: But it won't be about the Constitution.

LK: Because I don't think my constituency believes the Constitution is worth shit. Your nephew is not going to live because the Constitution has not extended the necessary rights to him that would force the NIH and the FDA and Congress to see that his disease is researched.
GV: Those things don't have anything to do with the Constitution, although there are many things wrong with the Constitution. It has to do with Congress.

LK: *Fuck* the Constitution, Gore.

GV: It has to do with the Congress. It has to do with the rulers. The *rulers* are the people you have to lean on.

LK: *Lean on?* We've done everything short of kidnapping them and if I knew how to do that, maybe we would have tried that too.

GV: Why don't you fuck Bush and give him AIDS? And say, "This will happen to the next President and the next President and the next."

LK: Don't think we haven't thought. . . . Bush has a nephew who's at the University of Pennsylvania. We talked around a few ideas of that nature. But, basically, the trouble with gay warriors is that, when it comes right down to it, it's very hard to rouse the anger past a certain pitch and we're a very small percentage of the gay community unfortunately. As is always the case.

GV: Well, my experience is with the left in America, but it's all the same. You get into a lot of divisiveness, theatricality, thwarted self-love. It's monstrous. I was co-chairman of the People's Party with Dr. Spock. I tried to get Spock interested in politics. He didn't have any—he was just against the war. We had the makings of a real party of the left. All the kids wanted was to avoid Vietnam. And I quite agreed with that. That's why I was helping out. But to try and interest them in any kind of real politics which might affect their lives—sexual politics, economic, racial—you couldn't turn 'em on. I don't know what it is. Something is done in the public educational system that just undoes their reception. They just can't pick up on it.

LK: Has there ever been a radical movement that's been well-organized and continuing?

GV: I suppose Lenin would say that *he* pulled it off, at least for his generation.

LK: What destroys, in the end, is the divisiveness. ACT UP has lasted longer than most.

GV: It has more reason for being than most.

LK: It's also on its last legs.

GV: And Queer Nation?

LK: Queer Nation is all but gone.
GV: I'm a great admirer of Jonathan Ned Katz. I love him on American history.

LK: Jonathan has not really been a part of either movement, ACT UP or Queer Nation. He's much more of an academic. Marty Duberman also hasn't been a part of either. Marty has sort of, in his own way, moved on to that quiet place that academics go when they reach a certain age.
GV: Called tenure.

LK: I don't know how to say this politely, but we miss him!
GV: Did you read his memoir? It was one of the funniest books I've read. I don't know that he would like my taking it that way.

LK: I don't think so.
GV: But going through all of that agony, to find Miss Right and then to find Mr. Right. Imagine going to somebody else for advice on these matters! I've never understood psychiatry. I mean there's no one's advice I want on anything to do with my life. And he took it so seriously—that white-picket-fence dream he has.

LK: Now, now, you're touching very close to home here. You're looking at another white picket fence . . .
GV: All right, it's a white picket fence with an *absolutely* straight boy inside.

LK: Well, I don't know about *that*. But you have all of that and you've had it all your adult life. You have a white picket fence in Ravello, and you have one in Rome, you have one in . . .
GV: In L.A.

LK: You have a very nice man who's been with you and loved you and looked after you tenderly and efficiently, for many years. I mean, that's everybody's dream. And you've managed to support yourself doing what you want to do.
GV: I don't deny the luck. But don't deny me the amount of shit that I've had to put up with.

LK: But surely you and I have welcomed the shit in some sort of perverse way because it fuels the engines.

GV: But I must say, it was rather startling a few years ago, to see a kind of great textbook come—five hundred novelists since the Second World War— and my name was never mentioned. Now I'm afraid it's all going the other way—altogether too many pieces about me in academe. It's all gone into reverse. But, um . . .

LK: Gore, so *what*? Who gives a shit what those people do with their fucking stupid idiotic lists? You do what you want to do and you're getting your rocks off every time you sit down at a typewriter, and screw them.

GV: Well, you have to have it in close-up so you *can* screw them.

LK: You're *too* slippery. As someone who's taken a lot of shit over the last ten years, after a while you just say, "Oh, fuck it." No matter *what* you say, X number are going to approve and X number are not going to approve, so you might as well say what you want to say.

GV: I'm really interested now in trying to destroy monotheism in the United States. That is the source of all the problems.

LK: A worthy cause. But I'd rather have you fighting for your heart—exploring what it means to be a gay man at age sixty-five in the world today—

GV: Sixty-seven.

LK: Sixty-seven in the world today and looking back . . . I've just written a play, which is basically an exploration of a journey.

GV: You're talking to your younger self—yeah, I remember reading about that.

LK: And, uh, the journey of my homosexuality. As you know, I started out in an entirely different way and certainly did not expect to be such a political animal.

GV: I never thought it was a big deal. Maybe that's the difference in the way we were brought up. [Homosexuality] was practiced quite widely in my adolescence. In schools, in camps, in the army. Some stayed with it and some didn't.

LK: But why is it so important for you—this notion that we are all bisexual? I keep coming back to this—it bothers me because I admire you so. I don't even think Freud went beyond the idea that all men had it in ourselves to, you know, fuck a woman or whatever, and that there was a scale, a Kinsey scale from one to ten. I think what we have now is millions and millions of people who just glory in being in love with, or drawn to, someone of the same sex. . . . We just want you, wholeheartedly and full-blown—if you'll pardon the pun—on *our* team.

GV: I *am* on your team. After all, I have been there all along. They have very good dessert here.

LK: What are you going to have?

GV: I'm not going to have any. I have to watch my weight.

LK: Do you read any gay literature or gay authors that you've liked?

GV: Jeanette Winterson is wonderful.

LK: Yes.

GV: I feel she's a discovery of mine. I read her first book and drew as much attention to it as I could. And I like Edmund White, particularly *Nocturnes for the King of Naples*—a lovely book. You know, Tennessee was asked these same questions: Why he didn't make his characters queer. And he responded very simply, "Why should I diminish my audience even more than it is?"

LK: Well, I think we're finding now that we have our own audience.

GV: You have to make the case for ghettoization. Maybe I'll agree with you. And maybe I won't.

LK: The ghetto is now so big that it's hardly a ghetto.

GV: But it's not the world and it's got a hostile government.

LK: But do you write for an audience or do you write for yourself?

GV: It's the same.

LK: I don't know if it is. I never think of going out to increase an audience or to decrease it. I write what I want to write.

GV: Playwrights do. And you're a playwright.

LK: I'm a novelist, too.

GV: Yeah, but when I'm talking about a playwright I'm speaking specifically of Tennessee, who wanted people to see his plays, and who didn't want to limit his audience any more than his romantic, subjective nature already did.

LK: You see, that's why I think it's a generational thing. I think that, if Tennessee were a young playwright today, he would write gay characters— just as I think that, if *you* were a novelist today, you would have carried on from *The City and the Pillar* and not have been diverted.

GV: Oh, no. I'm interested in so many other things.

LK: But that doesn't limit you from writing the other things.

GV: Well, I've written about those things, but it's not the center of my life.

LK: Well, I feel now this *is* the center of our lives and the center of *most* gay writers. That's how the world has changed. Because we found there were more of us or because AIDS made us learn that we have to fight for survival.

GV: Well, on solidarity, I am as one with you—in the matter of AIDS and in the matter of this very bad political system.

LK: Let me give you an example—you are an eminent biographer of Lincoln—it was Jonathan Katz who first presented it to me. There has been talk in gay historical circles that maybe Lincoln had some sort of gay relationship.

GV: I'm fairly convinced of it, yeah.

LK: Well, isn't it important that this be written about?

GV: Yeah, but you see, I wasn't covering that period of his life.

LK: He had an alleged affair with a man, Joshua Speed, and the letters that they exchanged were very . . .

GV: Very odd.

LK: Very romantic. And then when they got married, they each wrote to the other that they . . .

GV: Found it hard going, yeah.

LK: But, who better to tell the world than you?

GV: If I'd been writing about the young Lincoln I would have done it, but I'm writing about the Presidency during the Civil War.

LK: But I want you to write about the young Lincoln! Who better to tell the world than Gore Vidal? It would be ten times more useful than attacking the Constitution, to tell this fucking country that its most beloved President was gay, or had a gay period in his life—it would do so much to shake the notion of sexual freedom and rights.

GV: It's tempting. But, I've just written a book in which St. Paul is in love with Timothy, who is straight, to use that word, and puts out only to get on the road with him.

LK: I'm not going to in any way disparage that endeavor, I'm just going to choose your next one. I think it's important that we claim our historical characters. It took us so long, for instance, to get Walt Whitman acknowledged as a gay writer.

GV: And that only happened because the academics finally were shamed into it by the Europeans who said, "What is this nonsense? You exclude your greatest poet!" So they invented homoerotic.

LK: Don't you loathe that word?

GV: I do. Yes, Whitman had daydreams, but, of course, he wouldn't do anything. And, all you have to do is read the poems or the letters or look at some of the photographs of Walt with his young friends and it's very, very clear.

LK: Did you read the Ellmann biography of Oscar Wilde—the part when [Wilde] met with Walt Whitman?

GV: Yes.

LK: Wouldn't you have loved to have been there? Are there other gay historical figures that you know to have been gay that we don't?

GV: President Buchanan is generally agreed to be. And President Pierce is certainly an interesting case. I can't write about young, romantic love.

LK: Oh, I doubt that

GV: Well, I can't, not now. It's a matter of age. . . .

LK: That's exactly when one can write about it. You're too hard on yourself.
GV: I leave that to you. Anyway. . . .

LK: I'm fifty-seven, you're sixty-seven.
GV: So there was Franklin Pierce and Nathaniel Hawthorne, who was the most beautiful writer of his day. And Pierce was one of the most beautiful Presidents.

LK: You think Hawthorne was gay?
GV: Oh, yes! And I think Melville was in love with him.

LK: Oh, *that* I've thought.
GV: I don't think anything happened, because Melville was . . .

LK: There's a wretched piece by John Updike in *The New Yorker* this week about Nathanial Hawthorne and his "terrible secret." Not once is mentioned the possibility that he was gay.
GV: Oh, he would never do *that*. It wouldn't be Updikian. For him everybody's a cunt-hound.

LK: Gore Vidal has called John Updike a *cunt-hound*.
GV: No, I've called him an admirer of the cunt-hound in his novels. I know nothing of his private life.

LK: You know, that's almost too complimentary a term for John Updike.
GV: I can't read him . . .

LK: He's so boring. . . .
GV: He writes very well and he manages never to interest me. Which is *quite* a trick. A good writer can generally interest me.

LK: So Franklin Pierce, James Buchanan, Nathaniel Hawthorne, Lincoln and Joshua Speed . . .
GV: Well, there's also a great case to be made for George Washington and Alexander Hamilton.

LK: Really! Talk about that for a minute.

GV: I practically said it straight out in *Burr*. But if you don't have the evidence...

LK: But they don't have the evidence for Jesus!

GV: I can do anything I want to *him*. But I take Alexander Hamilton and Jefferson much more seriously than I do these Middle-Eastern freaks. Hamilton was an extremely randy fellow, very handsome. A cunt-hound and demonstrably so. Caught often, but with enormous talent. He was brought up by an older man in the West Indies. The older man was about twenty-eight, he was about fourteen. He was a mathematical genius trained by a Sephardic Jew. There was a whole bunch of them for some reason on this island. At fourteen, he was a first-rate accountant, working for this man—a bachelor of twenty-eight or twenty-nine from New York, who liked him so much he sent him to college. Hamilton made his way by making older men fall in love with him. A lot of guys do this. The sex isn't that great, but the emotion is just the same. And specifically in the case of George Washington, it's very clear that Washington was very much in love with him. Whether anything happened I rather doubt. First of all, there was a great deal of speculation about Washington's potency . . . er, activity. He might not have been able to do *anything*. But he certainly was in love with Hamilton, who treated him so rudely when he was his Commander-in-Chief and then when he was Secretary of the Treasury. In effect, Hamilton was prime minister for eight years. Washington was king. Hamilton treated him like a beautiful boy would treat a sugar daddy: standing him up, being rude to him. There was this whole pattern there. For a young writer coming along it's a lovely theme, the love affair between Washington and Hamilton—which invented the United States.

LK: But Gore, why not you?

GV: Because I'm out of historical novels. I'm done with it. But I'm throwing out some nice themes here. The ironies—which are the best fun: The United States is then formed, mainly to protect Washington's investment out on the Ohio River. Then they're separated. Hamilton's practicing law down in Mt. Vernon. Washington writes him a hysterical letter: "We've got to start a Republic, a strong federal government. We're about to lose our property. Because the guys who fought in the revolution got nothing out of it, and are being taxed and are angry." So Hamilton said, "All right, I'll give you a Republic." Now throw in the fact that it was a kind of love affair between these two men that started the whole country on this foundation—a more perfect union!

LK: That's what you should call it! "A More Perfect Union." You should do it as a play. You were a very successful and amusing playwright. It sounds like this would lend itself well to a play. Your return to the stage.
GV: "Where is my wig, Alex?" That will be the first line. . . .

LK: "Where are your teeth, George?"
GV: "I thought I had them in!"

LK: "They're still down around my crotch!" Did you not have *any* notion to write another play? I think if you wrote a play about a love affair between George Washington and Alexander Hamilton, we would find a way to get it on.
GV: But could you get the folks to come?

LK: I think. But you can't worry about that. Just do it. What are your next writing projects?
GV: I'm doing a movie with Scorsese. On Theodora and Justinian.

LK: I always find [Scorsese] to be an enormously homophobic man. Am I wrong?
GV: I wouldn't use *that* adjective. . . . A boy trained by Jesuits who is uptight about *a lot* of things. He's much more that, I think.

LK: There are few directors who are as gifted visually. I'm just getting a little tired of all his continued macho violence.
GV: So is he. More than "homophobic," you might say he's somewhat of a misogynist. He cannot deal with women in a serious way.

LK: And after the movie?
GV: I'm supposed to do a final summing up of the six American historical novels. It will be the final one, in which I'll be the narrator. I'll look back over my own life, bringing in some of the fictional characters and some of the real

characters I've known. It will center a lot on the foundation of the national security state in 1950 by Harry Truman, which made us a garrison state. Which made us what we are today—broke and unloved and with our military out of control.

LK: Does David McCullough say all this in his book?
GV: He says it, but he doesn't know what he's saying. He doesn't understand at all the politics of Harry Truman's life. He's a charming writer, McCullough, but it's part of the constant falsification of American life and American history. He's unrelenting. After that I'll let drop the feather.

LK: No! I think if anything you're getting sharper and wiser. Certainly no less angry.
GV: I'll say.

LK: And you must never stop.

America's Biographer: Interview with Gore Vidal

Richard Abowitz / 1999

From *Gadfly* 3.7 (July 1999). Reprinted with permission from *Gadfly*.

Most of his books are bestsellers, and as a public figure his fame extends far beyond even this substantial readership. Even as he predicts (as he has for decades) the death of the novel, Gore Vidal, the novelist, has thrived. For more than fifty years—from the publication of his first novel, *Williwaw* (Dutton, 1946), through *The Smithsonian Institution* (Random House, 1998)—Vidal's "inventions" have shown him to be a novelist not only of great imagination, but also possessing a vast technical range. He is staggeringly prolific: twenty-two novels, at least two hundred essays, various screenplays (including *Ben-Hur*), five plays, a memoir and numerous short stories.

Now, in his seventies, Vidal is working on *The Golden Age*, the final volume in a series of historical novels that, placed together, make up a biography of the nation that opposes prevailing national myths. If individuals can shape history, Vidal has known those who did and has watched them do it. There are, of course, many good vantage points from which to write about America, but Vidal's must be counted as one of the most unique: he is the grandson of a senator, an intimate of the Kennedys and a relative of the current vice president. Over the course of his life, Vidal has also kept company with the world's political, cultural, artistic and intellectual elite. Often the A-list didn't make a good impression, and Vidal's writing frequently depicts the failings of the self-declared best and brightest.

Vidal has twice run for office himself, but it is hard to imagine—especially if you share Vidal's view of the political process—that a man so given to notoriety and public candor could ever win an election. Imagine a senator who figures prominently in the diary of Anaïs Nin. Then there's Vidal's willingness to explore taboo subjects and the obvious relish he takes in public feuds. The homosexual relationship depicted in *The City and the Pillar* (Random House, 1948) created, as Vidal recalls in this interview, a public "firestorm." That pales next to the time *Myra Breckinridge* (Little, Brown,

1968) was attacked by William F. Buckley, Jr., on ABC: Mr. Reserve lost it and called Vidal a "queer" before the national audience. Vidal's feud with Norman Mailer almost turned *The Dick Cavett Show* into *Jerry Springer*. Vidal has also developed a small career as an actor with roles in recent films such as *With Honors* and *Gattaca*. All of this should make for lively reading in October when *Gore Vidal: A Biography*, by Fred Kaplan (Doubleday), is published. In addition to the first full biography of Vidal, Kaplan has also edited *The Essential Gore Vidal* (Random House, 1999), a good introduction to the work. Gore Vidal fielded *Gadfly*'s questions from his home in Italy.

Richard Abowitz: Has the pleasure you take in reading, the amount of time you spend reading or the speed at which you read changed significantly over the years?
Gore Vidal: The recent acquisition of glaucoma—every family should have one—has somewhat slowed me down. I've always been a slow reader; mistrust speed-demons. You cannot become a partner of a writer if you're conducting a one-night stand. On the other hand, there are writers one skims as opposed to reads. Biography is currently disdained largely because this has been a great age for biography and not much for history and literature (Creative Dept).

RA: What are your recent interests and enthusiasms?
GV: Strouse's *Morgan*—about J.P.—is splendid. Portrait of an age, etc. And how money works in the world. The only two novelists who ever had a sense of this were [Honoré de] Balzac and [Theodore] Dreiser.

RA: Do you use the Internet?
GV: No.

RA: Do you have any sense of what sort of president your cousin Al Gore might make? Will you vote for him?
GV: I haven't voted for president since 1964 when I voted for LBJ, "the peace candidate." Cousin Al is probably not as mediocre as he seems but that is the cross vice presidents must bear. Do anything interesting and the president takes credit. I think he lies more than he ought, out of compensation for not being in a position to do anything memorable. *Love Story*! Good God.

RA: In your memoir *Palimpsest,* you frequently discuss your own drinking and that of other writers. Has your drinking had any impact on your writing?

GV: My generation drank and so did everyone else in American history, literary and otherwise, until the stoned '60s, the white wine and coke '70s, and so on. Fitzgerald was dead at forty or so, Hemingway non compos, Faulkner incoherent after four good early novels . . . drink did not serve them well but Prohibition and its pressures contributed to their disintegration, along with a lot of others. Americans like to make laws forbidding people to do what they want to do. This produces lawlessness at every level. Ours is an intrusive and fundamentally evil state now heading for an all-out war against its own people since we had trouble defeating even Panama.

RA: Do you remember a moment during the writing of *The City and the Pillar* at which you considered or imagined how it would be received?

GV: I knew there would be a firestorm that I would survive, somewhat charred.

RA: Have you forgiven William F. Buckley for his behavior on ABC in 1968?

GV: He sued me for my response to a piece he had written about me in *Esquire.* Finally, he backed down; dropped the suit. I had to pay lawyers for his madness. One never forgives that.

RA: Do you have any opinion on Norman Podhoretz's recent book on his former friends?

GV: When he wrote *Making It,* I asked Poddy, sort of a friend, what on earth makes you think you've made it? Editor of *Commentary*? Come on. I haven't read his book. Runt of the litter complex who wants to be up there with the big guys—Norman [Mailer], Saul [Bellow], Gore.

RA: Did you have any reaction to Mailer's *The Time of Our Time* and the critical response to it?

GV: I don't read book-chat in general. I didn't read the book because I've read most of the pieces in it already. I gave *Advertisements for Myself* a good review when it was published.

RA: Harold Bloom writes, in *The Western Canon*, "Vidal's best fictions . . . are distinguished historical novels—*Lincoln, Burr* and several more—and this subgenre is no longer available for canonization . . ." Do you have any idea what Bloom means by this, and, if so, do you agree?
GV: Bloom's general point is well-taken. Americans hate history, which is why we do so badly in the present. From Aeschylus to Dante to Shakespeare to Tolstoy, reinterpreted history has been the backbone of the canon; I consider myself in that tradition, and so does Bloom, who includes *Lincoln* and *Myra Breckinridge* in his *Western Canon*. My satiric comedies, like *Myra* or *Duluth*, are too unsettling for school teachers, too funny as well, while the re-imagining of American history, which they know nothing of, falls outside their minute range. Bloom was thinking of current literary reputations and why I so trouble the mediocre—surely a proof of one's value!

RA: How have the editors with whom you have worked been most helpful? For example, what was it like to work with Jason Epstein?
GV: Jason's unusually intelligent and very interested in history. We parted company over my inventions like *Myra*, etc. He dislikes invention, satire, comedy. He gave me a manuscript to read. Short novel. He didn't like it. I said it's wonderful. Publish it. *The Breast* by Philip Roth. Then Philip left him for another publisher. Jason was upset. I said, "Writers know what you think of them."

RA: You write in *Palimpsest*, "Old age is turning out to be like youth." How so?
GV: Wool-gathering.

RA: Is there a reason you chose not to make the selections for *The Essential Gore Vidal* yourself? Is there anything you felt should have been put in that was left out? Is there anything in it that you would not have collected?
GV: I can't reread myself. I did help Kaplan get the point to some of the historical novels: key scenes that he had eerily missed.

RA: Do you intend to read Fred Kaplan's biography of you?
GV: Yes. For libel.

RA: Has being an actor brought you any benefit as a writer?

GV: I wish I'd done more acting earlier . . . for my dramatic pieces. Actors from Shakespeare to Noel Coward to Harold Pinter make splendid play-wrights and once you've been out there —or up there on the screen—you are in the belly of the beast in a way that no mere novelist can ever be. If nothing else you learn timing; a Pinter pause says more than most novels. But then just turning playwright without success made Henry James an even greater novelist when he came home to prose and wrote *Turn of the Screw, What Maisie Knew*, etc.

RA: Did you approach the writing of *The Smithsonian Institution* differently from your other "inventions"?

GV: I wrote it very slowly, page a day, like a poem, waiting for the inventions to find me. Tom Stoppard said he read it wondering how I was going to get out of all the traps I kept setting for myself, particularly in logic.

RA: Why do you think scholars (and other assorted pointy heads) have been quick to embrace the literary merit of your essays while ignoring your fiction? Considering your views on most critics and reviewers, were you surprised to win the National Book Critics Circle Award for Criticism?

GV: Essays are short and even they [scholars] can get through one. Novels take time. Thought. Since I don't write about marriage and/or getting academic tenure. I have cut myself off from the serious world. Did I win a prize?

RA: You've described yourself as the biographer of this country. If you were to write another historical novel set after *Washington, D.C.*, what years or events would you choose?

GV: I am writing the seventh and last volume. *The Golden Age*. It's 1940–1950: how we were got into World War II and then the Cold War; it runs alongside *Washington, D.C.*, with many of the same characters from different angles.

Gore Vidal on the "United States of Amnesia," 9/11, the 2000 Election, and the War in Iraq

Amy Goodman / 2003

From *Democracy Now*, 13 May 2003. Reprinted by permission.

Gore Vidal: The United States is not a normal country. We are a homeland now under military surveillance and military control. The president asked the Congress right after 9/11 not to conduct a major investigation. "As it might deter our search for terrorism wherever it might be in the world." So Congress obediently rolled over.

There was, I remember, Pearl Harbor. I was a kid then. And within three years of it I enlisted in the army. That's what we did in those days; we did not go off to the Texas Air Force and hide. I realize the country has totally changed, that the government is not responsive to the people. Either in protecting us from something like 9/11, which they should've done, could've done. Did not do. And then when it did happen, to investigate, investigate, investigate.

So I wrote two little books, one called *Perpetual War for Perpetual Peace*, in which I try to go into the why Osama Bin Laden, if it were he, or whoever it was, why it was done. And I wrote anther one, *Dreaming War*, on why we were not protected on 9/11, which ordinarily would have led to the impeachment of the President of the United States who had allowed it to happen. They said they had no information. Since then every day the *New York Times* prints another mountain of people that say they had warned the government, President Putin of Russia, he had warned us, President Mubarek of Egypt, he had warned us, three members of Mossad claim they had come to the U.S. to warn us that sometime in September something unpleasant might come out of the sky in our direction.

Were we defended? No we were not defended. Has this ever been investigated? No, it hasn't. There was some attempt at the midterm election, there was a pro forma committee in Congress which has done nothing thus far, and we're three years later. This is shameful. The media, which is controlled by the great conglomerates, which control the political system, has done an atrocious job of reporting, though sometimes good stories get in. I've worn my eyes out studying the *Wall Street Journal*, which despite its dreadful editorial policies is a pretty good newspaper of record, which the *New York Times* is not.

If you read the *Wall Street Journal* very carefully you can pretty much figure out what happened that day. At the time the first hijacking, according to law, FAA, it is mandatory within four minutes of a hijacking, fighter planes from the nearest air military base go up to scramble, that means go up and force the plane down, find out who they are, find out what's happening. One hour and 50 minutes I think it was, no fighter plane went up. During that hour and 20 minutes, we lost the two towers, and one side of the Pentagon. Why didn't they go up? No description from the government, no excuse, a lot of mumbling stories which were then retracted, new stories replaced them.

That to me was the end of the republic. We no longer had a Congress which would ask questions, which it was in place to do, of the executive. We have a commander in chief who likes strutting around in military uniform, which no commander ever did, as they are supposed to be civilians keeping charge of the military. This thing is surrealistic now and it is getting nastier and nastier, as we are more and more kept in the dark about those things which most affect us, which are war and peace, prosperity and poverty. These are the main things that the government should look after. And we the people should be told about them. We have been told nothing. And every voice is silent.

So I wrote two little books, which were then noticed by people who like to look at the Internet, and then a few hundred thousand people have bought them. And I don't come out with conspiracy theories, I never became a journalist, I am a historian. Because journalists give you their opinions. And pretend they're facts. I don't give you my opinions because they may be valuable to my mother, but they are of no value to anybody else. But I give you the facts as I find them, and I list them and they're quite deadly. This government is culpable of, if nothing less, negligence. Why were we not protected with all the air bases' fighter planes up and down the eastern seaboard? Not one of them went aloft while the hijackings took place. Finally two from Otis Field in Massachusetts arrived at the twin towers I think at the time the second one was hit. If anybody had been thinking, they would have gone on to Washington to try to prevent the attack on the Pentagon. They went back to Otis, back to Massachusetts. So I ask these questions, which Congress should ask, does not ask, which the press should ask, but is too frightened. It's a reign of terror now.

Amy Goodman: A recent expose shows that even a Congressional Committee that's looking into this can't get a hold of documents that are classified, and even public testimony is now being reclassified.
Gore Vidal: Well isn't it pretty clear that the dictatorship is in place. We're not supposed to know certain things and we're not going to know them. They're doing everything to remove our history, to damage the Freedom of Information Act. Bush managed to have a number of presidential papers, including those of his father, put out of the reach of historians, or anybody for a great length of time, during which they will probably be shredded, so they will never be available. And what I have always called jokingly the United States of Amnesia will be worse than an amnesiac. It will have suffered a lobotomy; there will be no functioning historical memory of our history.

AG: How has George Bush accrued so much power?
GV: Well, the election of 2000 was the end of the republic. It was the second time that it happened that somebody who got the popular vote did not get the election. Eighteen seventy-six, when Governor Tilden, a Democrat of New York, won the election. But they were able—we still had troops in the south—they were able to turn the election around, the electoral college, Tilden didn't want another Civil War, so he just withdrew, but there was no sinister group taking charge, it was just a party group of Republicans who wanted to continue the reign of General Grant. That was mildly sleazy. This is major corruption. This is corporate America, as one, putting in place a president who was not elected. Getting the Supreme Court to delay and delay, when under the 10th amendment, every decision about the voting in Florida, should be made by the Florida Supreme Court. Not the U.S. Supreme Court, which the Constitution rules out in matters of election.

AG: How did that happen? Well, isn't he your relative, Al Gore?
GV: That's nothing that I go through the streets boasting of no, but yes, he's my cousin. And very un-Gore. The Gores are known for their belligerence and he is not known for self-defense, let us say. He should have asked—it's easy to say he should've, but it was pretty clear at the time. I would've, and I've been in that situation—to count the total Florida vote. He has every right

to demand that, and they couldn't have played games, cause it's too big of a vote. Instead he asked I think three counties, Dade and Broward and one other, to do their count over again.

AG: Concern that he wouldn't win outside of those?
GV: No I think he figured that he had won those, Dade is certainly a large minority vote, which had all voted for him, there's a wonderful book by [John] Nichols, called *Jews for Buchanan*, and it's a marvelous shot of four Jewish gentlemen looking terribly alarmed, and you see Dade County goes for Buchanan. And even Buchanan goes, "These are not my votes down there, something's wrong." And it was stolen by the Secretary of State, that lady who now has been rewarded with a seat in Congress, the president's brother, the losing president candidate's brother, was governor, and he took part in it. And the court did by five to four.

Two of the five should have recused themselves, should have just withdrawn from the case when Gore vs. Bush came before the court. Why? One of them, [Anthony] Scalia, had a son, who was working for the Bush team of lawyers before the Supreme Court. Did Justice Scalia recuse himself as he should because his son is arguing? No. He wants to kill Gore. He wants to make sure that the bad guys win. Thomas's wife was busy, getting Curricula Viti of potential people to serve in a Bush administration. Clarence Thomas should have recused himself and withdrawn for the case, in which case it would have been 4 to 3 for Gore, who would now be president. And Iraq and Afghanistan I can guarantee would not have been knocked down, in order to benefit Halliburton and Bechtel.

AG: Scalia recently went to Cleveland. He spoke at the Cleveland City Club, which is known as the oldest free speech forum in the country. He allowed no press in, and the night before he spoke in the city, and he said that that vote, choosing George Bush, was his proudest moment.
GV: I would impeach him and in a well-run country the Senate should make a move toward the trial of Justice Scalia. And in back of that there's some interesting organization going on, which is hard to determine, Opus Dei. Both Scalia and Thomas have connections with Opus Dei, a secret Catholic order, originally fascist. General Franco in Spain was sort of a Godfather to it, and we don't know much about it, and it's all over the place, about 80,000 worldwide. Louis Freeh of the FBI at that time was a member, as was

Mr. [Robert] Hanssen, the spy, who had been giving all of our secrets. He was with the CIA; he had been giving our secrets to the Russians for many years. I make no charges, but I simply bring up questions. Why not ask questions of these people? Does it suit Opus Dei that Bush is president? Now we're getting into God territory, which I normally would stay away from as any good American should. It's not my business other people's religions. But Bush is Born Again, that's why he used biblical language. (imitating Bush)—He's evil! He's an evildoer!—Well that's theological language. You can say he's a bad man, a dishonest man, a ruthless man. Evildoer? And he believes the end of the world is coming. Born Agains believe in rapture. They don't care about this world. When it ends George W. Bush will be lifted up in a state of rapture into the bosom of our lord.

Also among the born-again category, not that kind of protestant, is Tony Blair, who has become like his wife, Roman Catholic, which is difficult for a British Prime Minister, since the Prime Minister is supposed to be an Anglican—what we would call Episcopalian—as he picks the Bishops of the Anglican Church, so you can't have a Roman Catholic picking Anglican Bishops, but he is. So now we have two boys who think, "Jesus wants them for sunbeams," who are willing to put at risk—I'm extrapolating on my own just from the evidence at hand. This is mostly humorous. You can judge it as you may—But two believers in our Lord's coming, an Armageddon and the end of the world—this is the way Reagan used to talk—and it made him very popular with the southern states, that's why this big thing was just about South Carolina that's the heart of it—why? Well those states don't have much in the way of population, but they have very strong born-again Evangelical Protestants, and they believe in our Lord returning at any moment, and you can collect them all by saying you hate abortion and this and that. They have a swing vote in those states because of the Electoral College. They don't have much population, but they have a lot of electoral votes among them. The Electoral College was devised—you call yourself democracy, you're very un-American, the founding fathers did not want democracy in the U.S. ever. They also did not want tyranny, a king or Hitler, they wanted a Republic. And they devised the Electoral College so the majority could never control any-thing. So you have a popular vote out there and in those days it was just for Congress, so there was one electoral vote per congressmen, one per senator and the state, and they get together and decide the election. So what Scalia was doing was going back to the Electoral College in order to put together a

majority to put in his candidate who will probably hasten the end of the
world. I don't know where Scalia will be during rapture. He may be [points
up and points down].

AG: You're talking about religion, you've written about Pat Robertson and
John Ashcroft.
GV: Yes I have, they are very religious men. The wall that Thomas Jefferson
thought that he had built, as did John Adams who was pretty much an antag-
onist of Jefferson, but they were both agreed that religion ought not to in any
way intrude itself into politics, it was something quite separate, whatever
your religion, you obeyed its laws, if you believed in those laws, and nobody
would stop you. But once you start raising money in tax-free institutions,
whose tax-free money you use to influence elections, like Mr. Robertson, and
Mr. Falwell, then you are out of the constitution, and you should be taxed
anyway before you use it, but they are free of taxation and with that the
whole country began to change and this very small minority of Evangelicals,
mostly in the south and southwest, have achieved great power, in states of
small population where their Electoral College count, state by state, adds up
to quite a lot, in fact added up to a Bush "victory."

AG: Gore Vidal, you've said, I don't see us winning this war, you've also said
that this will force Saddam Hussein to use whatever weapons of mass
destruction he may have. Maybe you were prophetic, and maybe in fact that
was true that if he had them he would have used them, and he didn't.
GV: Well, it's pretty plain he didn't have them, nobody in Europe thought he
did. The Europeans at least have a free press, which we don't, or most of the
countries there do. I said he probably would, if we pressed him hard enough.
You see when you live with nothing but lies being told to you in the media,
nothing but lies, and it's done the way they do advertising, it's repetition:
"Weapons of mass destruction! He's got weapons of mass destruction! Mass
destruction! Mass destruction! Mass destruction!" When you hear that
10,000 times a day, you finally think he must have, they can't go on like this
forever, well he didn't have them, now I'm sure we're busy planting them all
over the place, and we'll be: "Oh look what we found! Goodness me! Here's
an Atom Bomb! Made in USA. No, scratch that out, scratch that out. He
made that mark." I fully expect us to plant something or other, but as it's the
United States of Amnesia, why go to the trouble, it's expensive to have troops

going around looking for stuff. I think they think the public will have forgotten it, I think the public is forgetting it, doesn't much care.

I thought when I said that we would lose the war, I still think we will. Afghanistan the fighting is going on, rather rougher than it was during the so-called war. It will keep right on going as long as we have a presence in Iraq. And we will eventually be driven out. Somebody will have a bright idea, one of those neo-conservatives, we know what they're like, and will decide to kill everybody there, that this would be a very good thing to do. Gotta show force. And all these sissies, all of whom who ran from the idea of going into the army, talk so tough when they get together, we're gonna show our muscle, you look at Mr. Kristol, and Mr., who's the sidekick who rides with him? Fat Boys with Asthma, talking tough, it makes their blood run cold. So I think that we haven't a chance of winning in the Middle East, nobody has, nobody except the Turks, with the Ottoman Empire, which Woodrow Wilson, one of the great fools of our history, decided to break up at the end of WWI, so we get Turkey, which turns out to be really quite a formidable country now, and broke up bits and pieces, into Syria, and Jordan, into this into that, which became British and French mandates, and are now countries which are uneasy, with all sorts of warring religious groups.

AG: Gore Vidal, you developed a relationship with Timothy McVeigh. Can you talk about that?
GV: I never met him, nor did we talk on the telephone, but we did exchange letters. He read a piece I wrote in *Vanity Fair*, about the shredding of the Bill of Rights, which has been further shredded since his death, and he wrote me a letter, and I wrote him back, and he wrote me some very informative letters about himself. He was very smart, knew the constitution backwards and forwards. I was struck by reading about his trial. At first I had no interest. He was the lone crazed killer that our public must always have. Lee Harvey Oswald acted alone; we all know that. You can get the Warren Commission to say that. He was obviously not alone. But that worked so well that the people always fall for it every time, so they decided that Timothy McVeigh, a rather slight young man, with no knowledge of explosives, had put together this two-ton bomb, which he himself, and this guy called Nichols loaded on a Ryder truck—it took at least 9 people, it's been figured out, to get that bomb onto that truck, and then a very careful, experienced driver to get that thing, without blowing himself up,

into Oklahoma City in front of the building. He was not alone, and we have a pretty good idea of some of the people he was associated with who might have been in on it. The FBI began quite professionally. They had infiltrated a lot of these Patriot movements out there in the middle-west, people who don't like the government and others who were as angry as was McVeigh at what the federal government had done to the Branch Davidians at Waco. For McVeigh this was revenge upon what he regarded an odious government, a tyrannical government. He had gone out there and watched them using military, army stuff. And remember he was an army hero of the Gulf War, and he watched them break the law. The Posse Commitus Act of 1876. And in one of the letters to me, these are all reprinted in *Perpetual War for Perpetual Peace*, if you want to read McVeigh's actual words about it. He said, "You know soldiers are trained to kill. The police are trained to protect persons and property. These are two different functions. The justice department called in the army. They wanted tanks and all sorts of things, army material. With which they shot up the buildings that fired oil and people died." There was once again no proper investigation. In the course of McVeigh's trial, which was a kind of joke, the FBI behaved pretty well. They had a lot of interesting leads, 305s I think they're called. They take down the evidence that people give them, directions in which to look and so on. They followed up nothing. And I wrote Louis Freeh, who was then the head of the FBI, a letter which I include in the little book, a letter which I read aloud on the *Today Show*, just to make sure that he saw it. No answer. But I said there's certain very interesting leads here, and this is all from evidence at the pre-trials, which anybody can get at, and I said these should have been investigated, but they weren't, they decided it was McVeigh and that was it. Now a couple of days ago we find out that the FBI was faking it, some anti-McVeigh stuff in their labs, trying to prove that he built the bomb, that he had ammonia on his trousers or something. Well he may well have been in on it—I don't know, I'm not a prophet—but my impression is that he could not have done it alone. So there were others to follow up, and on television I said you've got to start doing your job, at the FBI, at the Justice Department. Your job is to protect persons and property. You didn't follow up. There may be 100 McVeighs out there, waiting to take another crack at us. And you did nothing, 'cause you want to unload Gray's killer, and you wanted the book shut [SHUTS A BOOK]. So what sort of government is this. I'd say a bad one.

AG: What effect do you think that the Persian Gulf War had on Timothy McVeigh? It said that he was involved with bulldozing people in the highway of death, as Iraqi soldiers retreated after surrender.

GV: Well he was shocked by it. He also got the Bronze Star. He was a great marksman, and he did his share of shooting soldiers, but he was appalled at the civilians, the children. That's why it's so ironic, "oh, he killed all those children," as though he got up in the morning to kill all the children in the nursery in that building. He says in one of his statements, he finally says I did it because he didn't want to spend the rest of his life in a box, he could live 30–40 more years and then as he wrote me, I'd rather have federally assisted suicide, which is how he termed the injection in the arm, than a lifetime in a box. Because he saw there was no way out. He could have sung, but he didn't. He could have said who else was involved in this, but he did not. He was a complex character, and endlessly interesting I thought, and he should have been kept alive, so we could find out who these other people were.

AG: Would you put Timothy McVeigh in the same category as Mohammed Atta?

GV: No, no, no. We don't know that story either. Mohammad Atta was obviously a Muslim zealot. Also in *Perpetual War for Perpetual Peace* there's another question that goes unanswered. The head of the Pakistan Secret Service was in Washington a week or so before 9/11. While he was there—it was just a ceremonial visit with the head of the CIA, they worked together—he sent back word to Islamabad about one of his henchman, to wire $100,000 to Mohammad Atta in the United States, which was duly done. The FBI, I think it was the *Wall Street Journal* where I got the story from, only said American Secret Services found out about this, and they complained to the Pakistani Government. Why is the head of the Secret Service in Washington telling somebody to send $100,000 to a guy that we now know was the lead bomber, lead hijacker just a week before 9/11? *Times of India* published the whole story. *Wall Street Journal* did a pretty good version for them. Now shouldn't that be examined? Wouldn't Congress be interested in this guy in Washington meeting with all our top secret people? Says ok, send him $100,000. Not one more word, not one more word. Now in a country with any curiosity, in a public that was informed of anything, there would be a great deal of outcry. I couldn't imagine this happening in England, maybe questions in Parliament, the papers would be full of it until it was solved. It couldn't happen in Italy, which dearly loves a conspiracy, or Germany. In the U.S., everybody listens to 19th Century Fox TV News, in which a bunch of loons just scream and scream and scream. And with each scream they tell another lie. How are we ever going to have an informed citizenry? Which means then how can we have an informed election?

AG: So what's it like for you, Gore Vidal, to go back and forth between Italy and the United States through this period.

GV: Let's clear up one thing. The right wing has been desperate to explain to Americans that I live in Italy, that I'm an ex-patriot. "He hates America." Just because I dislike them. I've had a house in California for 30 years. I've had a house in Southern Italy for 30 years. Sometimes I'm there when I'm working, but I've always been involved in American politics, and American history. You can look at a long line of books to attest to that fact. The idea of geography is very exciting to people, because I think it's only 7 percent of the American people who have passports, only 7 percent have been abroad. Not counting the ones who were sent in the military of course, but 7 percent have voluntarily gone abroad. It's a tiny percent of those in Congress who've been abroad. Bush had never set foot in Europe before he became president. He had spent 10 minutes in China when his father was Ambassador there, and obviously never went outside of the compound. What I have to do lot of times in Europe is explain to them that Americans are not stupid. When they meet them, they think they're very stupid because they don't know anything. I have to explain to them that we're not stupid. I think we're rather brighter than the average, but we're ignorant, which means not knowing. We have no information because it isn't given to us. Our public schools are a scandal. They stopped teaching geography in 1950 in most of the public schools, by which time we were a global empire. We have a global empire and nobody knows where anything is, nobody knows any languages, so our statesmen go abroad and people laugh at them, because they are so dumb, or seem to be so dumb.

Index